"If success always seems like tomorrow's goal, Ruth Gotian has written the resource for you. Distilling years of research into the world's most successful thinkers and doers into this engaging book, she offers concise and actionable ways to map their habits into your life."
Daniel H. Pink, #1 *New York Times* Bestselling Author of *When*, *Drive*, and *To Sell Is Human*

"Success has never been more beguiling, alluring, and elusive. Ruth Gotian cuts away the mystery and delivers an inspiring and practical take on success which will open your eyes to what it really takes to succeed. Filled with remarkable stories, *The Success Factor* gets to the heart of success."
Stuart Crainer, co-founder, Thinkers50

"Does success seem elusive to you? Ruth Gotian provides each of us with a roadmap to achieve success. Based on years of research, the book identifies the secret sauce to optimizing our success and provides us with practical tools to get us there. Your quest for success is a journey, and I highly recommend you bring *The Success Factor* along as your guide."
Laine Joelson Cohen, Director of Learning, Human Resources, Citi

"*The Success Factor* is a call to action to anyone who has the passion for success but needs a plan. Backed by research and interviews with the world's most successful people, Ruth Gotian reveals a powerful template for catapulting our own success. This book will be your inspiration and guide."
Benjamin Croft, founder and chairman, World Business & Executive Coach Summit

"An indispensable guide for leaders who realize that exceptional and continued success depends on their capability of understanding the needs, nurturing, and motivating a team of high performers. This book is like a well-equipped gym where you train your muscles and skills to continuously improve on the infinite game of success."
Fabrizio Parini, Member of the Board and former CEO, Lindt Chocolate and Sprüngli Italy

"What do high-achievers have in common? THIS BOOK. That's because peak performers are always searching for a secret sauce that will give them a competitive edge. You'll love the real-life success stories and best practices you can use immediately in your life, career and endeavors. Read it and reap."
Sam Horn, CEO of The Intrigue Agency, author of *Tongue Fu!*

"*The Success Factor* is truly a compelling must-read book for anyone who is looking to understand the blueprint for what makes a high-achiever and successful leader."
Faisal Pandit, President, Panasonic System Solutions Company of North America

"As someone who advises and mentors many high-achieving graduate students, scientists, and health professionals, I'm often struck by their inability to construct a roadmap for success. Building on cases studies from diverse fields including sports, science, law, and business, *The Success Factor* offers an important toolkit for that essential first step."
Peter Hotez, MD, PhD, DSc (Hon), Dean and Professor, National School of Tropical Medicine, Baylor College of Medicine

"The Success Factor makes success attainable to anyone who wants it, and is willing to work. Ruth Gotian has reverse-engineered the path to success, based on her research with extreme high-achievers, and offers useful tools and strategies which will give you a giant leap forward on your own path to greatness."
Dorie Clark, author of *The Long Game* and executive education faculty, Duke University Fuqua School of Business

"By providing a comprehensive path to move anyone, in business or in life, toward their own perception of success, Ruth Gotian's work will undoubtedly have a profound impact on readers. With this recent work, Dr. Gotian answers that question posed to her on her first day at Teachers College, Columbia University: 'In what area do you consider yourself a thought-leader?'"
Katie Embree, EdD, Vice President for Planning and Strategy and Chief of Staff to the President, Teachers College, Columbia University

"The Success Factor is a transforming book where you find the true stories of high-achievers and the foundations of their success. Ruth invested years to find out what their secret is and her research, perseverance and passion is raising the bar of excellence. Anyone can implement Ruth's ideas and tools, and improve their success!"
Darek Lenart, SVP, People and Capability, North America Markets and Strategic Growth Mastercard

"Ruth Gotian sets the record straight on how to take control of your career and reach success. *The Success Factor* showcases insights and personal stories of high-achievers from diverse fields to show—in a highly personal way—what works for different people. I gleaned something new from each different vignette. As an advisor and mentor to PhDs and MD-PhDs, I strongly suggest this book as a must-have for them."
Ushma S. Neill, PhD, Vice President, Scientific Education & Training, Memorial Sloan Kettering Cancer Center

"*The Success Factor* provides a playbook for the strategic pursuit of excellence, elite performance and ultimately success. Using compelling stories, Dr. Gotian provides insights into the commonalities and traits for high-achievers and emphasizes the role of mentoring in achieving success."
RC Buford, CEO, San Antonio Spurs, two-time National Basketball Association (NBA) Executive of the Year

"If you seek a guide to launch you on the path to true meaningful success, read this book. With keen analysis and compelling storytelling, Ruth Gotian unlocks the secrets of success and gives us actionable tools to achieve it."
Sanyin Siang, Thinkers50 #1 Coach & Mentor, and author of *The Launch Book*

The Success Factor

Developing the Mindset and Skillset for Peak Business Performance

Ruth Gotian

KoganPage

First published in Great Britain and the United States in 2022 by Kogan Page Limited

2nd Floor, 45 Gee Street	122 W 27th St, 10th Floor	4737/23 Ansari Road
London	New York, NY 10001	Daryaganj
EC1V 3RS	USA	New Delhi 110002
United Kingdom		India
www.koganpage.com		

Kogan Page books are printed on paper from sustainable forests.

ISBNs
Hardback   9781398602311
Paperback   9781398602298
Ebook   9781398602304

British Library Cataloguing-in-Publication Data

A CIP record for this book is available from the British Library.

Library of Congress Control Number

2021949054

Typeset by Hong Kong FIVE Workshop, Hong Kong
Print production managed by Jellyfish
Printed and bound by CPI Group (UK) Ltd, Croydon CR0 4YY

In blessed memory of my father
Arthur James Ginsburg, ל״ז
1932–2020

This book is dedicated to those who know that
"impossible" simply means "I'm possible."
Amnon, Benjamin, Jonathan and Eitan
The stars in my life who make everything possible. I love you.

You can download resources for *The Success Factor* at
www.koganpage.com/successfactor

CONTENTS

LIST OF TABLES

ABOUT THE AUTHOR

Ruth Gotian, EdD, MS has been hailed by the journal *Nature* and Columbia University as an expert in mentorship and leadership development. In 2021, she was selected as one of 30 people worldwide to be named on the Thinkers50 Radar List, dubbed the Oscars of management thinking, where she was described as a "Prolific mentor and educator, leading important research into the secrets of success." She is a semi-finalist for the *Forbes 50 Over 50* list and has coached and mentored hundreds of people throughout her career. In addition to being published in academic journals, she is a contributor to *Forbes* and *Psychology Today*, where she writes about optimizing success. She is the Chief Learning Officer in Anesthesiology and former Assistant Dean of Mentoring and Executive Director of the Mentoring Academy at Weill Cornell Medicine, where she is a faculty member. She is also the co-editor of a book on medical education. To learn more about her work, visit www.ruthgotian.com.

LIST OF NOTABLE LEADERS

Many thanks to the following people who shared their stories with me and are quoted in the book.

Peter Agre, MD, Physician-scientist, recipient of the 2003 Nobel Prize in Chemistry.

Michiel Bartman, Olympic champion, two-time silver medalist and three-time Olympian, Men's Rowing.

Dori Bernstein, Former Director of the Supreme Court Institute, Georgetown University Law Center.

Bonnie Blair, Five-time Olympic champion, one-time bronze medalist, and four-time Olympian, Women's Speed Skating.

Michael Brown, MD, Physician-scientist, recipient of the 1985 Nobel Prize in Physiology or Medicine.

Candace Cable, Three-time Paralympic champion, two-time silver medalist, three-time bronze medalist, nine-time Paralympian and Olympian, Wheelchair Racing and Para Alpine Skiing.

Charles Camarda, PhD, Astronaut.

Pablo Carrillo, JD, Former Chief of Staff to Senator John McCain.

Arturo Casadevall, MD, PhD, Physician-scientist, Professor and Chair, Johns Hopkins School of Medicine.

Maxine Clark, Founder and former CEO, Build-A-Bear Workshop

Victoria Clark, Tony Award winner, Broadway actress.

Lee Cockerell, Former Executive Vice-President, World Disney World Resort.

Jonathan Cohen, MD, Executive Chairman, BioReference Labs.

Caryn Davies, JD, Two-time Olympic champion, silver medalist, and three-time Olympian, Women's Rowing.

Colonel Travis Dolan, Colonel, US Army.

Anthony Fauci, MD, Director, National Institute of Allergy and Infectious Diseases, National Institutes of Health, and medical advisor to seven US Presidents.

Jeffrey Friedman, MD, PhD, Physician-scientist and Professor, The Rockefeller University.

James "Hondo" F. Geurts, Colonel (Ret), Formerly performing the duties of the Under Secretary of the US Navy.

Gary H. Gibbons, MD, Director of the National Heart, Lung and Blood Institute, National Institutes of Health.

David Ginsburg, MD, Physician-scientist and Professor, University of Michigan.

Scott Hamilton, Olympic champion and two-time Olympian, Men's Figure Skating.

Devon Harris, Three-time Olympian, Men's Bobsledding.

Kayla Harrison, Two-time Olympic champion, two-time Olympian, Women's Judo.

Deborah Heiser, PhD, Co-founder and CEO, The Mentor Project.

Helen Hobbs, MD, Physician-scientist, Professor and Chair, University of Texas, Southwestern.

Joe Jacobi, Olympic champion, two-time Olympian, Men's Canoe Slalom.

Erika James, PhD, Dean, Wharton School, University of Pennsylvania.

Jonathan Jarvis, Former director of the US National Park Service.

Thomas W. Jones, Former Chairman and CEO of Citigroup Inc's Global Investment Management.

Neal Katyal, JD, Former Acting Solicitor General of the United States, lawyer who argued 44 cases before the US Supreme Court.

Steve Kerr, Eight-time NBA champion and current head coach of the Golden State Warriors.

Kathy Kram, PhD, Mentoring expert and Professor Emeritus at Boston University.

Robert Lefkowitz, MD, Physician-scientist, recipient of the 2012 Nobel Prize in Chemistry.

Arthur Levitt, Former Chairman, US Securities and Exchange Commission.

Janice Lintz, CEO, Hearing Access and Innovations. Hearing advocate who initiated access in museums, taxis, baseball stadiums, and theaters.

Curtis Martin, Retired NFL player, was inducted into the Pro Football Hall of Fame in 2012.

Ryan Millar, Olympic champion and three-time Olympian, Men's Volleyball.

Ben Nelson, Former President of Snapfish, Founder, Chairman, and CEO of the Minerva Project.

Scott O'Neil, Former CEO of the Philadelphia 76ers and the New Jersey Devils.

Apolo Ohno, Two-time Olympic champion, two-time silver medalist, and four-time bronze medalist, three-time Olympian. Most decorated Winter Olympian, Men's Short-track Speedskating.

Zaza Pachulia, Two-time NBA champion.

Scott Parazynski, MD, Astronaut, Physician, Olympic coach, US Astronaut Hall of Fame.

Daryl Roth, Tony Award-winning producer of over 90 theater productions, including *Kinky Boots.*

Art Shamsky, 1969 MLB World Series Champion with the New York Miracle Mets.

Bert Shapiro, PhD, Former Director of Medical Scientist Training Programs at the National Institutes of Health.

Ian Siegel, Co-founder and CEO, ZipRecruiter.

Susan Silver, Comedy writer on classic sitcoms, *The Mary Tyler Moore Show, The Bob Newhart Show, Maude,* and *The Partridge Family.*

Haley Skarupa, Olympic champion, Women's Ice Hockey.

Nicole Stott, Astronaut.

Bert Vogelstein, MD, Physician-scientist and professor, Johns Hopkins School of Medicine.

Marie Volpe, EdD, Faculty member, Teachers College Columbia University.

Christopher Waddell, Five-time Paralympic champion, five-time silver medalist, two-time bronze medalist, seven-time Paralympian, Wheelchair Racing and Para Alpine Skiing.

Christopher Walsh, MD, PhD, Physician-scientist, Professor and Division Chief, Harvard Medical School.

Judge Paul Watford, JD, United States Circuit Judge of the United States Court of Appeals for the Ninth Circuit.

Phil Weiser, JD, Colorado Attorney General.

Peggy Whitson, PhD, Astronaut, former NASA Chief Astronaut, former Commander of the International Space Station.

Torsten Wiesel, MD, Recipient of the 1981 Nobel Prize in Physiology or Medicine, Professor and President Emeritus, The Rockefeller University.

Anne Wojcicki, CEO, 23andMe.

Lynn Wooten, PhD, President, Simmons University.

Iris Zimmermann, Olympian, Women's Fencing.

Huda Zoghbi, MD, Physician-scientist, Professor, Baylor College of Medicine.

FOREWORD

As an executive coach for over 40 years for CEOs at some of the world's largest and most successful companies, I'm no stranger to high achievers. In my coaching, I work with already successful people who want to get even better; similar to a champion tennis player working with a coach for the Olympics. These executives are not losers or lost causes—they are at the top of their game and looking to get better and achieve even more. This means that my clients have not only worked hard to be where they are currently, but are also willing to put in the exuberant amount of effort required to get to their next level of success.

While many people differ on definitions of success, no one can deny these leaders are high achievers. My clients come from different backgrounds, academic levels, and paths to the top of their fields. I've found that they do, however, have some similarities in common: they have drive, and passion for what they do.

This passion fuels their persistence against challenges and drives them to work harder and longer than their peers. Many of them never imagined they would become a CEO, a Michelin-starred chef, an astronaut, a Nobel laureate, or an NBA player when they first began doing something they loved. It started with an intrigue in their field and became what they pursued relentlessly to make it work.

One of my clients, Dave Chang, is the Founder of Momofuku, a Michelin-starred chef, and TV personality on Netflix's *Ugly Delicious*. Dave holds the accomplishments most chefs dream of, having opened restaurants internationally, coming up with new and inventive ideas for food and shows constantly. Yet Dave once shared with me that when he opened his first restaurant, Momofuku Noodle Bar, he didn't even know how to charge sales tax on purchases! He was plagued with doubt in his venture, and unsure of what his path forward would look like. But he was passionate about making good food and sharing it with others. So he pushed forward through the challenges, doubt, and obstacles.

The Success Factor perfectly captures the nuances of what took so many entrepreneurs, executives, physicians, scientists, and athletes to the top of their game. Ruth's stories and interviews from so many interesting people lend to the concept that no matter what your goal or in what profession you're trying to succeed, there are foundational keys to making it work. Throughout this book, you'll read about the intrinsic motivation, unparalleled work ethic, and continuous learning that led these fantastic people to their ultimate goals.

Ruth's unique position as an executive coach, educator, and author adds to her ability to pull back the curtain on the fascinating insights behind her interviewees. *The Success Factor* is brilliantly written to show you how to get from where you are now, to where you want to be.

Read on and be inspired to overcome what holds you back from achieving your next goal!

Marshall Goldsmith

Thinkers 50 #1 Executive Coach and *New York Times* #1 bestselling author of *Triggers, Mojo,* and *What Got You Here Won't Get You There.*

ACKNOWLEDGMENTS

How does one properly thank the army of people who helped me live out my lifelong dream of writing this book? It started with my Grandma Esther, who told me when I was a kid that I was a beautiful writer. I only wrote book reports at that point, but her words stayed with me forever. Dr. Marie Volpe, my mentor and doctoral dissertation advisor made me a better writer with her critical eye and unyielding support. She taught me to tighten every sentence so there is not even one superfluous word and make sure I address any potential gaps. Years after I earned my doctorate, she is still the person I turn to when I want someone to give me honest feedback on my writing. When I wrote the book proposal for this book, Marie was the person I turned to first.

The Covid pandemic was a time of incredible loss and isolation, but even among all of the devastation, there were silver linings, many of which eventually led to this book. Immense gratitude to my incredible editor, Kathe Sweeney, who found me, brought me into the Kogan Page family, and taught me about writing successfully to a mass audience. Heather Wood, thank you for making my words flow so that the reader won't want to put the book down, and for seeing this project over the goal line.

My Renaissance Weekend family, who are one of the most supportive group of high achievers I have ever met. I cherish our Saturday night Zooms during Covid which were the perfect distraction from the chaos all around us and created lifelong friendships. This incredible group even helped me come up with the title for this book! Special thank you to Dr. Susan Birne-Stone for getting the group together and helping me with my on-air presence, as well as Dr. Debbie Heiser and Janice Lintz, who responded to my countless emails, text messages, and phone calls with grace, incredible guidance, and humor (I love the GIFs!).

The Marshall Goldsmith 100 Coaches, or MG100, has been a bottomless source of encouragement, learning, inspiration, and opportunity. I am immensely thankful to Dr. Marshall Goldsmith and all of my fellow MG100 members who welcomed me with open arms. I learn so much from each of you every day. You are one of the best communities of practice I have ever been a part of.

My Weill Cornell Medicine family, who have been by my side for 25 years. My MD-PhD students were my original inspiration for my work on high achievers. Thank you to Drs. Hugh Hemmings and Kane Pryor for the continuous support and encouragement to let the ideas snowball and the residents, fellows, and faculty who motivate me to look deeper and find innovative ways to get the best out of every person.

To my initial community of practice, who started out as my competitors and became my good friends: the Royal Court—Arlene Kohler, Jana Toutolmin, Linda Burnley, Sharon Welling, Kathy Crawford, Nancy Malson, Dr. Bert Shapiro, and Dr. Mary Horton (you're an honorary member!). From our first initial meeting in Aspen, CO nearly a quarter-century ago, to where we stand today, your friendship, support, and celebration of all of life's small and big wins are what I most cherish.

My Mentor Project family, under the direction of Dr. Debbie Heiser. It is the only program I am aware of that allows a diverse group of mentors to learn from each other and get mentored by other star mentors. The focus on the mentor allows all of us to do our work better, energetically, and impactfully. Thank you to Dr. Debbie Heiser and Bob Cousins for creating something so magical.

Thank you to the incredible high achievers who openly, humbly, and honestly shared their stories with me. None of them believed they were high achievers and most were uncomfortable with that description. You are the kindest and most inspirational people I have met and am honored to now call you my friends.

Being a daughter, wife, mother, and sister means I have a built-in support system and sounding board who let me test ideas, talk endlessly during dinner about what I learned, and support me when I announce that I want to get a doctorate and write a book about extreme high achievers. Thank you, Amnon, Benjamin, Jonathan, and Ethan "Eitan" for the endless love, encouragement, support, hardwiring of the Internet, continuous Nespresso pod inventory, and blocks of silence so that I could write. A special thank you to Ben for reviewing my drafts and making comments which always enhanced the manuscript. To my brothers, Ron and Daniel, thank you for the support during this challenging year and to my mom, Dina, for always asking me how my writing was going. To my father, Arthur, ז״ל, of blessed memory, I only wish you were around to see this. I love all of you.

Introduction

I remember walking on the Teachers College Columbia University campus in New York City. A classmate stopped me to say hello, and we talked about school, our careers, and what we would like to do next after we finish our respective degrees: a master's degree for him, and a doctoral degree for me. I was not quite sure, but I knew I wanted my work to matter, to have an impact. He then posed a question that I have never been able to shake. He asked me in what area did I consider myself a thought leader? I was not even sure I knew what a thought leader was. He explained that it is what I am uniquely qualified to do and for what I am known. What theories, practices, or processes might I have conceived or know and understand better than most people? What would I be considered an authority in, to the point that others would seek out my expertise? I had no idea.

I thought about his comments a great deal. I had worked hard until then, but I am not sure I was considered a thought leader in anything. I knew right then and there that to move forward, that was a pivotal change I had to make. After all, high achievers are known for something specific, a niche topic, not everything and anything. They become the expert in the room.

I pursued my doctorate while working full time and raising my family. That meant I did not have time to waste. Every book, article, and conversation was building my fund of knowledge and I was a sponge, soaking in as much content, theory, and expertise as I could. On my commute to work, I would reflect on everything I learned and try to piece different ideas together. My doctoral advisor and mentor, Dr. Marie Volpe, and I would have phone conversations every day on my way to work, talking about what I had learned, whether or not I agreed with it, how I would envision applying it, and the limitations I viewed in certain theories and concepts. By the time I got to work, I was pumped. Those conversations with Dr. Volpe were better than any shot of caffeine. I was challenged, supported, inspired, and motivated.

When I entered graduate school, I pondered what topic I would focus on for my research. I knew I wanted to study physician-scientists, those who have the MD, and did research as well. I ran a program for future physician-scientists, a combined MD-PhD program, and saw firsthand that these students were terrific. The program had a 3.5 percent acceptance rate, so these students were the best of the best. They thought differently, worked harder than anyone I had ever seen or known, and the way they approached challenges was a textbook lesson in perseverance. They did all of this while being kind, humble, and always looking for a way to lend a helping hand to those who could benefit.

They were all fantastic students and humans, but there were always a few who were at the top of this highly competitive group. Continuing at this pace, which is akin to a lifetime marathon, is extremely challenging. Intellectually, they were trying to find treatments for diseases, and take care of their patients. They had to write grants to fund their research, publish papers in major scientific journals, and present at conferences in order to successfully communicate their work, teach, mentor, and handle administrative tasks. It is brutal but worthwhile. Sadly, not everyone can or wants to keep up with this pace. Nationally, a great deal of time, money, and effort was placed on preventing physician-scientists from leaving their chosen field (what we call a "leaky pipeline"). After looking at the leaky pipeline for nearly two decades, I wanted to look at the other end of the spectrum, those whose work was so spectacular and productive that it more than compensated for anyone who left the field. I was interested in finding a new way to solve the problem that had plagued those in my industry for decades.

Another mentor of mine, Dr. Bert Shapiro, who oversaw all of the MD-PhD programs at the National Institutes of Health (NIH), gave me wise counsel. When discussing potential dissertation topics, he told me, "Do something important, not just interesting." He explained that my research was going to look at this group from a completely different angle, and I was in a position to make an impact. So that is what I set out to do.

I interviewed the most successful physician-scientists of our generation, ranging from Nobel Prize winners, institute directors at the National Institutes of Health (NIH), to a US former US surgeon-general. I learned that they all had four elements in common which they continually develop in tandem. When I finished my doctorate, I thought I was done with research, but the idea kept nagging at me. If the four mindsets for extreme achievement that I found explained the success factor for the physician-scientists, would the same process be true for other top performers and leading experts in their respective fields?

I decided to find out. I interviewed over sixty extreme high achievers, including astronauts, Olympic champions, NBA champions, Tony Award winners, CEOs, and other luminaries. The four factors that led to the physician-scientists' success also held true for the other extreme high achievers. Eureka! I learned that the astronaut's path to success is very similar to that of an Olympic champion. If that was true, it meant to me that success could be learned and, equally as important, it could be taught. I reverse-engineered the high achievers' methods to success and created a blueprint for others to follow (Friedman, 2021).

I became captivated by success. I started writing articles about the topic for *Forbes*, *Harvard Business Review*, *Psychology Today*, and academic journals. Many of those articles appear in this book. I started teaching the principles and methods and speaking about them all over the globe. By 2021, Teachers College Columbia University, the institution where I earned my doctorate, presented me with an alumni award, and Thinkers50, dubbed the Oscars of management thinking, named me on their Radar List as one of thirty management thinkers to watch due to my work on mentorship and high achievers. Shortly after, I learned that I was a semi-finalist for the *Forbes* 50 over 50 List. The world was telling me that I was a thought leader.

High achievers are not humdrum in their approach to work in their field or industry; they push it forward. They are known for breaking barriers, looking at problems differently, and identifying solutions. The most prominent identifier of success is someone who advanced their field, really pushed the confines of what we know to be true. They did things differently, faster, better, or more efficiently than others. Successful people take what we know to be true, turn it on its head, and reexamine it. They consider how to make it better, more efficient, safer, faster, or more dynamic (Friedman, 2021, Gotian, 2017).

Throughout all of my research, what became evident was that you cannot copy someone else's habits, but you can emulate mindsets with customized applications. That is what this book does. I found the success factor, and this book will teach it to you in a manner that allows you to take actionable steps immediately. Real stories from extreme high achievers are used to underscore your learning. It is a masterclass where you will learn from a diverse group of luminaries ranging from astronauts, Olympic champions, Nobel laureates, CEOs, Tony Award winners, and high-ranking government officials. You will learn success gleaned from over sixty interviews with everyone from the former NASA Chief Astronaut, Dr. Peggy Whitson, to the CEO of 23andMe, Anne Wojcicki, Nobel Prize winner, Dr. Mike Brown, the most decorated winter Olympian, Apolo Anton Ohno, and NBA champion and coach, Steve Kerr.

How to use this book

The Success Factor was written as a tool to help you optimize your success. This is a book that you can leave on your nightstand, pick up any chapter and enhance and improve your journey to success immediately. No more talking about one day; you can learn new skills and make today day one. This is not a book you read once and put away; instead, refer back to it as you wish to try new skills.

You will learn about the four mindsets extreme high achievers use in order to reach optimal levels of success. There are different ways of approaching this, and the book will give you multiple options from which you can choose. The important thing is you have to activate all the tenets in tandem; you cannot pick and choose which you want to do and when.

The book is broken down into three sections. Part One (Chapters 1–3) sheds light on my fascination with success and high achievers, why I think you should try to become one, what can hold you back, and why and how organizations should recruit, lead and retain these top performers. Part Two (Chapters 4–7) explains each of the four pillars of success and underscores their message by sharing the journeys of many extreme high achievers, some of whom are household names and others you may not have heard of before, but I am sure their stories will inspire you. Part Three (Chapters 8–12) offers customizable applications for each of the four markers of success. You will learn how to assess your passion, develop a mentoring team, and find informal learning opportunities and people who will understand and empathize with your work and journey.

My goal is that this book serves as your mentor, guide, light, and motivator. You can succeed. This book will give you the tools to do so. Keep it close by and refer to it when you need a boost or reminder. Like a good friend and expert mentor, it will always be there for you and offer you suggestions, without telling you which choice to make. The decision will always be yours. I am excited about your journey. Let's roll.

References

Friedman, R (2021) *Decoding Greatness*, Simon & Schuster, New York

Gotian, R (2017) *Optimizing Success of Physician-Scientists*, EdD, Teachers College Columbia University

PART ONE

High achievers and success

01

What defines a high achiever?

Growing up, I never thought of myself as a high achiever. High achiever was a term applied to other people—Olympic athletes, astronauts, award-winning writers, global figures among others at the top of their field. In my mind, they had traits and characteristics that were distinct. Because they were extraordinary, they had different training and advanced pedigrees that allowed them to be perceived as all-knowing. As a result, they could achieve accolades that were utterly unattainable to the average person. In short, I was mesmerized by high achievers, but I was also very wrong.

As I grew older, I realized that high achievers are no different than the rest of us in that they have challenges, opportunities, fears and stressors, and they work hard, really hard, to overcome them. But what they do have that is different—and what can be learned—is their mindset (their motivation) and their approach (the how). High achievers have found something they are really good at and have invested their energy into studying, perfecting and refining it to the best of their ability. They are intrinsically motivated and passionate about pursuing this dream, driven by their own desire and curiosity, not an external judgment such as a diploma, promotion, or award.

They have three approaches to their success that are done in unison and build on their intrinsic motivation. High achievers have: 1) a strong work ethic, 2) a solid foundation that is constantly being reinforced, and 3) commitment to lifelong learning through informal means. The high achievers' unyielding work ethic and perseverance drive them to work smarter and harder than everyone around them. Despite all of their achievements and accolades, they still practice and reinforce the basic techniques that have led to their success. It worked for them at the beginning of their career, and they still practice the same process and procedures decades later as they know that it is a necessary and pivotal part of their foundation and success. Finally, while being considered the experts in their fields, the best of the best, high achievers realize there is always someone who knows more than them, and there is always something new to learn. High achievers are committed to lifelong learning, usually outside of the formal classroom.

Getting an 'A' in any academic class is difficult but not impossible. The same idea holds true in the workplace. If you put in the time, ask questions when you are unsure about something, you can do 'A' level work. You can achieve a grade of 90–95 percent. As Tom W. Jones, former Chairman and CEO of Citigroup's Global Investment Management, told me "Go for 100 percent, that is 5 percent more than everyone else. Compounded, that will make you stand out over time. Give 100 percent effort in the workplace, and people will notice your effort and achievements." That is how you become a high achiever. Most people who do well do not go for that extra 5 percent effort, which separates high achievers from the rest of the pack. That leaves the space on the top of the pyramid of success open and available to you if you are willing to put in the work.

What motivates high achievers?

Why strive to be a high achiever? I think a better question to ask yourself is why not? The high achievers I have studied strive for a life of significance where their work inspires others. Hopefully, the accolades of promotions, high salaries, and recognition will follow, but with all the exemplars, that is not why they went down this road. It was not for the Nobel or Olympic medal; it was because they found purpose in what they did, which led them to love the journey. They could not picture themselves doing anything else. Their motto—"Make your mark to leave this world better than you found it."

For most of my adult life, I surrounded myself with high achievers. I observed everything they did, how they converged upon new experiences, who they collaborated with, what calculated risks they took, and how they handled inevitable challenges. After studying high achievers for so long, I realized that most people who find purpose in what they do want to achieve more and be successful in their efforts. My mentor, Dr. Bert Shapiro, told me, "Do something important, not just interesting." In other words, if I was going to make an impact, I had to focus on something meaningful to many people, not just fascinating to me. Interestingly, Dr. Tony Fauci, who led the US response to the Covid-19 pandemic, told me the same thing when he shared how he decided which projects to pursue. Nobody starts their career aiming for a Nobel prize or Olympic gold medal or for the opportunity to fly to space. They know it exists, but those who make it do not usually have that as their initial goal. High achievers aim to make a difference, push boundaries, look into the unknown, and make positive changes.

But the path to being successful in something you care about can be daunting. This may be because the "how" of high achievers seems obscure and not apparent to most people.

Getting to the "how" of high achievement

To accomplish more, you need to overcome the "hidden curriculum" of unwritten rules and traditions that you are supposed to know, but nobody tells you (Sostrin, 2013). People will often rise to expectations, but they need to know what they are first. That is why I wrote this book, to reveal the "rules" or practices that high achievers abide by so that you can understand and apply these practices to your own career and achieve more.

Blending adult learning and management theory with the insights gleaned from over sixty interviews with extreme high achievers from multiple industries, I outline the success factors—the self-management traits that you can develop in order to become a high achiever in your chosen discipline. If you are reading this book, I have to believe that you want to succeed and are willing to put in the work. You just need clarity on what to do.

You will hear directly from Nobel laureates, astronauts, Olympic and NBA champions, Tony Award winners, senior military and government officials about what it took to achieve their success. As you hear what they say about their own experiences, consider their achievements as the tip of the iceberg and understand for yourself the motivation and approach they took to get there. Like an iceberg, their achievements are what lies above the waterline. What I uncover is everything you could not see but need to know if you are going to find your own success.

Obstacles for high achievers

Nearly every organization conducts annual performance evaluations of their employees. But what are they measuring (Wilson, 2012)? Human Resources and Compensation departments in organizations base their performance evaluations and rewards programs—and spend an inordinate amount of energy—on establishing baselines and getting people to average levels. In many companies, yearly objectives and goals are set, merit increases are awarded to those who achieve them based on an average score, and corrective action plans are developed for those below the baseline (Bloxham and Boyd, 2007; Kasworm et al, 2010). On grants, we report average scores, ages, and time to completion of goals. The baseline should not be a goal, but somehow that is what it has become. This level of mediocrity becomes frustrating to high achievers who never want to settle for being average. If everyone's goal is to aim for average, and you come in showing your potential as a high achiever, you will stand out.

Countless conference sessions, energy, and untold dollars are spent on the "leaky pipeline," referring to the predicament organizations face concerning the mass exodus of those who leave a specific career path. We seem to be so focused on holding on to people who do not want to be there. Instead, or in addition, we should spend more time on developing and retaining the high achievers, those whose work and productivity can more than compensate for those who leave the pipeline.

Nature versus nurture

Is success based on nature or nurture? The answer is that it is both. One thing is clear; you need to have a natural talent and passion for something. What you do with your untapped gift is up to you. You cannot force something that is not there, so being intrigued and proficient at something is a critical first step. Being lazy or wasting time will not make you successful, and it might be your first sign that this is not your true passion. If it were, you would not need pushing and prodding to get to work. It might take you a while to figure out where your natural talent lies, but that is where practice and exposure are paramount. With children, we often enroll them in countless after-school activities, buying uniforms for every athletic team they join. With time, they will shed most activities and gravitate toward others. As an adult, you need to do the same thing. Try many things out, and see what sticks.

You may start by finding an area that interests you, such as marketing, science, or entertainment. It should come naturally to you and be fun. You love everything about it, learn anything you can get your hands on, and think about it often. You read about it, talk to experts, watch YouTube videos, or listen to podcasts, to learn more. You do this because you want to, not because you have to. You are nurturing your natural talent. With incredibly arduous work, you can get to the A+ part of the pyramid of success. Reading this book will help you identify what you are passionate about versus simply really good at doing. There is a difference. You can be good at many things, but you will compromise your success if you do not enjoy doing them. We will talk more about this in Chapter 4 and there will also be a Passion Audit that you can complete to help you clarify what you enjoy doing. Once you do, you can identify goals and specific plans to achieve them. There are many talented people around, but few nurture their natural gifts with the focus and intention of becoming an elite high achiever.

Success is a moving target

Can you define success? While we often claim certain people are successful, putting words and labels to their success is not as easy as it may appear. I learned that the definition changes based on who you ask. Success is a moving target. Lots of research, interviews, and surveys that ultimately led to my doctoral dissertation made me realize that success is measured differently based on who you ask (Gotian, 2017). Years later, that tenet still holds true. To add to the conundrum, the definition of success also varies based on gender and rank in an organization (Gotian and Andersen, 2020). Ultimately, we recognize it when we see it. Success early in your career looks different than success later in your career. It is a moving target.

There is no one definition of success in many fields, thereby making it difficult to track, plan training, or predict success. If we cannot even come up with a commonly agreed-upon definition of success, how can we develop more people to reach these undisclosed markers? This is another segment of the hidden curriculum. Knowing that success is a moving target, exemplars approach things methodically, working to achieve one milestone at a time, every step carefully planned and executed. They are laser-focused on what is needed to reach the next objective, beat their latest time, get one more thing accomplished. It is not about doing everything; rather, it is about doing one thing exceptionally well.

I started my research with the population I knew best, namely academic physician-scientists. To consider success, I asked these academics to think forward and backward. Who do they consider successful? What would a person need to do to be considered successful? The answers turned out to be a mixed bag of variables with some common themes. The more junior faculty listed measures of success they would need to get promoted, such as publish more papers or get more grants. The more senior faculty I interviewed offered answers that they would want to be known for, namely their legacy. They mentioned awards, impact, national recognition (Gotian, 2017; Gotian and Andersen, 2020). This finding is interesting, as they likely would not have gotten to consider their legacy if they had not done what the junior faculty had first to accomplish.

The idea that what is measured is managed is often attributed to Peter Drucker, the prolific management thinker and author. Unfortunately, you cannot always calculate success. While a Nobel Prize or Olympic medal is an obvious measure of success, not all success attributes are quantifiable. There is only one Olympic gold medal at each of the Games and up to three Nobel Prizes in each category per year. There is a limit to how many flights go to space and how many astronauts can fit in a space shuttle. What about everyone else, including those who did not get to compete on an international stage or fly to orbit? Are they any less successful? This book will share the stories of many luminaries who won national and international accolades and are household names. Conversely, others did not win the most famous awards but moved the needle in their field, so much so that their work impacts thousands, often millions of people. They are unsung heroes.

While we can quantify objective measures of success, such as the number of awards or grants, they are not always an accurate definition as there are people who did not win famous prizes who had a profound impact on their field. Subjective measures of success are equally tricky, sometimes even impossible, to measure. It is essential to identify and recognize the value in both. If we can recognize and label the achievement, we hope to attain or impact we would like to have, it gives us something we can work toward. It offers something tangible which we can identify and develop into a goal.

The journey is more telling than the destination

I quickly learned that the path to success was significantly more interesting than the achievement. How the success was achieved unearths the power of mindsets that can be replicated. The journey to success for physician-scientists was fascinating, and I quickly found myself curious to learn if the mindsets for success were transferable to other industries: they were. I realized that an astronaut is not much different from an Olympic champion. That was my a-ha moment. That is when I realized that we could all learn to be successful if we just have a blueprint, if only we knew what to do. This book will share the four mindsets and skillsets for success found among high achievers. The stories of Nobel laureates, astronauts, CEOs, Olympic, Major League Baseball (MLB), and National Basketball Association (NBA) champions, as well as some high achievers you may not have heard of, will all underscore the four important lessons.

The extreme high achievers share a similar mindset and approach.

Their mindset

High achievers are intrinsically motivated to pursue their chosen profession. They cannot visualize themselves doing anything else. They love it and would do it for free if they could.

Their approach

STRONG WORK ETHIC

High achievers have a deep-rooted work ethic and are always looking to get better at their craft. They recognize perfection, like success, is a moving target, but they put in more time and effort than anyone else to produce the best work they can do within the constraints before them. In martial arts, it is said that a black belt is just a white belt that never quit. There is no such thing as an overnight success. It takes incredible focus and determination, and there are many trials and errors, and times filled on the mat of falling and getting back up again. While people may dabble in multiple areas of concentration early in their career, it is sustained focus on one specific area that has led them to greatness.

STRONG FOUNDATION

High achievers have a strong foundation which they are constantly reinforcing. They do not rest on their laurels, nor do they ever think basic tasks are beneath them. High achievers still do the same fundamental drills and tasks they did early in their careers, albeit with better equipment.

LIFELONG LEARNING

Despite all of their accomplishments and terminal degrees, high achievers are constantly learning from everyone and everything around them. They are observing, reading, listening, and talking to anyone who could provide valuable information. They rely on a mentorship team that has always been by their side. Today, all of them pay it forward by helping others in the best way they know how, from individual mentorship to running programs and non-profits.

Motivations of high achievers: love what you do

Apolo Anton Ohno, with eight Olympic medals, is the most decorated winter Olympian. Before he graced the Olympic stage, he was a state champion swimmer, a baseball player, and a roller skater. All of this was done before he ever made indoor short-track speed skating his domain. He told me that while he was athletic and good at all of these other sports, he never loved them. But he *loved* everything about short-track speed skating. As he made the turns at lightning speed, putting his body nearly parallel with the ice, he truly felt as if that was where he was supposed to be. He found his passion early and dedicated his life to it from the age of fourteen. He lived, breathed, and slept short-track speed skating. At fourteen, he moved away from his single-parent father, who raised him, and went to live with other speed skaters, years his senior, at the training center in Lake Placid. He competed nationally and internationally, including at three Olympic Games. He was all in; he did not do anything else. He missed out on traditional teen years as he was skating with the team. He missed his high school graduation ceremony and never got to go to prom and don a tuxedo. He was constantly training for the next big race.

The approach of high achievers: always learning

How many times have you been told to play nicely in the proverbial sandbox? Learning to work with others and, more importantly, to collaborate with others is critical to success. There is an African proverb that says, "If you want to go fast, go alone. If you want to go far, go together." If your goal in being successful is to make an impact and have a life of significance, you need to surround yourself with others. Be the least interesting person in the room. Open yourself up to learn from anyone around you. All of the high achievers underscored the need to work with and learn from others. You know your niche well, but teaming up with others who can show you your blind spots or give you ideas on enhancing your work is pivotal. Being open to joining forces is a crucial variable on the road to success. The isolating feeling of success, which can be haunting at times, can be mitigated by having partners in your pursuit.

It was a true collaboration that led Drs. Mike Brown and Joe Goldstein to win the 1985 Nobel Prize in Physiology or Medicine. They met in the mid-1960s as internal medicine residents, the training you do after medical school, at Massachusetts General Hospital (MGH) in Boston (Nobel Prize, nd). They quickly became friends and were drawn together because they were both interested in the underlying physiology. They questioned why a particular patient would have a specific disease.

During the midnight meals at MGH, the residents would gather and embrace the quiet time. Brown and Goldstein would discuss the patients they admitted, their diseases, what the literature said, and the underlying science. They became friends and were both accepted into research roles at the National Institutes of Health (NIH) during the Vietnam War. Goldstein was in the Heart Institute and had to care for two patients at the NIH: two little children, a six-year-old girl and her eight-year-old brother. They were both hospitalized at the NIH because they had had heart attacks due to the cholesterol level in their blood which was ten times above normal. The high cholesterol in the children was a very rare situation. Brown and Goldstein knew it was genetic because the patients were brother and sister. They tried to lower their cholesterol and put them on a cholesterol-free diet. "They had nothing but rice and vegetables and fruits for six months," said Brown.

The cholesterol did not decrease, so Brown and Goldstein doubled down on their growing partnership. Together, they decided they were going to figure this out. This was a question they could not ignore. What was the cause? Nobody knew anything about what controls the level of cholesterol in the blood. Goldstein had already committed to returning to Dallas after his stint was over at the NIH. "If we were going to work together and solve this problem, I had to move to Dallas. Dallas, Texas in 1971 was not high on my list," Brown said.

It was even less high on his wife's list. Brown and his wife were New Yorkers. When they were at the NIH, they thought Bethesda, Maryland, where the NIH is located, was the deep South. The idea of moving to Texas seven years after President Kennedy had been shot and killed in Dallas was not enticing. Brown went to visit the University of Texas, Southwestern, and was impressed by what he saw. He was quickly surrounded by physician-scientists: his people.

Brown moved to Dallas, and the research on solving the problem of this genetic disease continued with intense fury. Brown and Goldstein were able to figure out how the body controls cholesterol and what went wrong in this disease. Those insights led to the development of drugs to lower cholesterol. "We had the rare, rare, rare but extremely rewarding privilege of not only doing basic science but also doing something that had great medical relevance and helped to develop a treatment for the disease," exclaimed Brown. That collaboration led Brown and Goldstein to win the Nobel Prize in Physiology or Medicine in 1985. They were passionate about their work, traveled to what seemed like the ends of the earth, all so that they could make an impact and do something of significance.

When you collaborate, you learn from others and enhance your success. Joe Jacobi won the Olympic gold medal in canoeing at the 1992 Summer Olympics in Barcelona. He told me that the time he trained with the world champions in Washington, DC, along the Potomac River, made all the difference. He said:

> They were elite in the sport, and they were good people who I learned so much from. Everyone contributed something to the team culture. All kinds of people can make contributions to a performance culture and community. They need to enjoy being there and the principles on which the group is formed. Our group was formed on the idea that we wanted to be the best in the world. We did that by competing with each other, the best in the world, world champions. Ultimately, competitions were easier than practices.

Try anyway

Trying to do something that no one else has done takes guts and requires you to be bold and courageous and is a defining feature of a high achiever. It takes self-confidence, the belief in yourself that you can do it because you have a track record of doing similar things. It also takes self-efficacy, the belief that you can do something even though you have never done it before. It means making a decision, going with it, and not backing down, no matter what the external naysayers or the voice in your head tells you to do. It allows you to approach challenges differently and stick with it, which ultimately helps you become a high achiever.

Remember Dr. Mike Brown, the Nobel laureate who moved to Dallas with his friend Joe Goldstein? That pairing almost did not happen. Brown made a bold move that changed the trajectory of his career. Brown attended the University of Pennsylvania for medical school. At the time, he knew little about science. He needed to earn money during the summer, so he found a job at SmithKline, a pharmaceutical company in Philadelphia. He had what he referred to as a "trivial study looking at intestinal motility in rats." He was envious of his friends who did not need the money and worked in interesting labs at the medical school. By his own admission, "It turned out that job, doing that stupid project was the secret of my future success." He spent every summer during medical school at SmithKline. They were trying to find a drug that would be a treatment for ulcers. Brown did experiments where he measured how far charcoal had gone in the intestines of rats.

Brown's friends were all doing sophisticated projects and submitted abstracts to the prominent and prestigious scientific meetings. Brown felt he had nothing. So he went over all of his data and realized he was able to write a mathematical equation predicting the location of a meal in the digestive system after food consumption. He felt it was trivial but wrote and submitted an abstract to a small conference in Atlantic City. In science, if you do not present and later publish your work, it is as if it never happened. His proposal was accepted and he presented his work in front of a tiny audience of twenty people.

Two years after that presentation, he applied to work at the NIH. It was the most competitive position to get because everybody wanted to be there instead of going off to fight in the Vietnam War. At the time, the NIH had a matching system to pair people. Each applicant completed a form listing their top thirteen choices of which labs they would like to join. Brown wrote his top thirteen choices and then at the bottom decided he was going to write in a fourteenth choice. There was not an option to list fourteen labs; he just wrote it in. Bold move. Ultimately, thirteen labs rejected him, but the fourteenth lab invited him to join; the lab was a write-in and technically was not a legal part of the process. It was a courageous move that paid off.

After working in the lab for a while, he asked the professor, "Why did you pick me? Nobody else picked me." The faculty member had been one of the twenty people in that small audience in Atlantic City and thought that the project and solution Brown proposed using math to measure food in the digestion process was important and showed promise. He remembered Brown and his project.

If Brown had not had the fortitude to apply to present at a conference he thought at the time was insignificant, he might never have had the opportunity to work at the NIH. He would have been sent instead to Vietnam to fight in the war. He had the confidence and self-efficacy to write in an additional name on his intake form. He was all about doing things in non-conventional ways. It was that courage and tenacity that served him well his entire career.

It is one chapter, not the whole story

You would think with all of the awards they won, honors they received, and television appearances, the egos of these extreme high achievers would be enormous. That was not the case with the exemplars I interviewed. They were extremely humble. The Olympic champions told me that winning the gold medal was *a* day in their lives, not their entire lives. The years leading up to it were spent in training, falling and getting up, getting hurt, and working on getting healed. The Nobel laureates were excited about their prize but more emphatic about the journey, failed experiments, and the long line of people who helped them along the way.

When I interviewed 1981 Nobel prize winner Dr. Torsten Wiesel, he had an unframed photo of himself with former US President George W. Bush laying on the bookshelf—not framed, not on display. It was just sitting there among other books and papers like it was no big deal.

When I interview Olympians, I always ask them to show me their Olympic medal. None of them have a trophy room, nor are the medals out on display in their home or office. Short-track speed skating Olympic champion, Apolo Anton Ohno, kept his medals for years in a sock drawer. I was shocked they were not on display. When I asked which was his favorite, Ohno grabbed his silver medal from the 2002 Olympic Games in Salt Lake City. I was surprised he did not show me one of his gold medals; after all, he is the most decorated winter Olympian. He explained that the silver was his first Olympic medal: "It was supposed to be gold. I was knocked down two seconds before the finish line. It was parallel to the state the country was in, six months after 9/11/01." Ohno got up and scrambled. He did not lose the gold; he won the silver (Gotian, 2020a).

Most of the Nobel laureates in medicine and chemistry whom I interviewed are physicians. Most have not seen patients in decades as they are dedicated full-time to their research. Ironically, none of them gave up their medical license. They still pay the annual premiums. When I asked them why, they gave me two reasons. The emotional toll of getting a medical degree and finishing the multi-year training is not something that you ever forget or can easily discard. The hard work, sleepless nights, and missed family engagements left an invisible scar. The medical license is a reminder of the journey (Gotian, 2020b).

Second, they hold on to the medical license as a form of a back-up plan. Even with the Nobel Prize and their place in scientific history cemented, they are continuing their work, writing grants and papers. There is still a tinge of a feeling that it could all disappear one day. The federal funds can dry up, or their research can go out of vogue. If they have their medical license, they can always go back to seeing patients, their initial motivation, their roots. That job will always be there.

The high-achieving mindset makes them good mentors

In his book *Management Challenges for the 21st Century*, Peter Drucker suggested that people do what they see (Drucker, 1999). Further research by Anna-Lucia Mackay in her book *The Four Mindsets* suggests that high achievers are looking for positive role models (Mackay, 2015). It was therefore important that the high achievers featured in this book could serve as role models for the next generation. They are good people who are paying it forward.

High achievers like to support, mentor, and train the next generation of high achievers. Although one person often gets the medal, high achievers recognize that their path to success was not a solo journey. Many believed in and supported them long before they realized their own talent. It is, therefore, no surprise that so many of them train the next generation of high achievers.

Olympic champion Joe Jacobi lives outside of Barcelona, overlooking the river where he won his gold medal in canoeing. On that same course where he won his gold medal, he is now teaching future Olympic paddlers. Jacobi knows every corner and depth of that river. He trained with the absolute best and brings those experiences to a whole new generation of canoers and kayakers.

Nobel laureate Dr. Bob Lefkowitz lectures at Duke School of Medicine with a talk titled *How To Deal With Failure and Rejection*. Lefkowitz is most vulnerable in his talk as he shares what he calls "the meanest spirited, nasty letters of rejection and reviews of papers" that he ever received. Once the sting of the harsh words wears off, he takes a closer look at the criticism. Lefkowitz teaches the students what he learned from these comments and how he rebuilt the papers based on the feedback. Ultimately, he shows the students the final version of the article, which he revamped based on the commentary he received. The paper was eventually published in a high-profile journal.

There are many objective and subjective metrics of success. Those we can see and those we cannot. Those we recognize and measure and those that cannot be calculated but are equally as integral. As I looked for elite high achievers, I was cognizant that while they had measurable success metrics, some of which I described above, many are more challenging to recognize. Still, without them, they would not have succeeded. Not every award equals success. It is the journey that is the most telling. Most people know the success stories, but not always the failures they endured and how they came back from them.

I wrote this book with the intention that you can pick up any chapter and learn something new. Keep it by your nightstand and thumb through the inspirational stories and tips you could use to elevate your success or give your motivation a boost. You can learn to achieve success. It is up to you to take the first step.

COACHING QUESTIONS

What is one thing you feel you are intrinsically motivated to pursue? Can you make that your next goal?

KEY TAKEAWAYS

1 High achievers are intrinsically motivated to pursue their passion.

2 Success is a moving target, so it needs to be reevaluated and redefined on a regular basis.

3 Extreme high achievers have a similar mindset and approach to achieving success.

4 High achievers are not afraid to fail and feel they always need to at least try.

5 High achievers are humble and do not let their accolades define them.

6 High achievers actively mentor and pay it forward.

References

Bloxham, S and Boyd, P (2007) *Developing Effective Assessment in Higher Education: A practical guide*, Berkshire, UK, Open University Press

Drucker, PF (1999) *Management Challenges for the 21st Century*, New York, Harper Collins Publishers, Inc

Gotian, R (2017) *Optimizing Success of Physician-Scientists*, EdD, Teachers College Columbia University

Gotian, R (2020a) Olympic champion Apolo Ohno explains how to reevaluate after a loss, *Forbes*, https://www.forbes.com/sites/ruthgotian/2020/11/10/olympic-champion-apolo-ohno-explains-how-to-reevaluate-after-a-loss/ (archived at https://perma.cc/FFW8-QQ82)

Gotian, R (2020b) Why I Stand, *Academic Medicine*, 95(2), p 175

Gotian, R and Andersen, OS (2020) How perceptions of a successful physician-scientist varies with gender and academic rank: toward defining physician-scientist's success, *BMC Medical Education*, 20

Kasworm, C, Rose, AD and Ross-Gordon, JM (2010) *Handbook of Adult and Continuing Education*, United States of America, SAGE Publications, Inc

Mackay, A-L (2015) *The Four Mindsets*, Australia, John Wiley & Sons Australia, Ltd

Nobel Prize (nd) *The Nobel Prize: Michael S. Brown, Biographical* https://www.nobelprize.org/prizes/medicine/1985/brown/biographical/ (archived at https://perma.cc/JTX8-SAL2)

Sostrin, J (2013) *Success Stories from the Hidden Side of Work*, New York, Palgrave Macmillan

Wilson, JP (ed.) (2012) *International Human Resource Development*, United Kingdom: Kogan Page

02

Controlling your destiny

"Do something important, not just interesting." My mentor's words are etched in my brain and have become my guide. After studying all of the extreme high achievers, it became evident that, subconsciously, they had the same guiding light. Their reason for achieving more was an unquenched curiosity, drive, and ability to have a significant impact.

Every day I ask people what it means to them to be successful. Most people recognize successful people when they see them, but you have to press them for a definition. My initial research helped me crystalize the three areas of excellence one must achieve to be identified as a high achiever. Namely, they need to advance their field, mentor the next generation and receive recognition for their accomplishments. Rarely, if ever, will anyone say that you need to win the Nobel Prize or compete in the Olympics, let alone win a medal, to be successful. You do not even need to fly to space. It is so much deeper than that. It is about connecting the dots, seeing what others do not yet see or appreciate, paying it forward, building relationships, and being a good citizen. To be successful, you need to make an impact. Along the way, you need to appreciate that success is a moving target and there is always more to try and achieve. As executive coach Dr. Marshall Goldsmith taught me, it is the difference between having a time-bound ambition and a long-term aspiration.

Control your work, time, and career

By being a high achiever, you get to have greater control over your work, time, and career. You select which projects you wish to pursue, who you want to work with and, equally as necessary, to whom and what you will say "no." Your passion for the topic or idea and ability to make an impact becomes your driving force. When you become a high achiever, you have greater control over your destiny.

In 1984, Dr. Tony Fauci became the National Institute of Allergy and Infectious Diseases (NIAID) director at the National Institutes of Health (NIH), a position he still holds today. To many during the Covid pandemic, he was the face of reason and truth. He led a nation through a challenging time as a member of the Trump Administration's Coronavirus Taskforce and Chief Medical Advisor to President Joe Biden, and a member of the White House Covid-19 Response Team. However, to scores of physicians and scientists, Fauci was well known long before this latest global crisis.

President Joe Biden is the seventh president Fauci has advised through various pandemics. I once heard Fauci deliver a riveting presentation describing the various global health crises since he took office in 1984. In detail, he reviewed each global pandemic, shared how many people and which countries were impacted, which president had to deal with which pandemic, and the aftermath of each crisis. Fauci had a hand in responding to every significant crisis, including HIV, SARS, Ebola, and Zika. By the time Covid rolled around, I knew it was not his first rodeo.

Long before Covid, Fauci made essential contributions to understanding how HIV destroys the body's defenses, causing it to be vulnerable to deadly infections. He was a critical player in developing treatments for people with HIV. Fauci was one of the lead architects of PEPFAR—President's Emergency Plan for AIDS Relief—a program that saved millions of lives. He studied HIV and helped to develop treatments. That is a perfect example of pushing boundaries and changing the status quo. He advanced his field in ways that will benefit the current and future generations in immeasurable ways.

Fauci is one of the top-cited scientists in the world. That means other people in their published work reference Fauci's published scientific work. Do this enough times, and you get what is called a high *h-index*. Most scientists and physician-scientists aim for an h-index in the double digits. If you want the Nobel prize, aim for 70. Fauci's h-index is 221—triple digits (Schreiber, 2019; Cybermetrics Lab and Consejo Superior de Investigaciones Científicas (CSIC), 2021)! According to the NIH's website, Fauci is ranked as the 32nd most-cited living researcher. According to the Web of Science, in the immunology field, Fauci ranks seventh out of more than 1.8 million authors by total citation count between 1980 and January 2020 (National Institutes of Health, 2021). Generations of physicians and scientists have studied Fauci's work. Next time you go to your doctor, ask her if she has the book *Harrison's Principles of Internal Medicine*. Good chance she will, as it is one of the foundational books every medical student and resident uses and has used for generations.

In 2008, Fauci was awarded the Presidential Medal of Freedom by President George W. Bush but has yet to win the Nobel Prize. Fauci has done work he is proud of, passionate about, and has made an enormous impact on the world. He could stop if he wanted to, but he loves what he does and finds the work important.

Imagine being one of the people who gets to work with Fauci. Consider how much you would learn and the scientific progress you could make. Since Fauci has set such a high bar for himself, it elevates the expectations and culture for those around him. If you are successful, it becomes an unwritten expectation that everyone around you should strive for more. You can single-handedly change the culture of a department or organization so that instead of aiming for average, the group norm is to aim for excellence each and every time. Being average becomes the floor, not the ceiling.

Work because you want to

While most people try to avoid failure, high achievers are strongly motivated to achieve and fully understand that setbacks are part of the path to success. They are natural problem-solvers and enjoy the challenge of solving a dilemma that everyone else finds daunting. If it were easy, everyone would do it. They instead live for the challenge of finding a solution that has eluded everyone else. The more complex the problem, the more excited they get (Tobak, 2015). The chase becomes almost as exciting as the win.

Fear of success is legitimate because, for many, it is an unknown and can lead to imposter syndrome, the fear of being exposed as a fraud (Clance and Imes, 1978; Gotian, 2020a, 2021e; Gotian and McGinty, 2020). Those who avoid failure are more focused on protecting themselves from embarrassment and a sense of incompetence. They may shield themselves from uneasiness and a sense of ineptitude by procrastinating, as they would rather people doubt their effort than their ability. Worse yet, they may participate in behaviors that can hinder their success, such as partying the night before a big deadline (Beuke, 2011; Boyes, 2018). Conversely, those who focus on high achievement do their best to control their environment and recognize their success is dependent on their effort, persistence, and initiative. They outwork everyone.

The odds were against National Football League (NFL) Hall of Fame running back Curtis Martin ever making it to a national stage. He grew up under the worst circumstances, where even coming home alive or unscathed was a significant accomplishment. His father was abusive and later absent. At fifteen years of age, Martin was held at gunpoint, and by the age of nineteen, over thirty of his friends and family members had been murdered. The NFL was not something on his radar and not something he could even begin to consider. Staying alive was his main focus.

At his mother's insistence, Martin was partaking in after-school activities just to be able to stay off the streets. These extracurricular programs kept him out of danger and away from people who were looking for trouble. His mother told him to pick any sport when he was in high school; he picked football as a default. The more he played, the better he became. His natural skill and ability led Martin to earn an athletic scholarship to play at the University of Pittsburgh. He did not take football very seriously back then as for him, it was solely a way to get an education and have a place to live.

Recognizing his reality, Martin did not believe he would live to adulthood. One day, he went to his church and asked God to help him stay alive past his 21st birthday. In Martin's world, that would have been a significant accomplishment. When that wish was fulfilled, Martin began to take his life more seriously. He realized God had held up his end of the bargain, so he needed to take control of his life and make success a default outcome. His mindset shifted, and he became a different type of person and athlete. Instead of football being part of his routine, it now became his commitment. During practice, Martin was all in. He worked out vigorously in the weight room and paid close attention to his nutrition, hydration, and sleep cycle.

Sadly, injuries prevented him from playing many games in college. He knew football would be his ticket to a better life, so he kept looking for ways to improve his workouts and techniques. He met a trainer who pushed him harder than he had ever worked before. The trainer took him to a remote location, free of distractions, to focus on his goals. In the woods of Pennsylvania, as he trained with someone who believed in his potential, Martin's internal fire was ignited, and he was doing everything he could to keep the flames blazing.

Martin managed to get the attention of the person who organized the Senior Bowl, which brought top college students to play against each other. Martin did not initially earn a spot on the team but was told he could join the practice. He decided to stand out by out-practicing everyone. When finally allowed to play, Martin was placed in the fullback position, a role he had never experienced before. He was way too small to play that position but did not care. He played so hard and put so much effort into his practice and performance that the talent scouts had no choice but to notice.

Realizing someone talented was on the field, the scouts asked to see Martin play in the running back position, the role he played all throughout college. He was completely in his comfort zone. Martin played hard and shined. He was later invited to play in an All-Star game, where again, he pushed himself harder than ever before. This time, the NFL scouts noticed Martin.

Coach Bill Parcells of the New England Patriots sent a trainer to give him what Martin calls the "workout from hell." He was evaluated based on that regimented training. Martin knew that the scouts, trainers, and coaches examined everything he did with a magnifying lens; he also knew that it was done to make him better, stronger, and faster. Martin did what he does best— outwork everyone. He was never going to be faulted for not trying hard enough. His work ethic was unwavering.

One day, Curtis Martin received a phone call from Bill Parcells asking him if he would like to be a New England Patriot. "Yes, sir," said Martin. Curtis Martin, the boy from Pittsburgh, Pennsylvania, who grew up with a plagued upbringing, was drafted in the third round of the NFL draft.

Martin's pastor taught him that football was how Martin was going to have an impact, and it was the vehicle to do well in the world. From that moment on, Curtis Martin took football more seriously than ever before. He played professionally for eleven years on two different teams and only missed one game. In his first year in the NFL, he won Rookie of the Year. He retired in 2006 and in 2012 was inducted into the NFL Hall of Fame. The Super Bowl was never Curtis Martin's focus. He wanted to do the best he could and outwork everyone else. "Whatever you fear in life become your boundaries," Martin said. He grew up with too many predetermined barriers and knew he would have to work extra hard to overcome the overt and covert hurdles. Curtis Martin wants his name and reputation to be his biggest asset. He wants to be known for his work ethic and for succeeding despite the circumstances of his upbringing.

Be part of the solution

Being around such people is inspiring and quite a learning experience. Watching them diagnose a problem and work through various potential solutions is a lesson that can only be learned by observation. Being a high achiever affords you an opportunity to be a role model to an entire generation of people. People will watch how you approach a problem, find a solution and deal with difficult situations. They will observe to see if you respond or react. In turn, they will learn to control their own destiny by being part of the solution instead of waiting for others to solve the problem.

Being a high achiever means you are able to do things others find daunting or avoid doing. You see a gap in knowledge or achievement and you work toward filling that need. Waiting for others to solve a problem you have the ability to handle is inconceivable. You are not afraid to put in the work if it means finding the right solution. Often, you will take the knowledge that is already being used and apply it differently.

Throughout the book, you will learn about many extreme high achievers who devoted their lives to being part of a solution. You will meet physician-scientists who made discoveries because they could not allow a problem to be overlooked, government officials who brought people together to lead innovation, astronauts who reimagined space travel, Olympic champions who forever changed the face of their sport, and Paralympic champions who use their gold medal platform to drive change for people with disabilities. High achievers do not hear the words "no," "can't" or "won't" (Gotian, 2020c). Instead, they hear "not yet." Their drive to a solution is not about one day, it is about making today day one.

Love your job

When you get to be that creative physically, emotionally and intellectually, you tend to be happier. High achievers tend to be more content at work and less likely to leave their employers (Willyerd, 2014). When treated well, you will see high achievers have a strong loyalty to their organization. Astronauts tend to stay with NASA for years, decades even. Top NBA and NFL players become household names because they stayed with the organization and continued to play the game for years, despite the grueling workouts and travel schedule. NFL Hall of Famer Curtis Martin played for over a decade with only two teams. Former Chief Astronaut Peggy Whitson joined NASA in 1989 as a research biochemist. In 1996, she was selected as an astronaut candidate. She retired in 2018, twenty-nine years after first starting to work at NASA. There is an immense sense of loyalty when high achievers are recognized and allowed to flourish.

High achievers tend to be more self-directed in their learning, reaching out to appropriate resources such as people or programs to fill in any gaps in their knowledge (Merriam et al 2007; Knowles, 1980; Brockett and Hiemstra, 1991; Brookfield, 2009). They are not afraid to say "I do not know" or "This is not clear to me." Being vulnerable, learning more, and asking for guidance is completely natural to them, as they believe that they still have more to learn. They do not focus on what was; instead, they work toward what can be.

Fear not trying more than you fear failing

As a high achiever, you likely do not suffer from "status quo bias," the idea of being comfortable with the status quo; the belief of leaving well enough alone (Fleming et al, 2010; Gotian, 2021b). Quite the opposite: you are charged by challenge and change. High achievers tend to seek out environments that offer the additional challenges they need to develop even higher levels of competence and differentiate themselves from others (Czikszentmihayli, 1975; Spence and Helmreich, 1983; Kanfer and Heggestad, 1990; Rynes and Connerley, 1993). They place a higher priority on interesting and challenging work (Trank et al, 2002).

Not trying is not an option for high achievers. They fear not trying more than they fear failing. Not achieving success immediately or even failing is considered a learning opportunity for the high achievers. They recognize that success is a moving target. It is never about the ultimate goal; the focus is always on the *next* goal.

A recent study of entrepreneurs, scientists, and even terrorist organizations found that people who experience failure early often become more successful than their counterparts who achieve early success (Yin et al, 2019). Embrace the challenges that come your way, as there will be a learning opportunity embedded within each hurdle. Ultimately, you will realize that as a high achiever, you will start to believe that you can overcome the obstacle. Your focus will then transfer from *if* you will succeed to *how* you will achieve more. It becomes a complete shift in mindset which then allows you to focus on solutions instead of dwelling on the problems. Your ability to overcome previous hiccups serves as a reminder of what you can achieve with focus and determination. Every obstacle will teach you something new and introduce you to new people and opportunities.

That desire to find the answer or hit the next milestone is a fire that burns deeply within high achievers. They work hard to quench the eternal thirst for knowledge and to do better today than they did yesterday. The process produces meaningful experiences and memories, which are a constant source of support (Lafair, 2016). Each of the high achievers remembers exactly where they were when they achieved something amazing, from a scientific breakthrough to an Olympic medal. They can vividly recall where they were and what they felt. Decades later, they still have a visceral response to the memories.

When they are ready to leave, high achievers have more options open to them in the marketplace and have a faster track to the C-Suite (Willyerd, 2014; Wong, 2017; Lafair, 2016). Not satisfied with average, they seek out environments where they can surround themselves with other equally motivated high performers. Being surrounded by other high achievers makes the work and learning environment more stimulating to them (Stross, 1996). They enjoy attacking challenges together with others who enjoy the pursuit of solutions and new knowledge, as opposed to fearing them. Together, they have shared values and social identities (Mael and Ashforth, 1995; Freiberg and Freiberg, 1997).

For high achievers, feedback is an opportunity for enhancement so they place a high value on getting reactions in real time (Gotian, 2020b). For them to enhance their work, feedback is critical and worthwhile (Ashford and Cummings, 1983). Every piece of information is viewed with an opportunity to get better, stronger, faster, and more creative; it is never a critique. It allows them to think differently. Any edge is considered beneficial and they constantly seek this additional source of advice. They are thinking beyond the immediate milestone to the long term. They know they are all in as far as their career is concerned, and will do anything they can to be better.

GROW model

Subconsciously, high achievers are always accessing what coaches call the GROW Model (Alexander, 2006; Alexander and Renshaw, 2005). They work through the steps of identifying their goals, recognizing the limitations and opportunities in their current situation, and strategically deciding on their next steps. Note, the 'O' can have two meanings:

Goals: What are your short- and long-term goals? What do you want to achieve in one, three, and five years?

Reality: What is the current reality? What is occurring right now?

Options: What are the options before you? What could you do?

Obstacles: What obstacles are standing in your way?

Will: What will you do next? What steps have you decided to take?

Deciding when to walk away from it all

High achievers have an unwavering determination which lets them decide when they need to back down or walk away from an opportunity or even their career, which they love. Having the power to make that decision for themselves might be reason alone to try to become a high achiever. Your future, destiny, and legacy are within your complete control. Every athlete and astronaut knew when it was time to retire. They felt it in their bones and left the career they loved without any regret. They used their high-achieving career as a launching pad for their second career.

Nicole Stott is a retired NASA astronaut, aquanaut, aeronautical engineer and painter, who spent 104 days in space. She was in line to fly to space again but asked herself three questions first:

1 Did she *need* to fly to space again?

2 The astronaut job on the ground allowed her to travel to incredible places and have unusual experiences. Would she be satisfied without doing those things?

3 She realized the people she worked with were creative, technical, and doing life-changing work. Would it be okay if she did not get to work with them side by side regularly?

Stott recognized that she would take on a new adventure by stepping away from the current one, which is precisely what she did. She now combines her love for space and art as the founding director of the Space for Art Foundation. Stott did not leave a career she loved; she took what she had learned and experienced and used it in a new dimension. It fueled her passions in new and creative ways.

Curtis Martin, the NFL Hall of Famer, retired in 2005 due to an injury. He played for over a decade and knew he had given it his all. Martin always wanted his name, reputation, and relationships he built over his life to be his most valuable assets. He leveraged that in his post-football career to launch new businesses in the insurance and private equity market.

Your network is your net worth

High achievers amass a massive network, which includes countless people both within and outside their industry. Many of those contacts are high achievers as well. There is a level of trust and understanding between them, which allows them the opportunity to gather together, collaborate, ask questions, and hear perspectives. Every single high achiever mentioned their network as a source of potential prospects, including jobs and mentors. They call upon each other for speaking, investing, and consulting engagements, allowing them to travel the world. High achievers enjoy surrounding themselves with people from their network as they are always learning something new. It is not a competition; instead, it is camaraderie. They are consistently helping others, paying it forward, and involving people from their network to contribute to great causes ranging from teaching our youth to financial endowments.

Being at the forefront of change

High achievers can produce up to 400 percent more than the average employee (O'Boyle and Aguinis; 2012; Willyerd, 2014). They positively impact productivity, innovation, and motivation. Being part of this elite group lets you be at the forefront of change and surrounds you with all the movers and shakers on a similar mission. You will be engulfed by people who find solutions to problems, not whine about what did not go their way. As a litmus test to see if you are a high achiever or a dreamer, consider the following (Denning, 2017; Gotian, 2021a):

1 Dreamers talk about what they should do; high achievers just do it. Dreamers talk about "one day," while high achievers focus on "day one."

2 Dreamers over-plan; high achievers act and adjust as the situation changes.

3 Dreamers babble; high achievers are clear and concise in their message. They know their audience and message and can get to the point quickly.

4 Dreamers have many unrelated goals; high achievers are laser-focused on their one goal.

5 Dreamers talk more than they listen; high achievers listen more than they talk.

6 Dreamers give up when faced with a challenge; high achievers know they will overcome the challenge. It is never a question of "if," so they focus on "how" to overcome the latest hurdle.

Helping others at scale

As a high achiever, your accomplishments, knowledge, and network will let you help others at scale. You are in a position where your words and actions matter, people will listen, and you can serve as a role model for an entire generation. Two-time NBA champion, Zaza Pachulia, opened a basketball academy for 1,400 children in his home country of Georgia. Nobel laureates routinely give keynote speeches that inspire young scientists. Olympic champion Apolo Ohno wrote a motivational book, and Paralympic champion Candace Cable uses her notoriety as an athlete as a platform to fight for disability access around the globe. Founder and former CEO of Build-A-Bear Workshop, Maxine Clark, started foundations and mentors new entrepreneurs. I have spent countless hours interviewing those who appear in the book and found them to be humble and always looking for opportunities to pay it forward and serve as role models.

Downside to being a high achiever

It is not always a bed of roses when you are a high achiever; there are downsides as well and if you are aiming for this path, you should be aware of them now. As a high achiever, you are so passionate about your pursuit that you are all in, and get frustrated when others around you do not show the same level of care, effort or attention. There are few around you who know exactly what you are doing, which means it can be isolating at the top, especially if people get envious. Your focus is unrivaled, which can make you appear misunderstood. When you start getting well known for your achievements, some people might get envious. They do not understand that a spotlight on you does not diminish the light on them. Your closest friends may start to become distant as you no longer have a common language and experiences as your connection.

While becoming a high achiever is something you can learn how to do, you likely had natural abilities this whole time. Unfortunately, schools and the workplace tend to teach to the middle as it is the path of least resistance, and teachers are able to impact the most people. As a high achiever, this means you may not have the stimulation and challenges to help you cultivate your ability to achieve more. The best of the high achievers seek out these challenges on their own and do not wait for these opportunities to come to them. Thankfully, since the internet and virtual learning opportunities exploded, there are limitless options to advance your own knowledge independently (Gotian, 2021c).

As you become more successful, you have more people and projects depending on your expertise, which means stepping away spontaneously becomes more challenging. If you are not careful, every minute becomes scheduled, which means if you do not manage it, you will miss out on meaningful family experiences. You need to get this under control quickly before outside sources control your time and purpose (Gotian, 2021d; O'Neil, 2021). When they do, it will quickly lead to burnout. Recognizing the downfalls of being a high achiever means you can be on the lookout for the pitfalls and work proactively to put systems in place to prevent them from taking over your life.

High achievers did not set out to be the best when they started their journey. They put in an incredible effort, listened to wise counsel from everyone around them and wanted to learn from the process at every turn. The more they succeeded, the more they became hungry and curious for what was next. There is always another milestone to achieve, another goal to be met, another person to help. They are on the hunt, trying to determine how to have the biggest impact. They get to have enormous power and privilege doing what they love. Years and decades later they still get unbridled joy from their work. Their words matter and have power so they use them carefully and for the greater good. You can be average and have a very fulfilling life. If you want to have a life of purpose and significance, consider doing the work and trying to be a high achiever.

COACHING QUESTIONS

1 What is one thing you believe you can start doing today to put you on the path of being a high achiever?

2 What is one way you can use your success for a greater good?

KEY TAKEAWAYS

1 Not trying because something is hard is not an option for high achievers. They fear not trying more than they fear failing.

2 When there is a problem or a better way to do something, high achievers cannot leave it alone. They need to find a way to make it better, faster or more efficient.

3 High achievers crave being at the forefront of change. They despise the status quo and want to find new and innovative ways of accomplishing something.

4 There are multiple downsides to being a high achiever, including being misunderstood, unchallenged and frustrated by those without matching focus.

References

Alexander, G (2006) Behavioural coaching: the GROW model, in J Passmore (ed.) *Excellence in Coaching: The industry guide*, 2nd ed. London: Kogan Page

Alexander, G and Renshaw, B (2005) *Super Coaching: The missing ingredient for high performance*, London, Random House

Ashford, SJ and Cummings, LL (1983) Feedback as an individual resource: Personal strategies of creating information, *Organizational Behavior and Human Performance*, **32**, pp 370–98

Beuke, C (2011) How do high achievers really think? *Psychology Today*, https://www.psychologytoday.com/us/blog/youre-hired/201110/how-do-high-achievers-really-think (archived at https://perma.cc/HGB6-MUFS)

Boyes, A (2018) 4 ways busy people sabotage themselves, *Harvard Business Review*, https://hbr.org/2018/09/4-ways-busy-people-sabotage-themselves (archived at https://perma.cc/GE2V-4VHB)

Brockett, RG and Hiemstra, R (1991) *Self-direction in Adult Learning: Perspectives on theory, research, and practice*, New York, Routledge

Brookfield, S (2009) Self-Directed Learning, in R Maclean and D Wilson (eds.) *International Handbook of Education for the Changing World of Work*, Germany: Springer Science + Business Media B.V

Clance, PR and Imes, SA (1978) The imposter phenomenon in high achieving women: Dynamics and therapeutic intervention, *Psychotherapy: Theory, Research & Practice*, **15**, pp 241–47

Cybermetrics Lab and Consejo Superior De Investigaciones Científicas (CSIC) (2021) Highly Cited Researchers (h>100) according to their Google Scholar

Citations public profiles, https://www.webometrics.info/en/hlargerthan100 (archived at https://perma.cc/6SQH-XY6Y)

Czikszentmihayli, M (1975) *Beyond Boredom and Anxiety*, San Francisco, Jossey-Bass

Denning, T (2017) How to go from being a dreamer to a high achiever, https://addicted2success.com/success-advice/how-to-go-from-being-a-dreamer-to-a-high-achiever/ (archived at https://perma.cc/3R2E-KYEV)

Fleming, SM, Thomas, CL and Dolan, RJ (2010) Overcoming status quo bias in the human brain, *Proceedings of the National Academy of Science U.S.A.*, **107**, pp 6005–09

Freiberg, K and Freiberg, J (1997) *Nuts! Southwest Airlines' crazy recipe for business and personal success*, New York, Broadway Books

Gotian, R (2020a) Don't let imposter syndrome derail your career, *Psychology Today*, https://www.psychologytoday.com/intl/blog/optimizing-success/202010/dont-let-imposter-syndrome-derail-your-career (archived at https://perma.cc/6PJ3-KLMU)

Gotian, R (2020b) How to turn feedback into an 'opportunity for enhancement', *Forbes*, https://www.forbes.com/sites/ruthgotian/2020/08/14/how-to-turn-feedback-into-an-opportunity-for-enhancement/ (archived at https://perma.cc/PDH2-VUEM)

Gotian, R (2020c) Why some people don't take "no" for an answer, *Forbes*, https://www.forbes.com/sites/ruthgotian/2020/11/27/why-some-people-dont-take-no-for-an-answer/ (archived at https://perma.cc/B5XD-42W5)

Gotian, R (2021a) 6 reasons why some people dream and others achieve, *Forbes*, https://www.forbes.com/sites/ruthgotian/2021/05/11/6-reasons-why-some-people-dream-and-others-achieve/ (archived at https://perma.cc/R7LC-R4ZV)

Gotian, R (2021b) Disheartened by lack of progression at work? Here's how to turn displeasure into success, *Forbes*, https://www.forbes.com/sites/ruthgotian/2021/04/20/disheartened-by-lack-of-progression-at-work-heres-how-to-turn-displeasure-into-success/ (archived at https://perma.cc/ME5G-KMPJ)

Gotian, R (2021c) Pandemic professional development looks different, And it is here to stay, *Forbes*, https://www.forbes.com/sites/ruthgotian/2021/04/13/pandemic-professional-development-looks-different-and-it-is-here-to-stay/ (archived at https://perma.cc/AB78-FF2C)

Gotian, R (2021d) Too distracted? Learn how to be where your feet are, *Forbes*, https://www.forbes.com/sites/ruthgotian/2021/06/01/too-distracted-learn-how-to-be-where-your-feet-are/ (archived at https://perma.cc/R36T-9V72)

Gotian, R (2021e) Why you earned the right to have imposter syndrome, *Psychology Today*, https://www.psychologytoday.com/us/blog/optimizing-success/202104/why-you-earned-the-right-have-imposter-syndrome (archived at https://perma.cc/5JZG-EZX2)

Gotian, R and McGinty, G (2020) How to fight imposter syndrome in the time of coronavirus, *Harvard Business Review Ascend*

Kanfer, RM and Heggestad, ED (eds.) (1990) *Motivational Traits and Skills: A person-centered approach to work motivation*, Greenwich, CT: JAI Press

Knowles, MS (1980) *The Modern Practice of Adult Education: From pedagogy to andragogy*, New York, Cambridge Books

Lafair, S (2016) The pros and cons of being a super achiever, *Inc.* https://www.inc.com/sylvia-lafair/the-pros-and-cons-of-being-a-super-achiever.html (archived at https://perma.cc/NGR2-6CFA)

Mael, FA and Ashforth, BE (1995) Loyal from day one: Biodata, organizational identification, and turnover among newcomers, *Personnel Psychology*, 48, pp 309–33

Merriam, S, Caffarella, R and Baumgartner, L (2007) *Learning in Adulthood*, San Francisco, CA, Jossey-Bass

National Institutes of Health (2021) *Anthony S. Fauci, M.D.*, https://www.niaid.nih.gov/about/anthony-s-fauci-md-bio (archived at https://perma.cc/5N2X-PV45)

O'Boyle, JE and Aguinis, H (2012) The best and the rest: Revisiting the norm of normality of individual performance, *Personnel Psychology*, 65, pp 79–119

O'Neil, S (2021) *Be Where Your Feet Are*, New York, St. Martin's Essentials

Rynes, SL and Connerley, ML (1993) Applicant reactions to alternative selection procedures, *Journal of Business and Psychology*, 7, pp 261–77

Schreiber, WE (2019) Scientific Impact and the H-Index, *Clinical Laboratory News*, https://www.aacc.org/cln/articles/2019/september/scientific-impact-and-the-h-index (archived at https://perma.cc/GN27-UZQR)

Spence, JT and Helmreich, R (eds.) (1983) *Achievement-related Motives and Behaviors*, San Francisco: Freeman

Stross, RE (1996) Microsoft's big advantage—hiring only the supersmart, *Fortune*, 134, pp 158–62

Tobak, S (2015) 10 Behaviors of High Achievers, *Entrepreneur.com*, https://www.entrepreneur.com/article/245843 (archived at https://perma.cc/M8FZ-GVNU)

Trank, C, Rynes, S and Bretz, R (2002) Attracting applicants in the war for talent: Differences in work preferences among high achievers, *Journal of Business and Psychology*, 16

Willyerd, K (2014) What high performers want at work, *Harvard Business Review*, https://hbr.org/2014/11/what-high-performers-want-at-work (archived at https://perma.cc/A37Y-DABM)

Wong, K (2017) How to identify and retain top performers with rewards and recognition, *Engage*, https://www.achievers.com/blog/identify-retain-top-performers-rewards-recognition/ (archived at https://perma.cc/L3EU-V82P)

Yin, Y, Wang, Y and Evans, JAEA (2019) Quantifying the dynamics of failure across science, startups and security, *Nature*, 575, pp 190–94

03

Leading, supporting, and retaining high achievers

Some people are exhausting. You know who I am referring to: those who have a problem with every solution. While some people have a "no problem too small" mentality, high achievers simply get the job done. In doing so, they send a bolt of charge and reinvigorate the team and organization. They do not question *if* they will solve the problem, as they know that they will. Instead, all of their focus is on *how* they will deal with the challenge and find a resolution. It is an entirely different mindset. High achievers are born problem-solvers and view a challenge as a puzzle to be solved. To get the job done they need space, with limited bureaucratic red tape and high degrees of autonomy. High achievers will finish the task quickly and efficiently, but not if you stand in their way. They are constantly fighting for a cause and are always a flight risk if they do not feel appreciated or supported for their work.

Every organization should be tripping over themselves to recruit these high achievers, and doing whatever is necessary to retain them. Research has shown that high achievers can quickly take on a leadership role and develop a high-performance mindset within an organization (Mackay, 2015; Huselid, 1995). High-achieving employees, those who routinely blow benchmarks out of the water, can be the most productive colleagues yet challenging to retain. While a higher salary might be their stated reason for departure, for high achievers, the lack of mentorship and murky path to leadership is a major reason they walk out the door.

Employees who fall below average and do not meet prescribed metrics, often get corrective action plans detailing their areas that need improvement. But that is just the beginning of organizations supporting their under-performers (Goldsmith and Carter, 2010). Below-average employees are sent on courses to develop their skills to meet the baseline and even have regular check-ins with their supervisor to discuss their progress. Conversely, those who continuously excel do not get nearly the same attention, if any at all. This action, or inaction, is unfortunate, as high achievers can provide 400 percent higher productivity than an average employee (O'Boyle and Aguinis, 2012). Most organizations do not have formal programs to recognize and develop high achievers as a pipeline of future leaders. So what is the result? The high achievers get frustrated by the lack of advancement and innovation and leave the organization. The company is then left with average or, even worse, below-average employees. Ultimately, there is a real business case for actively working toward retaining high achievers.

To understand high achievers, you must first understand adult learners. I do not mean whether they are visual, kinesthetic, or auditory learners. I am referring to the focus on adult learning as it interacts with your life situation. While pedagogy refers to the theory and practice of teaching and learning for children, andragogy, developed by Malcolm Knowles in 1968, focuses on the same ideas but through a lens of adult learners (Knowles, 1970, 1980, 1968). Adult learners often have a full and often overflowing plate and whilst some are only responsible for themselves, many are also responsible for others, including a spouse or partner, children, and parents. No longer relying on others to pay their bills, they have to find a job to support themselves and their dependents. They do not always believe everything they hear and read and value relationships with others.

Malcolm Knowles, one of the founding fathers of adult learning, coined the term andragogy and considered it the "art and science of helping adults learn" (Knowles, 1968). Knowles had six assumptions that he developed to guide the understanding of adult learning. They have become the cornerstone of this field and need to be understood to build more high achievers:

1 As a person matures, they advance from a dependent personality to a self-directed human being. They like to choose how they will learn, such as in a formal classroom or webinars. The adult learning environment needs to be a place where a culture of respect, support, and acceptance is fostered. There needs to be a level of psychological safety to leverage the maximum learning potential (Edmondson, 2019).

2 An adult compiles a growing stockpile of experiences, which serve as a rich source for learning. Every experience is an excuse to learn. That is why high achievers view feedback as an opportunity for enhancement, not a critique (Gotian, 2020c). They understand any insight can make them better, faster, stronger, more efficient, or innovative.

3 The readiness of an adult to learn is firmly related to their social role. If your role does not provide any opportunity or expectation for growth or innovation, why try harder? If, however, you are always expected to be curious and original, you are more likely to seek opportunities to learn.

4 As people age and mature, their perspective shifts from the future application of knowledge to its immediate use. As a result, an adult is more attuned to a problem-centered approach than a subject-centered focus on learning. They want to know how their knowledge will be helpful to them and their work or life.

5 Intrinsic motivation, which is focused on the person and their internal desire to learn, is more potent than external motivations governed by other people and can be seen when it is driven by recognition such as promotions, diplomas, and awards (Deci and Ryan, 1985, 2000).

6 Adults need to know why they are learning something. They do not want to memorize random facts that are not anchored in anything useful.

These ideologies and assumptions are at the cornerstone of adult learning and need to be recognized and fulfilled if you will recruit, lead and retain more high achievers. To maximize their ability to learn, involve them in the process, offer different ways to learn, make them feel safe with you and their environment, and be sure they understand why the content is crucial and relevant to them. Without having Knowles' andragogy principles in place, everything else you do will simply be small talk, or worse yet, background noise. Once you have these foundational conventions in place, you can leverage the productivity and increase recruitment and retention of high achievers in your organization.

Two powers are constantly at odds with each other in an adult's life and it is a continuous and relentless feeling of tug-of-war. The first is a *load of life*, such as child or elder care, cleaning the home, or preparing meals, which sucks our time and energy. The second is the *power of life*, which allows one to deal with the load, such as a nanny, housekeeper, or the ability to order takeout for dinner. Howard McClusky called this the Theory of Margin (McClusky, 1963a, 1963b; Merriam et al, 2007). The greater the power, the higher the margin to participate in learning. The ability to pay for conveniences opens up your bandwidth to learn new things. Adults have external loads—such as family, work, community responsibilities—and internal loads, which are the pressures we put on ourselves such as the need to look or act a certain way or achieve specific things by a certain age, such as marriage, children or professional rank. High achievers find alignment and an appropriate ratio of load to power, which frees their time to think creatively, find collaborators, listen to mentors, and succeed.

Reward your high achievers

While it may appear to be the most elementary concept, you need to reward high performers for their hard work and achievements. Do not ignore their repetitive good work and think it is sustainable to ignore their achievements. They are not volunteers and, like everyone else, they want their diligence and achievements to be noticed. This is not an unreasonable request and should be automatic. In group work, which is a critical function of every organization, the high achievers think differently, produce more, and often carry the group. As a result, they prefer a payment structure that is based on individual rather than group performance. Peak performers want to be paid competitively, but that is not all (Cable and Judge, 1994).

Research by Daniel Pink demonstrates that for high achievers, extrinsic values such as bonuses or salary increases do not improve productivity at nearly the same rate as intrinsic motivators such as adding value to an organization (Pink, 2009). High achievers want to see examples of creative innovation, curiosity, and passion for raising the bar. They want to know that the organization is investing in their professional development and their path forward within the company. There are several things an institution can do to develop its high achievers.

While everyone wants to receive top dollar for their work, high achievers want to know that you are recognizing their achievements throughout the year, not just when it is time to distribute merit increases or bonuses. More so, they want to see that excellent work is appreciated, as seen by a wide delineation in pay increases between low, average, and high performers. They need to receive financial, non-payment, and social benefits and recognitions in addition to their annual increase. High achievers are relentless in their pursuit of excellence and need to know that the organization values this in their top employees. Make sure the recognition you offer aligns with the superior performance. Do not recognize baseline activities such as arriving on time or keeping a clean work area. That is a basic expectation and you will lose credibility with your team if this is what you highlight. Make sure you recognize major achievements or hurdles that were overcome.

Just as you are recognizing the talent of your top performers, they are seeing fire in others. High performers are the first to recognize and sponsor other rising stars (Wong, 2017). They like people who push the envelope, are creative in their thinking, and do not fear failure. They will recommend those people for awards and recognition and create a network of other high achievers which they will mentor and sponsor. Take a careful look at who they are nominating as that is your future pipeline of top performers.

Engage your employees

A report by *Harvard Business Review* illuminates that two-thirds of executives understand the need for employee engagement but struggle to make it happen successfully (Harvard Business Review Analytic Services, 2013). Just a quarter of the study respondents in their organization are highly engaged. This is the time to listen to what your high performers want and need. Conduct a careful and focused analysis of employee survey data from top performers. It can identify the factors that influence the engagement of these elite employees and what might lead to their departure (Baldoni, 2013). Use the findings to understand what drives high achievers and develop corresponding programs that demonstrate the organization's commitment to and investment in this valuable resource. Ultimately, your high performers want to know that you recognize their value beyond the bottom line and see them as people. This must be done with authenticity and sincerity, or else the high achievers will see through your synthetic veil and you, as the leader and the organization, will lose credibility.

Those who supervise high performers need to know how to corral and engage with these unique employees. What works for everyone else will not work for them. Research has shown that irrespective of industry, job function, or status, the common denominator that high achievers seek in a boss is a caring nature, a good communicator, authenticity, results-oriented, and a strong inclination to help and develop others (Mackay, 2015; Sutton, 2010).

To develop these high achievers, it is critical to find a leader who can sniff out talent; they can see potential in even the highest performers, a budding promise which these elite employees do not yet recognize in themselves. They might be high achievers, but that does not mean they are immune to losing confidence or developing imposter syndrome, the fear of being considered a fraud, or downplaying their achievements (Gotian, 2020a, 2021b; Clance and Imes, 1978).

Offer opportunities for exposure

High achievers have intrinsic motivation and passion for the work they are doing and problems they are solving, but an extrinsic motivation for competitive excellence and the yearning to be distinguished from others (Frank and Cook, 1995; Kanfer and Heggestad, 1990; Spence and Helmreich, 1983). Let the high achievers show their leaders and others what they are capable of accomplishing by provide them with ongoing stretch assignments and projects where they have greater exposure and visibility to senior leaders and other teams. For example, allow them to head up a task force, lead a cross-functional team, conduct an analysis, or develop a proposed solution for a pervasive challenge. Give them a lead role in presenting these ideas to the executive leadership team. If you want to prevent your top performers from relocating, allow them to lead global teams (Willyerd, 2014).

High achievers want to know that their work adds value. They thrive off of feeling like they are respected and have a seat at the decision-making table. Offer them domains of ownership where they feel empowered to think like CEOs. For decisions that impact high performers but lie outside of their responsibilities, provide ample context and transparency while treating them like decision-making partners, not simply employees who will execute orders from the leadership.

Provide autonomy

High performers live for the challenge of solving a problem (Tobak, 2015). To do this effectively, they need the right conditions where they can quench their craving for autonomy and avoid being micromanaged. They need the freedom to be creative in their thoughts and processes while having the authority to complement their responsibilities. If this does not match, high achievers start to look for other opportunities that are better aligned with their needs.

Part of being creative and innovative is trying things out that others may view as too risky. High achievers can make connections that others do not yet see or appreciate. They crave finding the unknown and going down a path that others have not. For high achievers, the chase is as exciting as the win, which is likely why they fear not trying more than they fear failing. The path to success is paved with many failures, hiccups, bumps, challenges, craters, and hurdles. The high achievers stand out among the pack because they do not get deterred by these challenges. They fully recognize that they will have multiple losses before they reach their goal. From each mistake or failure, they learn something new and apply that new knowledge to their next iteration (McGrath, 2011). Having the latitude to try without penalty for failing, needs to be actively encouraged.

Create advancement pathways

High achievers prefer rapid promotion opportunities and will balk at doing the same types of tasks for years on end (Kanter, 1977). They do not wish to sit in the same chair doing the same type of work just because the person in the role senior to them is stuck in their career. The high achievers recognize that the faster they get promoted, the better opportunity they will have to work on challenging assignments, which they crave. Promotions and fast-track career opportunities would be expected and increase the likelihood of retention of the high achievers.

When a position is open within an organization, high achievers should be considered and proactively told about it and recruited. This will provide an understanding that their employer is consistently looking to develop them within the organization. Do not decide for them if this is too big or small a job, or if they are too busy with outside commitments; that is their decision to make (Smith and Johnson, 2020).

Offer further training

Despite all of their accolades and advanced degrees, high achievers are always on the hunt. They look for opportunities to enhance and broaden their knowledge. Often the developmental programs offered through human resources are not appropriate for what they need and are too generic to be of interest to them. Consider offering them opportunities to further their training, learn new skills, and broaden their career pathway. These courses can be in person or online and might be provided outside of your institution. Provide flexible working conditions so that they can go to class or work on assignments as needed (Trank et al, 2002). High performers are engaged when they learn new skills and immediately recognize their application in their daily work. The learning will lead them to get more excited about projects. Do not worry about them working less because they are not in the office; high performers will work until the job gets done, likely long after you went to sleep.

Professional development allowance

High performers tend to direct their learning through formal and self-directed learning options and are looking for an organization that will actively support that growth (Willyerd, 2014). Consider offering a professional development budget for high performers. Letting the employee have control over which course to take or conference to attend is essential. A culture of psychological safety and encouragement is critical to ensure that they take advantage of this opportunity and don't feel it is a benefit that is offered but should not be used (Edmondson, 2019).

Now you recognize what makes adult learners tick and how they process information. Because it varies for each person, offering options is empowering for adults. Alternatives are especially needed for high achievers who do not like to be bound by rules often made for the majority, which is inherently the middle of the group: those who are average. This does not work for high achievers who routinely work along the liminal edge. As a rule of thumb, adult learners remember (Mackay, 2015):

- 10 percent of what they read;
- 20 percent of what they hear;
- 30 percent of what they see;
- 50 percent of what they see and hear;
- 80 percent of what they say;
- 90 percent of what they say while they are doing the task.

Some of these measures cost money; however, the benefit of retaining a high achiever far outweighs the start-up costs of replacing one. There needs to be a concerted effort to keep high achievers, as like attracts like. Given the law of attraction, these valued contributors will draw more of the same to fuel a company's vision. In today's economic reality, where leaders need to do more with less, you can be sure that your business will achieve greater returns by investing in your high achievers (Gotian, 2020b).

In his book, *Choosing Courage*, Jim Detert explains that those who are courageous at work, especially those in leadership roles, can galvanize others to increase their loyalty, work harder and do things that benefit the organization (Detert, 2021). To create an institution filled with courageous high achievers, you need to recruit the right people whose skills and mindset align with what you hope to achieve. As Jim Collins stated in his book *Good to Great*, you want to get "the right people on the bus" (Collins, 2001).

Steve Kerr, the head coach of the Golden State Warriors NBA team, knows a great deal about high-performing teams. He was a member of many high-performing teams and now coaches them to greatness. He played for fifteen years on six different teams and is an eight-time NBA champion, having won the title five times as a player (three with the Chicago Bulls and two with the San Antonio Spurs) and three times with the Golden State Warriors as their head coach. Kerr is the only NBA player to win four straight NBA titles after 1969.

Before becoming a head coach, Kerr spent a great deal of time visiting other teams and learning from their coaches. He also benefited from being coached himself by numerous Hall of Fame coaches. Kerr thought about everything he knew, read, or observed and wrote it all down. When working with his high-performing team and pushing them to achieve even higher levels of greatness, he focuses on a few principles that have worked for him repeatedly.

What are your values?

Consider how you will incorporate your values into your team culture. Think about how you want your team to feel when they walk into the building and consider, what is the plan to ensure that happens? How will you build the team and organizational culture? This process cannot be reactive; you need to put intentional thought into it. As a leader, your team and organization need to feel your humanity and know your values. If you do not stand for something, then you do not stand for anything.

When Kerr was asked by a fellow NBA coach what his values are he realized he had never stopped to think about that before. He paused to reflect and focus on his values and developed a process to make them part of his daily work and life. Kerr suggests taking a well-intentioned pause to think about what is important to you and get that list down to three or four items. Next, figure out how to achieve those values daily. When you actualize your values, that will be your team culture.

Asking someone to identify their values is challenging. You will likely come up with some random list of values that sound good, but are they real?

How do you know what you stand for and consider essential and integral? In her book, *Design the Life You Love*, designer Ayse Birsel recommends listing all of your heroes (Birsel, 2015). Then write down what it is about your heroes you so admire. Look carefully at those traits as you may find them in yourself. That is an excellent first step to identifying your values (Gotian, 2021a).

Kerr identified his values as joy, compassion, competition, and mindfulness. At its core, it is about loving the game. That is why he started playing in the first place, and he knows the rest of the players did as well. "Keeping that joy as part of the everyday workout is a constant reminder of why we started playing," shared Kerr. "It is easy to forget because you can get injured, booed by fans, or traded."

Your values need to come alive every day when you are at work. It needs to be part of the tapestry of the culture. Kerr brings in joy by using his sense of humor, laughter in the gym, music during portions of practice, harmlessly mocking each other, and partaking and creating a brotherhood. The entire group celebrates achievements. "For someone's birthday, we find footage from throughout their life and create a montage," shared Kerr. "There is no jealousy because accomplishments are celebrated for every single member of the group."

Mentor your high performers

There are fifteen players on a basketball team, and every single one plays a strategic role. The high-performance team needs to be strategically constructed with the right balance of veterans, rookies, and some mid-career players. With this structure, mentorship organically develops instead of a hierarchy.

Of the fifteen players, everyone has a unique story; there is always something to gain and something to lose. All of the players are under immense pressure. Even the best player on the team needs to live up to the constant pressure of being the best. The fifteenth player on the team is trying to keep his job. "The top player will not lose his job, but might lose his standing as one of the best players," exclaimed Kerr.

Each player has their own circumstances and to keep a high-performing team functioning at peak performance, you need to know how to keep this machine humming. The roster construction is crucial, and mentorship plays a key role in keeping the high-performing team cohesive. Having senior members who are truly professional and become the nucleus, the fabric of the team, is pivotal. "A third of the team usually becomes the backbone of the team. They are top players, professional, and hard-working. They take the younger guys under their wing," shared Kerr.

Avoid the copy and paste strategy

Just because something worked at a previous organization, does not mean it will be effective with your new team, so try to avoid the "copy and paste" strategy. Do not try duplicating other people's methodologies or cultures and embedding them into your organization as it will likely fail (Gotian, 2018). The culture and group dynamics are different so they will not translate well. Instead, be yourself and develop something that is uniquely yours and aligns with the organization's culture. Your employees will feel your authenticity. The copy and paste method is especially ill-advised if you are bringing successful strategies from one organization and simply embedding them, with a complete disregard to the history and culture of the new organization. You will be viewed as a one-trick pony, someone who does not have original thoughts or ideas. Eventually, you will be resented for discounting or ignoring positive traits, people, and traditions that people have come to cherish.

What makes you tick?

Figure out who you are, what makes you tick; those ideas and vibes that get your adrenalin pumping while keeping you whole and authentic. Knowing who you are and what you stand for is absolutely critical if you are going to lead a team. Next, you need to figure out how to ingrain those ideologies into your team. Excitement is contagious, so how you choose to come in every morning is not to be overlooked. If you identify it first in yourself, your team will follow in kind. If you walk in lethargic, with the mindset that you have to be there instead of wanting to be there, your team will see that, be uninspired by you and respond in kind. The high achievers want to be around people who are excited to do their work; it is the reason they get out of bed in the morning. Model it and watch the high achievers soar.

Management thought leader Peter Drucker famously said that "people do what they see." (Drucker, 1999). They will mirror behavior and rise or fall to the expectations they observe. In her book *A Higher Standard*, General Ann Dunwoody, American's first female four-star general, reinforced the idea that you have set a new lower standard for what is acceptable if you walk by a mistake (Dunwoody, 2015). If that is the case, then the opposite should be true. If you recognize high performance as the new normal, it raises the bar for everyone and can develop into the new cultural norm.

COACHING QUESTIONS

1 Who are your heroes? What do you appreciate about them? What does that say about your values?

2 How can you implement your values into your work?

KEY TAKEAWAYS

1 High achievers are 400 percent more productive than the average employee. Every organization must work to hire, lead and retain these top performers.

2 High achievers want to know that they and their work are valued. They are seeking organizations where they can learn, grow, and be inspired and innovative.

3 There are numerous ways to develop high achievers, including giving them stretch assignments, offering them professional development inside and outside the organization, extending opportunities for exposure, and providing mentoring opportunities.

4 High achievers know others like them. Developing a team of high achievers requires putting together a blend of senior, junior, and mid-career top performers so that they can learn from and support each other.

References

Baldoni, J (2013) Your least engaged employees might be your top performers, *Harvard Business Review*, https://hbr.org/2013/04/your-least-engaged-employees-m?autocomplete=true (archived at https://perma.cc/NP8F-FPLX)

Birsel, A (2015) *Design the Life You Love*, New York, Ten Speed Press, an imprint of the Crown Publishing Group, a division of Penguin Random House LLC

Cable, DM and Judge, TA (1994) Pay preferences and job search decisions: A person-organizational fit perspective, *Personnel Psychology*, **47**, pp 317–48

Clance, PR and Imes, SA (1978) The imposter phenomenon in high achieving women: Dynamics and therapeutic intervention, *Psychotherapy: Theory, Research & Practice*, **15**, pp 241–47

Collins, J (2001) *Good to Great*, New York, NY, Harper Business, an imprint of Harper Collins Publishers

Deci, EL and Ryan, RM (1985) *Intrinsic Motivation and Self-determination in Human Behavior*, New York, Plenum

Deci, EL and Ryan, RM (2000) The "what" and "why" of goal pursuits: Human needs and the self-determination of behavior, *Psychological Inquiry*, **11**, pp 227–68

Detert, J (2021) *Choosing Courage*, Boston, MA, Harvard Business Review Press

Drucker, P F (1999) *Management Challenges for the 21st Century*, New York, Harper Collins Publishers, Inc.

Dunwoody, A (2015) *A Higher Standard*, Boston, MA, Da Capo Press, a member of the Perseus Books Group

Edmondson, AC (2019) *The Fearless Organization*, Hoboken, NJ, Wiley

Frank, RH and Cook, PJ (1995) *The Winner-Take-All Society*, New York, The Free Press.

Goldsmith, M and Carter, L (eds.) (2010) *Best Practices in Talent Management*, San Francisco, CA: Pfeiffer, an imprint of Wiley

Gotian, R (2018) Integrating cultural perspectives into organizational learning: Anecdotal evidence for organizational effectiveness, in D Peltz and A Clemons (eds.) *Multicultural Andragogy for Transformative Learning*, IGI Global

Gotian, R (2020a) Don't let imposter syndrome derail your career, *Psychology Today*, https://www.psychologytoday.com/us/blog/optimizing-success/202010/dont-let-imposter-syndrome-derail-your-career (archived at https://perma.cc/3VBU-XK38)

Gotian, R (2020b) How to attract, retain, and lead high achievers, *Forbes*, https://www.forbes.com/sites/ruthgotian/2020/06/29/how-to-attract-retain-and-lead-high-achievers/ (archived at https://perma.cc/X553-68Z9)

Gotian, R (2020c) How to turn feedback into an 'opportunity for enhancement', *Forbes*, https://www.forbes.com/sites/ruthgotian/2020/08/14/how-to-turn-feedback-into-an-opportunity-for-enhancement/ (archived at https://perma.cc/PDH2-VUEM)

Gotian, R (2021a) Tell me your heroes and I'll tell you your values, *Psychology Today*, https://www.psychologytoday.com/us/blog/optimizing-success/202103/tell-me-your-heroes-and-i-ll-tell-you-your-values (archived at https://perma.cc/T2J3-MGJG)

Gotian, R (2021b) Why you earned the right to have imposter syndrome, *Psychology Today*, https://www.psychologytoday.com/us/blog/optimizing-success/202104/why-you-earned-the-right-have-imposter-syndrome (archived at https://perma.cc/5JZG-EZX2)

Harvard Business Review Analytic Services (2013) The impact of employee engagement on performance, in press, H. B. R. (ed.)

Huselid, MA (1995) The impact of human resource management practices on turnover, productivity, and corporate financial performance, *Academy of Management Journal*, **38**, pp 635–872

Kanfer, RM and Heggestad, ED (eds.) (1990) *Motivational Traits and Skills: A person-centered approach to work motivation*, Greenwich, CT: JAI Press

Kanter, RM (1977) *Men and Women of the Corporation*, New York, Basic Books

Knowles, MS (1968) Andragogy, not pedagogy, *Adult Leadership*, **16**, pp 350–52,386

Knowles, MS (1970) *The Modern Practice of Adult Education*, New York: New York, Association Press

Knowles, MS (1980) *The Modern Practice of Adult Education: From pedagogy to andragogy*, New York, Cambridge Books

Mackay, A-L (2015) *The Four Mindsets*, Australia, John Wiley & Sons Australia, Ltd

McClusky, HY (1963a) Course of adult life span, in Hallenbeck (ed.) Chicago, IL. Adult Education Association of U.S.A.

McClusky, HY (1963b) The demand for continual learning in modern society, *University of Michigan School of Education Bulletin*

McGrath, R (2011) Failing by design, *Harvard Business Review*, **89**, pp 76–83

Merriam, S, Caffarella, R and Bamgartner, L (2007) *Learning in Adulthood*, San Francisco, CA, Jossey-Bass

O'Boyle Jr, E and Aguinis, H (2012) The Best and the Rest: Revisiting the norm of normality of individual performance, *Personnel Psychology*, **65**, pp 79–119

Pink, DH (2009) *Drive*, New York, NY, Riverhead Books, an imprint of Penguin Random House LLC

Smith, DG and Johnson, WB (2020) *Good Guys*, Boston, MA, Harvard Business Review Press

Spence, JT and Helmreich, RL (1983) Achievement-related motives and behaviors, in J Spence (ed.) *Achievement and Achievement Motives*, San Francisco, Freeman

Sutton, RI (2010) *Good Boss, Bad Boss*, New York, Business Plus, an imprint of Grand Central Publishing

Tobak, S (2015) 10 Behaviors of High Achievers, *Entrepreneur.com* https://www.entrepreneur.com/article/245843 (archived at https://perma.cc/ M8FZ-GVNU)

Trank, CQ, Rynes, SL and Bretz JR, RD (2002) Attracting applicants in the war for talent: Differences in work preferences among high achievers, *Journal of Business and Psychology*, **16**

Willyerd, K (2014) What high performers want at work, *Harvard Business Review*, https://hbr.org/2014/11/what-high-performers-want-at-work (archived at https://perma.cc/A37Y-DABM)

Wong, K (2017) How to identify and retain top performers with rewards and recognition, *Engage*, https://www.achievers.com/blog/identify-retain-top-performers-rewards-recognition/ (archived at https://perma.cc/L3EU-V82P)

PART TWO

Four elements of success

04

Intrinsic motivation

The journey to success is never straightforward. Understanding the often-uncharted path and how to deal with challenges paves the road to achievement. Exemplars achieved their notoriety by doing four things in unison, and actualizing these four principles helped the high achievers stay the course, even when a detour was tempting. While the ideas may not be revolutionary, how the high achievers sought them out and fine-tuned them over time made them stand out and achieve success. Learning these lessons from high achievers can help you elevate your success. It is time to take ownership of your life.

The first of these pillars of success is intrinsic motivation. I am referring to the kind that is your North Star. It is an unrelenting passion that reminds you of why you do what you do, even when times are tough and things do not go according to plan. It gives you great joy, purpose and is your driving force. High achievers explored multiple avenues before they found their passion. Once they did, there was no use trying to pry them off. They were like a dog with a bone. With a laser-like focus, high achievers fixate on achieving their next goal. Finding your motivation is the first and most critical step to optimizing your success.

This chapter aims to help you identify your intrinsic motivation by identifying what you are naturally good at and enjoy doing. I will introduce several tools and a systematic process to help you determine your intrinsic motivation, and then provide strategies to help you apply that motivation to your success. I will introduce ideas such as surrounding yourself with people who are smarter than you, understanding and remaining true to your core values, becoming a role model for others, and creating a network of similarly inspired professionals.

Is your motivation intrinsic or extrinsic?

Have you ever felt unmotivated? You know you need to do something, but you cannot find the fuel to get started or maintain momentum. You would rather watch useless videos on your phone or even clean your house instead of getting to the task that needs your attention. When you finally get around to doing it, you are lackluster in your approach. You are doing something because you *have* to do it instead of *wanting* to do it. What you need to do is find the right type of motivation. There are two sources of motivation: extrinsic and intrinsic. To optimize your success, you need to tap into the right one (Deci and Ryan, 1985).

When I was getting my doctorate at Teachers College, Columbia University, one of the last formal classes doctoral students took before embarking on their research was a proposal development seminar. At the beginning of the first class, my professor, who was also my doctoral advisor, Dr. Marie Volpe, asked each person why they were getting their doctorate. What was their reason for embarking on this long, often isolating process? It is a relevant question as upwards of half of those who start their doctorates in the humanities do not finish (Winerman, 2008; Bloomberg and Volpe, 2008). They usually complete the coursework and pass the candidacy exam, the multi-hour cumulative test to check your knowledge of everything in your field of study. But they never do the research, which they have to defend later; a requirement to change their status from 'All But Dissertation' (ABD) to doctor. The path from ABD to PhD, a doctorate in philosophy, or in my case EdD, a doctorate in education, moves the student from the passenger seat to the driver's seat. You are no longer following a predetermined track of taking classes and being told where to go, what to do, and in which progression. Instead, you are now making decisions on your own, motivating yourself, and setting your schedule. This independence can be liberating for some and paralyzing for others, especially those who prefer the scripted plan of taking a set number of classes in a particular sequence.

I sat there and listened to the responses of my classmates. Some wanted the degree as they hoped for a promotion and felt an additional degree would help that pursuit. This idea makes sense. With more people attending college and going to graduate school, a higher degree would make them stand out from their competitors. Other students wanted a doctorate for prestige. That is not too surprising. Less than two percent of Americans have a doctoral degree, so it is a pretty elite group (Wilson, 2017). Worldwide, that number is even smaller, at 1.1 percent (OECD.org, 2020).

Other classmates wanted to learn something new. They had a burning question that needed answering and hoped to learn the tools to investigate it.

In essence, classmates were sharing their motivation. Those who wanted the degree for a promotion or prestige were extrinsically motivated. I noted that years later, many never finished their degree: they remained ABD. Those who expressed their curiosity, their need to solve a problem or answer a question were "intrinsically motivated" and completed their degree, usually in record time.

Extrinsic motivation is fueled by external forces, such as grades, diplomas, degrees, performance appraisals, awards, or tips. It is how *others* judge you. You might be extrinsically motivated to get the respect and admiration of others, so ultimately, others control the rewards and therefore govern us. I find that those who are driven by extrinsic motivation tend to burn out or fail out. Their goal is simply to finish, and they often aim for average.

Intrinsic motivation means your drive for doing something comes from internal sources such as your core values, interest, morals, and passion. You find it enjoyable and inherently interesting. It results in high-quality work and creativity. When intrinsically motivated, you find joy and challenge in your pursuit and are liberated from the pressure resulting from external measures such as awards.

When you have identified your intrinsic motivation, it becomes a source of burning passion. It becomes your reason for waking up in the morning and why you will burn the midnight oil as you consistently push yourself to do more. You know you are passionate about what you do when you are so motivated that you would do it for free if you could. Time stands still, and you are in a state of flow. You are completely mesmerized by your work. You do not notice the minutes and hours ticking by. You do not have hunger pain, you are not stiff yet, you feel no pain, you are entirely in the zone. You are intrinsically motivated to succeed.

Motivation gives you focus and energy and drives your perseverance. In adult learning and social psychology, we use social determination theory (SDT) to examine motivation and what it would take for it to be realized. Edward Deci and Richard Ryan, who came up with SDT, state that to be genuinely intrinsically motivated, you need to satisfy your need for competence, autonomy, and relatedness (Deci et al, 2001; Deci and Ryan, 1985, 2000; Ryan and Deci, 2000).

Selecting what you are good at

Competence refers to having the ability to succeed and excel at what we do. It would be hard to be motivated to do something you were not good at, let alone something you did not master. All Olympic athletes referenced their natural talent and ability to compete at a higher level than their peers. The scientists mentioned that they were good at science, and the concepts made sense to them. If you watched *The Queen's Gambit* on Netflix, you recall the scene where she would visualize chess moves on the ceiling as she was lying in bed. She was able to think several moves ahead. It all made sense to her, and she had a natural ability for the complex game of chess.

Elevating your relationships

Relatedness refers to the ability to connect with people through networking, collaborating, or communicating with others. Sometimes, no words need to be exchanged between the people as they understand each other so well. They know what needs to get done. It is that special relationship between team members such as astronauts aboard the shuttle, a coach and athlete, and a scientist and trainee.

Building your autonomy

Autonomy implies the ability to direct our own lives, have independence over our own decisions, control over our creativity, and having the necessary tools and skills to do so. Can you decide what projects to work on, which order to do them in, or with whom you get to work? How would you react if your work was scripted? On a space shuttle, mission control regulates every task and the timeline to see it to completion. Astronaut Peggy Whitson turned these assignments into a competition to finish them faster than the timetable allowed. That is how she exerted her autonomy over a very controlled situation.

Finding your purpose

In his 2009 book *Drive*, Daniel Pink suggested that having a sense of purpose is critical to motivation, thereby adding a fourth dimension.

Purpose relates to the opportunity to make a contribution or difference. One successful physician-scientist told me that the work was so draining that he often thought of quitting. But then he thought of the patients who were dying unnecessarily. He realized he did not have what he called "the luxury" of taking the easy way out. He realized he could not stop working on treatments to help patients. It was his purpose.

Your purpose could be saving one life or millions of lives. US President George W. Bush asked infectious disease expert and director of the National Institutes of Allergy and Infectious Diseases at the National Institutes of Health, Dr. Tony Fauci, to serve as the principal architect of the PEPFAR program, the President's Emergency Plan for AIDS Relief. That initiative saved over eight million lives. Fauci recognized the impact of PEPFAR, which is why he worked so diligently to bring it to fruition. "There's nothing better than that feeling of knowing that you played a major role in something like that," shared Fauci.

Ultimately, when people find their intrinsic motivation, they have found the locus of their joy. Loving what you do is such an integral part of finding your passion and, ultimately, success. So much so that it is in the Olympic Charter: "Olympism seeks to create a way of life based on the joy of effort" (International Olympic Committee, nd).

There is a thrill in achieving something that has not been done before. As Nobel laureate Dr. Mike Brown shared with me, "What I love most about being a physician-scientist is that moment when you solve the problem in the laboratory." It is about discovering the unknown.

Dr. David Ginsburg recognized that feeling when he discovered something new with a trainee in the laboratory. He told his student, "Here's a fundamental fact of nature, that is a truth of nature, and only two people in the world could know this, you and me. And there's something very cool about that. That's part of the joy of this discovery too." Ginsburg shared that you get a real buzz out of it. He asserted that getting to know how things work is what makes the career so fun. He found his joy and his intrinsic motivation.

Finding your intrinsic motivation is a process. You do not wake up one day and realize what you were put on this earth to do. The high achievers I spoke with tried many things before realizing what they truly excelled at, which put a fire in their belly. These are all paths you could consider when embarking on the search for your intrinsic motivation.

High achievement is not about the prize or medal. It is about achieving what you set out to do. There is a bigger purpose. Janice Lintz lived in

New York City, regarded by many as a cultural capital. Museums and Broadway theaters surrounded her. When her daughter was diagnosed with hearing loss at the age of two and a half, Lintz felt her world crumble. Her daughter could not enjoy the shows New York City was famous for, nor could she hear the docent at the world-famous museums on Fifth Avenue.

A doctor recommended to Lintz that she send her daughter to a special education school. Lintz vehemently disagreed. Rather than have her daughter accommodate herself to the hearing world, Lintz moved to accommodate the world for her daughter. In the process, she changed the world to accommodate millions of people with hearing loss. Her advocacy work, for which she was rarely paid, pushed the world to be more hearing accessible. One fight, one conversation, one project at a time, she was making a dent and making the world more equitable for those with hearing loss.

First, she started by creating New York City as a model. Lintz's tireless work made all New York City taxis, Broadway theaters, US national parks, baseball stadiums, several Delta terminals, and Apple stores more accessible to those with hearing loss. From there, she thought bigger and wanted her work to spread out throughout the United States. To do this, she testified before Congress and spoke to US Senator Elizabeth Warren to break the hearing aid oligopoly, which led to her introducing and passing with Senator Grassley the over-the-counter hearing aid law. She connected with half a dozen commissioners of the Federal Communication Commission to regulate standards for closed captioning. After that, it was world domination. She spoke to Ban Ki-Moon, the UN Secretary-General, to make the UN more accessible to people who are hard of hearing. She reached out to former vice-president and now president of Ecuador, Lenin Moreno, to equip museums in his country with the technology needed for people who are hard of hearing to engage with the exhibits actively. She even wrote to Queen Elizabeth, the monarch of England, to make Buckingham Castle more usable to those with hearing loss, and engaged in dialogue with a staffer who initiated the necessary changes (Gotian, 2020). Lintz was relentless in her pursuit to enhance hearing access throughout the world.

Now a world expert on hearing accessibility, Lintz did not know a thing about this field when her daughter was first diagnosed. She researched the subject, talked to people, and thought about the problem day and night. She understood that every call she made, every meeting attended, and every person she spoke to could help make the world more accessible for her daughter and the 466 million people worldwide who suffer in silence (World Health Organization, 2021).

When you are intrinsically motivated, you work tirelessly toward your goal. You get into a natural rhythm and just cannot stop. There is no beginning and no end. Everything blurs as you are laser-focused on your goal. Everything you do, every action and decision you make, is in service to that goal. When you get into this flow state, all outside distractions are muted, and you are in the zone. If you achieve that flow state even once, take note and identify what you are working on; that is your clue that you just might have found your passion, which you are intrinsically motivated to pursue.

Try a few things out

Do not expect to wake up one morning and figure out what your passion is. You will likely need to try a few things out to see what you gravitate toward, what you are naturally good at, and what piques your curiosity. You get this idea in your head, and you just cannot let it go. You think about it and often research the topic. You try to learn everything you can about it and are constantly searching for more intel. It becomes like a good book that you just cannot put down; you want to learn more, do more, achieve more. Time stands still as you work on your passion.

David Ginsburg, a preeminent physician-scientist, tried a few paths before he found his calling. As a child, he wanted to be president of the United States. As he grew older, he considered being a mathematician and then a physicist, but neither was the right fit. In college, he caught the research bug and knew this was what he needed to do. Ginsburg was an undergraduate at Yale and took a required science course with a young assistant professor, Dr. Joan Steitz. He liked the subject matter and wanted to learn more. After class one day, he asked if he could join her laboratory and do research, and to his excitement, she agreed. Ginsburg relished working in the laboratory. He loved discovering things and thinking about problems in new ways. He loved doing research so much that he continued working in Steitz's laboratory and published his first academic paper with his mentor after graduation.

Ginsburg went to medical school at Duke, then did a residency in internal medicine followed by a fellowship in hematology at the Brigham and Women's Hospital in Boston and oncology at Dana Farber Cancer Institute. All of this clinical work left little time to do research and he missed it desperately; it was always gnawing at him. He had unanswered questions swirling around in his head.

Physicians undertake patient rounds, the morning event where trainees and their attending physician visit every patient to get an update and recommend a course of action moving forward. It was on these morning rounds that Ginsburg met Dr. Stu Orkin, a young physician-scientist. As he did with his undergrad mentor, Ginsburg approached Orkin and asked to do research in his lab. Orkin agreed, and Ginsburg continued pursuing his passion. He kept learning more and getting better and was eventually offered several jobs in high-profile institutions where he could open his independent laboratory and do the research he found interesting. He was appointed as a Howard Hughes Medical Investigator simultaneously with his first independent faculty position, which gave him an enormous financial safety net to feverishly and independently pursue his passion.

Every year, Ginsburg gets a vivid reminder of why pursuing his passion is valued. Why those late nights, early mornings, and failed experiments are worthwhile. Early in his career, Ginsburg was working with one of his mentees, a hematology fellow, to take care of a University of Michigan undergraduate student who had cancer. The college student had acute leukemia and a horrible prognosis. They treated him at the time with an experimental new protocol, and with what Ginsburg refers to as incredible luck, the college student did exceptionally well. It has been over thirty years since Ginsburg treated that Michigan college student, and he is in great shape and presumably cured at this point. Every year at the anniversary of his diagnosis, the former student writes to Ginsburg and his mentee. Ginsburg shared that having such an impact that cured a patient is profound and motivates him to keep doing his work. He realizes that his work is helping to save lives.

Finding your flow state

When you are doing the work that fuels your purpose and is what you are intrinsically motivated to do, all of the outside distractions become background noise. You are laser-focused and time melts away. You enter a state of flow. In positive psychology, a flow state is achieved when you are fully immersed in what you are doing. You are in the zone, entirely focused on your work and getting immense joy from it. You are completely engrossed in your task and lose track of time. The ego subsides, and every thought, action, and move you make seamlessly flows into the next. The concept of flow was first introduced in 1975 by psychologist Dr. Mihaly Csikszentmihalyi

(Csikszentmihalyi, 1990). To achieve a perfect flow, you must attain a balance between the task and level of skill. If it is too challenging or too straightforward, the flow will not transpire; the skill and level of complexity must be high and aligned for actual progress to be made. If it is too simple, it will result in apathy (Csikszentmihalyi, 1997); if it is not in equilibrium, it will result in frustration.

Olympic gold medalist Apolo Anton Ohno knows the feeling too well, as he spent his entire career chasing it. It was the fuel to his motivation that led him to be the most decorated winter Olympian. He loved to win and hated to lose. He excelled at indoor short-track speed skating. It was his passion and love, and he was extremely competitive. For him, it was an obsession with perfection and progress. Ohno felt outstanding on the ice and achieved the elusive flow state. The edges were blurred between his foot, blade, boot, and contact with the ice. He said it often happens in practice but not in competition; he only had that feeling twenty times in his competitive career. Chasing that feeling motivated him and it became addictive. That drive, charged by his intrinsic motivation to succeed, ultimately led him to eight Olympic medals, the most of any winter Olympian.

Strategies to maintain your motivation

Now that you have identified your intrinsic motivation, here are strategies for maintaining that motivation that will lead to peak performance.

Strategy 1: Surround yourself with people who are smarter than you

If you are the most intelligent person in the room, do not sell yourself short; find another room. Surrounding yourself with smarter people than you can open your eyes and mind to opportunities you did not know existed. Sometimes you may know early on what you want to do, but it could take years or even decades to actualize it. You may not have the competencies, knowledge, skills, and attitudes to bring your goal from the dream state to reality. Being surrounded by those who are doing what you ultimately want to do helps fuel motivation.

Dr. Charles J. Camarda watched seven men go on America's first space flight and knew right then and there that he wanted to be an astronaut. A college professor told young Camarda about an internship at the National Aeronautics and Space Administration (NASA). He applied, got accepted, and packed his bag. He loved his NASA internship and could not get enough of it. He was surrounded by such brilliant people and wanted to absorb everything he could. He kept a notebook, which he still has today, decades later, of all of the codes he learned. He came to the internship to learn engineering but feels he learned so much more. Upon completion of the training, Camarda knew he had to return to NASA. These were the people he needed to be around.

Camarda returned to school, finished college, and subsequently earned a master's and doctoral degree. In 1978, NASA permitted non-pilots to apply to be astronauts, and Camarda ran to apply. He was rejected. He still loved everything about the space program and wanted to remain at NASA as he felt he could be helpful and loved being around the intelligent people there. He became a leading NASA engineer instead, which aligned perfectly with his degrees. He spent his entire career at NASA, initially researching their heat-pipe-cooled sandwich panel and then reusable launch vehicle programs. He later oversaw the thermal structure laboratory, where he led numerous component developments for the space shuttles.

Camarda loved being an engineer and working at NASA, but there was an itch that needed scratching. He wanted to go to space. It was a decades-long dream since he had first seen the initial seven astronauts on television. Eighteen years after he first applied, a mentor encouraged Camarda to apply again. Camarda was a single dad, so living out his dream was not so simple anymore. He consulted with his third-grade daughter, who told him it would be an adventure. They packed their bags and moved from Virginia to Texas. Camarda was going to be an astronaut. In 2005, Camarda put on his space-suit and boarded his first space flight, the STS-114, the space shuttle *Discovery*. The world was watching this launch, dubbed "return to flight", as it was the first launch to space since the 2003 *Columbia* space shuttle disaster where seven astronauts had lost their lives.

Camarda was a challenging child, always getting into trouble. By his admission, he was no different as an astronaut. He was always looking for things that could go wrong. He felt he had no choice as he and others had lost friends on the *Columbia*. He was intrinsically motivated to ensure another disaster did not occur. On his flight, Camarda and his good friend, Peter Gnoffo, an aerodynamics expert, found a problem with the belly of the space shuttle. Something was sticking out an inch. They had to do an emergency spacewalk and remove the part sticking out, or else the space shuttle would catch fire. Camarda was not going to let that happen; he was not going to let any more astronauts die.

Camarda was always finding mistakes in the mechanical systems. His performance appraisal said, "He has a low tolerance for stupidity." He felt he had no choice. Lives were at stake. His intrinsic motivation was not just to get to space anymore; it was to do so safely so that space exploration could continue. Surrounding himself with bright, diligent, and forward-thinking people helped Camarda bring his dream to fruition.

Strategy 2: Stick to your core values

Dr. Bert Vogelstein is a leading physician-scientist based at the Johns Hopkins University School of Medicine in Baltimore, Maryland. As a toddler, his parents inculcated in him the Jewish core value of *tikun olam*, repairing the world. Being true to his beliefs, Vogelstein knew he had to do his part to fix the world. He wanted to do this by helping people. He was a mathematics major in college and did well in his science class. After graduation, he went to medical school, figuring it would be a direct way to assist people.

It was in medical school that Vogelstein had his first experience working in a laboratory. That changed everything. He realized he had a passion for research and found it fascinating. He finished medical school and started his residency. In his first year, called intern year, he continued doing research. Intern year is perhaps the most challenging year of training; the hours are long and the work is hard. After taking care of patients all day, Vogelstein would sometimes go to the laboratory at night and help solve problems that others were stumbling on during the day. He worked hard but could not get enough of it.

Vogelstein realized he had to make a decision. He never did research full time; it was mostly in the summers. At times he got in trouble at the clinic as he was absent and in the laboratory instead. He continued doing research at the National Institutes of Health for his postdoctoral fellowship, and there he made the critical decision to pursue research full time in lieu of clinical practice. It was not an easy choice, but it was one that he made by following his passion:

> I had no idea whether I was going to succeed in research. I wasn't arrogant
> enough to think that I could discover something new. I was hoping I could.
> I knew I enjoyed the activity, but certainly, I wasn't confident. The only thing I
> was confident about was that if I looked back twenty years after I started,
> I would want to know that I had given it my best shot. I thought, if I'm going to
> try to do it, I'm going to do it right, with every part of my being.

Strategy 3: Find and become a role model

Finding your passion requires you to try many different things before one sticks. The challenge is that you do not know what you do not know. There is a whole world of options that you might not have considered just because you did not get exposure. Having role models, people who have done it before you, can open your mind to new possibilities.

When she was nine years old, Dr. Peggy Whitson saw the first moon landing and got inspired. By the time she finished high school, NASA had selected their first female astronaut. They also picked a biochemist, and Whitson was interested in both biology and chemistry. When she was ten, Whitson's father got his pilot's license, and she thought, "Astronauts fly, so why not me?" By the age of 12, she told her mother she wanted to be a pilot. Her sister laughed and told her, "You mean a flight attendant, right?" When Whitson pushed back and said she wanted to be a pilot, her mom encouraged her to pursue this noble goal.

In college, Whitson's biology professor was full of energy and motivated her to pursue a career in the sciences. There were not too many women in science then, so the encouragement was well placed. Whitson selected a similarly mannered PhD advisor who continued to inspire her. Women in science surrounded Whitson, so continuing down this path was more natural to her than most.

Whitson still wanted to be an astronaut. She applied to NASA and was accepted, but not as an astronaut. Undeterred, she applied for ten years before finally being accepted. In the end, having other responsibilities at NASA during those ten years qualified Whitson to be a commander. As the lead for the joint shuttle Mir science program in Russia, Whitson was in charge of leading a team under unknown conditions, never knowing when the next shoe would drop, or what unpredictable event was around the corner. She had to find the right person to pay off to get their things out of customs, unload and haul thousands of pounds' worth of hardware up three flights of stairs when the elevator was broken, and work in rooms that were bugged. These experiences made her better qualified for her leadership role years later when she was selected to be the commander of the International Space Station.

Whitson worked tirelessly for decades to achieve her goal; it was what she had wanted ever since she was a little girl. Even when she was told she was not accepted as an astronaut, she kept trying. She kept her focus and became an astronaut, a two-time commander, chief astronaut, and holds the US record for the most days in space.

Strategy 4: Find your tribe

Being different can be very isolating. Finding people who see your difference as a gift, instead of a threat, is inspiring. Discovering an entire group of people who want to work together toward a common goal is the ultimate reward. You are all intrinsically motivated toward a shared objective. You lift each other, inspire one another, and provide a sense of belonging.

At the age of 12, Olympic champion rower Caryn Davies was already six feet tall. She was lanky and awkward. When she went to the supermarket one day with her father, a scruffy man walked up to her, assertively pointed at her, and said, "I want you for rowing." She was a little intimidated. What Davies did not know was that the man was a rowing coach, and tall people are favored for rowing. The coach spoke with her dad, and a few days later, Davies was rowing. It would take another year before she could train competitively as the training schedule did not align with her junior high school schedule.

Davies was suddenly part of a team with others who were just like her. She was accepted, valued, and even popular. Surrounded by rowers, she came out of her shell and blossomed. These were her people, her tribe. She knew she loved it so much that when it was time to look for college, Davies knew she had to continue rowing. She looked for a school where she could excel academically and continue her competitive rowing. She went to Harvard, and the rowing team became her social group. Being part of this team gave her a sense of belonging and self-confidence. She loved it. In her mind, there was never a question of not rowing. She had found her tribe.

By the time I spoke to her in 2020, she was training for her fourth Olympics. She had already won the silver and back-to-back golds at three previous Olympic games. Each time there was a new team, she had to form new bonds. Inevitably, they always gelled and worked together toward that common goal. They inspired each other and helped each other regain focus after a race that did not end with the result for which they were aiming. While training for the 2021 Olympics in Tokyo, she told her new teammates that "Everything matters and nothing matters. No one poor performance will take you out of the running" to make the Olympic team. That attitude and self-compassion remind Davies why she works so hard, taking a year off from her work as an attorney to train. She loves rowing in the purest sense and remembers that with every stroke. That mindset led her to be the most decorated female rower in Olympic history (Koenig, 2012).

Working toward a goal can be a tremendously difficult journey and incredibly isolating. Late nights, early mornings, and countless hours spent working on your craft, finding a treatment, correcting an error. There are many hurdles and mistakes along the way. That is to be expected. Those who are intrinsically motivated know that the challenges, bumps and bruises are all part of the process. They need to meet their goal, and they have an unyielding desire to make progress. They passionately love what they do, and all the high achievers told me they would do it for free if they could. Many do.

We have all seen the motivated person outperform the less motivated person both in performance and outcome. This is true even when the opportunities and skills are identical. The difference is the source of motivation. We have all seen this reality. In essence, it is the intrinsically motivated person who surpasses the extrinsically motivated person. We do not need to see research on this, even though plenty exists (Gallup, 2020). Identifying your passion is a critical first step to achieving your success. Consider what you are good at, what skills you have, what types of things you enjoy doing, what you procrastinate doing, who you like to do it with, either alone or with others. See the online resources which accompany this book for a passion audit worksheet that can help you determine what you are passionate about and intrinsically motivated to pursue.

When I oversaw admissions for a combined MD-PhD Program, students would often get frustrated and overwhelmed by the sheer volume of work. At times, they lost their motivation. With the hopes of being reminded of their purpose, they would come to me, and I would pull out their essay from the admission application where they had written why they wanted to become a physician-scientist. The admissions committee were seeking their "why," their motivation for pursuing the combined degree. They were trying to determine if they were intrinsically motivated. You might study cancer because someone in your family died from it, and you want to prevent others from experiencing that heartbreak. Perhaps you want to be an astronaut because you were always fascinated by space. Extreme high achievers searched and found their intrinsic motivation and pursued it relentlessly. Keep a visual to remind yourself of your cause.

Over time, your intrinsic motivation may change. As you go through life, you may find yourself interested in other things. That is to be expected. Go through the same process to identify your new intrinsic motivation. Throughout the process ask yourself, whose goals are you working toward? Are they your goals or someone else's? Make sure you are not living out someone else's dream. When you tap into your intrinsic motivation, find your flow state, and get to work. The feeling will be liberating.

COACHING QUESTIONS

1 What is one strategy you will implement to find your intrinsic motivation?

2 What is one approach you will use to make your intrinsic motivation stick?

KEY TAKEAWAYS

Identifying and pursuing your intrinsic motivation will help you become a high achiever. Its pursuit will nourish and sustain you as you face challenges, and they will surely come:

1 Use the tools provided in this book to help you identify your intrinsic motivation. This may change as you face transitions in life, so feel free to go back and repeat the process when you need to get back to your "why."

2 Often, your love and passion for a project will far surpass your initial goal. It gives you purpose. Work to pinpoint what gives you purpose.

3 Sample several things before you decide on the area where you will focus. See where you are able to maintain a flow state and where you get distracted.

4 Utilize the strategies offered in this chapter to help your intrinsic motivation stick.

References

Bloomberg, LD and Volpe, M (2008) *Completing Your Qualitative Dissertation, A Roadmap From Beginning to End*, Thousand Oaks, CA, Sage Publications, Inc.

Csikszentmihalyi, M (1990) *Flow: The psychology of optimal experience*, New York, Harper and Row

Csikszentmihalyi, M (1997) *Finding Flow: The psychology of engagement with everyday life*, New York, Basic Books.

Deci, EL, Koestner, R and Ryan, RM (2001) Extrinsic rewards and intrinsic motivation in education: Reconsidered once again. *Review of Educational Research*, **71**, pp 1–27

Deci, EL and Ryan, RM (1985) *Intrinsic Motivation and Self-determination in Human Behavior*, New York, Plenum

Deci, EL and Ryan, RM (2000) The "what" and "why" of goal pursuits: Human needs and the self-determination of behavior, *Psychological Inquiry*, **11**, pp 227–68

Gallup (2020) Gallup Q12® Meta-Analysis, https://www.gallup.com/workplace/321725/gallup-q12-meta-analysis-report.aspx (archived at https://perma.cc/L64Z-ZK3Q)

Gotian, R (2020). How Complaining To The Right Person Can Influence Change. *Forbes* https://www.forbes.com/sites/ruthgotian/2020/08/18/how-complaining-to-the-right-person-can-influence-change/ (archived at https://perma.cc/3RFX-Y5NF)

International Olympic Committee (nd) *Olympic Charter* https://olympics.com/ioc/olympic-charter (archived at https://perma.cc/7VBJ-JUGW)

Koenig, A (2012) Day 6 at the London Olympics: Gold for Davies '05 and Lofgren '09. *The Harvard Crimson* [Online]. Available: https://www.thecrimson.com/blog/the-back-page/article/2012/8/2/day-6-london-olympics-lofgren-davies-harvard-gold/ (archived at https://perma.cc/UC6H-DVZ4)

Oecdorg (2020) Education at a Glance, OCED, https://www.oecd.org/education/education-at-a-glance/ (archived at https://perma.cc/PT6C-GVG6)

Ryan, RM and Deci, EL (2000) Self-determination theory and the facilitation of intrinsic motivation, social development, and well-being, *American Psychologist*, 55, pp 68–78

Wilson, R (2017) Census: More Americans have college degrees than ever before, *The Hill*, https://thehill.com/homenews/state-watch/326995-census-more-americans-have-college-degrees-than-ever-before (archived at https://perma.cc/P7EL-NBUD)

Winerman, L (2008) Ten years to a doctorate? Not anymore, *gradPSYCH Magazine*, American Psychological Association

World Health Organization (2021) Deafness and hearing loss, https://www.who.int/news-room/fact-sheets/detail/deafness-and-hearing-loss (archived at https://perma.cc/SAZ6-L8E9)

05

Perseverance

How you approach adversity is what distinguishes high achievers from those who are average in their pursuits. High achievers approach challenges differently (Gotian, 2020a). They know they will prevail over the latest hurdle that is sure to come their way. High achievers believe that no matter the obstacle, they will go over, through, under, or around it. Being motivated to succeed is a good start, but success does not happen based on motivation alone. You need to mix in a strong work ethic, a sense of tenacity, and a dose of stubbornness. Perseverance infused with motivation is a combustible combination in the most positive of ways. It makes you almost limitless in your pursuits. For some people, no problem is too small. Others see challenges as nothing more than a bump in the road. For them, it is not a question of *if* they will overcome a challenge, as they know they will. Instead, they focus on *how* and *when* they will overcome the obstacle. They have a laser-like focus to control what they can control. They have the self-confidence and the self-efficacy that they will prevail. They are not afraid to take on calculated risks and challenges and they are fixated on their goal. For them, it's not that they want to meet their goal; they need to, with every fiber of their being. Ultimately, high achievers fear not trying more than they fear failing.

Bonnie Blair, a five-time Olympic gold medalist in speed skating, trained for the pack-style short-track races. In December 1979, right before the 1980 Olympic trials, she went to Wisconsin to partake in a pack-style meet. The day after her event, there was a different type of race; instead of racing against a pack, you compete against one other person and the two of you race against the clock. Blair had never competed in that race before and did not even have the right equipment for it. However, she was not afraid to fail and with every fiber of her being she felt she needed to try. She borrowed someone's uniform, used for the longer races. Her one competitor did not show up.

The Olympic trials were the next week, and Blair knew that if she could finish the 500-meter race in 47 seconds, she could compete in them. There was a clock at the end of the straightaway and she was fixated on the time; she felt that the race was between the clock and herself. She finished at 46.5. Never having trained in this race before, but fearing not trying more than she feared failing, she did it. Bonnie Blair realized she was going to be in the Olympic trials. She was only 15 years old.

Blair went back the next weekend and competed in the race she had only skated once before. She was used to competing in the short-track pack style, so racing against one competitor and trying to beat a clock was completely new to her. That year the US team took five women in the 500 meters for the Olympics. Blair placed eighth overall; she was so close to making the team. That was when she realized she had a shot at a future Olympics. It only happened because she feared not trying more than she feared failing.

In this chapter, I outline the key practices of high achievers that allow them to overcome difficult obstacles. These practices include a strong work ethic, a sense of humility that allows them to recognize failure but the boldness to push past those limits. The view of being told "no" is converted to an opportunity to work harder, an optimistic outlook, and pure love and passion for what they do.

A strong work ethic

High achievers work until the job gets done to a level with which they are satisfied. Dr. Tony Fauci, director of the National Institute of Allergy and Infectious Diseases at the NIH, was on television multiple times a day during the Covid-19 pandemic, as he led America's response. Having advised every US President since Ronald Reagan, he said that if you tell yourself, "I can't wait until it's 5 o'clock so that I can go out and do what's fun," that simply will not work. That is not the work ethic needed to achieve success. That work ethic led him, at eighty years old, to work more than eighteen-hour days during the Coronavirus pandemic (Young, 2020). Arturo Casadevall, MD, PhD, a professor at Johns Hopkins School of Medicine who worked on convalescent plasma for the Covid pandemic, summarized it perfectly: "The single most important characteristic is persistence... Sticking with it, persistence, don't give up."

Extreme high achievers have an unrelenting worth ethic (Duckworth, 2016). When there is a problem that needs solving, days and nights get blurred. They stop at nothing to get the job done in a manner in which they are proud. After Justice Ruth Bader Ginsburg passed away, I interviewed several of her former clerks for a *Forbes* article to find out what professional and life lessons they had learned from the legal giant (Gotian, 2020b). They all had many of the same things to say, one of which was her recognizable work ethic. She was notorious for leaving five-minute-long voicemails at 3 am.

An optimistic outlook

Dori Bernstein, who clerked for Justice Ginsburg from 1991–92, told me that she learned a valuable lesson from working with the notorious RBG:

> Justice Ginsburg did not waste precious time or energy on regrets, or allow disappointment to fester into bitterness. Instead, she always looked forward with hope to the future, continually striving to do the best she possibly could— and her best was nearly always perfect. Through her example, the Justice taught me a lesson that has been particularly helpful in absorbing the sorrow of losing her. Meaningful work can strengthen and sustain you; it was at the core of her indomitable spirit and the best way to honor her memory.

Love for what they do

Having unanswered questions and needing to know why something hap-pens pushes the highest achievers to work relentlessly toward their goal, fueled by their passion. Dr. Gary H. Gibbons, a cardiologist and director of the National Heart, Lung and Blood Institute at the National Institutes of Health, said:

> You're driven to pursue something because you love the pursuit and are fulfilled by it. The mastery fulfills you, and you want more. That propels you even when you get rejected manuscripts, you are doing experiments at 3 am, or have grants that don't get funded. You're intrepid in your pursuit. Even if you weren't paid for this, you'd probably find some way to do it.

As Dr. David Ginsburg, a high-achieving physician-scientist, shared with me, "You need to have a hunger in your belly. You want to do this; you become driven and possessed a bit. The most successful people are those who are driven and just *need* to do this work."

Dr. Peggy Whitson, NASA's former chief astronaut, is a record breaker. On 24 April, 2017, Whitson broke the record for spending the most cumulative days in space by any NASA astronaut. The count was 534 days! Overall, she is the most experienced NASA astronaut of any gender, having spent 665 days in space during her multiple missions. That is equivalent to a hypothetical trip to Mars. She was the first female commander of the International Space Station, a role she held twice. At 57, she holds the record for the oldest female astronaut.

Having led multiple teams in space, Whitson, who is extremely competitive by nature, knows a thing or two about work ethic and loving what you do. She told me that halfway through the missions, people often get depressed. They are away from their family and friends for long periods. They are in a small area with the same people all the time. Every minute of their workday is structured and scripted by mission control. Whitson said she never felt despondent as she loved what she was doing. It probably helped that she turned everything into a competition, from unloading supplies to fixing the toilet (yes, astronauts need to do everything onboard the shuttle themselves). When mission control gave her a timeline of what to accomplish, Whitson always tried to finish the tasks in less time. By her admission, Whitson said she competed with herself a great deal and always pushed herself to do more. When mission control extended her time in space, Whitson did not complain. She saw it as an opportunity to advance her pursuit. She loved what she was doing and felt it was her calling.

Failure and rejection

For high achievers, failure and rejection are separate concepts. Rejection or "no" comes from external sources, those who judge us somehow. Extreme high achievers need to be able to bounce back from external rejection. But it is a bit different when they fail to reach their own goal: it becomes more personal. Seeing where you failed and pushing past it takes a different level of resilience than coming back from an external rejection.

If there is one sport where you lose more than you win, it is baseball. You statistically fail more than you succeed and worse, there is someone who is always calculating and announcing these statistics for everyone to hear. Before the 1969 New York Mets won the World Series and became the "Miracle Mets," they did so poorly that they were known as the "Loveable Losers." Art Shamsky was a member of that fateful team, and said:

> In baseball, you fail more than you succeed. It's great for developing relationships and learning to depend on your teammates. It teaches you humility and how to survive the losses. It's a great step that teaches you many life skills. You go to practice every day and give it your all because you love the game and have a deep respect for your teammates.

Throughout the 1969 season, the Mets' Manager, Gil Hodges, was "platooning" players, putting certain players against the right- or left-handed pitchers. The players did not like it as it did not help their careers, but they did it willingly because they had the upmost respect for Hodges and the technique was working. At game one of the World Series, the Mets were playing against the Orioles and were losing. Shamsky walked to the on-deck circle to get ready for his at-bat. The Orioles manager went up to the mound to talk to the opposing pitcher. Shamsky had an unanticipated extra minute and reflected on his upbringing and the endless times he had been with his friends to play baseball in the summer, all the amateur games where he had competed, the bumpy bus rides to games, all the hours of practice on his days off, and the immense effort that led up to batting at the World Series. Shamsky realized that he was getting to live out every kid's dream. He spent that moment thinking about his journey. His life memories flashed before him. He thought about the tremendous road to get to the World Series. Decades later, he remembers it vividly. It was constant practice. There were injuries and operations along the way to get there. "There were lots of curveballs and a great deal of pressure," Shamsky said. An audience of 55,000 people watched the game in the stadium, and an additional 100 million people were watching him on TV. He knew that he was not going to make every at-bat, and everyone would see it. But he focused on the opportunity to get to play in the World Series. Shamsky went to home plate and grounded out to second base. Ultimately, the Mets won the World Series.

No means not yet

When told no, you are not selected, your proposal will not work, your grant is rejected, manuscript not accepted, or your idea does not have merit, you have two choices. You can give up and decide you are not cut out for this path, or alternatively, you can reframe "no" and choose to hear "not yet." High achievers choose the latter option (Gotian, 2020c). Adding the word "yet" means you are still in the game; there is more you can do to change the outcome and meet your goal (Dweck, 2016). That puts you in control of when this journey is over. You get to decide when to continue and when you have had enough. The choice becomes yours, not someone else's. To start, you need to normalize rejection.

By not taking no for an answer, Dr. Deborah Heiser, a developmental psychologist and aging specialist, revolutionized how depression is assessed in nursing homes. Her graduate school assigned Heiser to a 705-bed nursing home for her practicum (Gotian, 2020c). According to the staff, very few residents suffered from depression, but that was not what Heiser observed. She noticed residents who sat in chairs with their heads down for hours, stayed in their room by choice, without a television, book, or any other stimulation. She inquired if everyone was assessed for depression and was told, "Yes. We use the Minimum Data Set (MDS), a government standard measure for clinical assessment of all residents in Medicare- or Medicaid-certified nursing homes."

Despite what the government form said, Heiser felt that many residents were undiagnosed for depression and wasting away in the nursing home. As a graduate student, she was intrepid enough to raise the issue but was dismissed. Heiser could have readily admitted defeat then, but chose not to. Hoping to probe deeper, she challenged the status quo and was permitted to distribute a questionnaire to the residents, which she did. What she found changed the lives of countless senior citizens. Her analysis of 700 question-naires found a significant number of residents who screened positive for depression—the exact opposite of what the government form said.

Heiser found a discrepancy between those who were positively assessed for depression by psychologists and the MDS results. Needing a "gold standard" for comparison, Heiser reached out to the creator of the Schedule for Affective Disorders and Schizophrenia-Research Diagnostic Criteria (SADS-RDC), the gold standard measure for depression. She recruited graduate students to help her conduct further research and found the SADS results were on a par with the self-questionnaire she had distributed and did not correlate with the MDS the nursing home was using. Her find-ings were published and featured as the lead article in a journal, won an international award, and changed how staff assessed nursing home residents for depression (Heiser, 2008). She did this as a graduate student! One person from her dissertation committee said, "I never thought anyone would try to add to the gold standard measure—it was so much work!" When Heiser was told "no," she reframed that comment and said to herself, "What is the strategy to make this happen?"

When people are told no, it may be more about them than you. It is possible and even likely that the naysayer does not understand how to make it happen, and cannot or will not take on additional responsibility. If you feel a project can be done or a goal achieved, think broadly and creatively about what actualizing it would involve. Strategize what would need to happen and who you would need to talk to to help you achieve your goal. The word "no" is not forever. For high achievers, no means not yet.

Humility to recognize limits and boldness to push past them

For Olympic champion speed skater Apolo Ohno, the higher the stakes, the more he worked at it. Not succeeding one year was the fuel he needed to succeed at his next chance: "My goal was to be the best. It was a series of failures that caused me to reevaluate and push harder. I never wanted to taste that failure again. I cranked up my training. The skates became a part of my feet, a natural extension."

Failure is part of the process

Failure and rejection are just the first steps of a very long process, and high achievers know they are in it for the long haul. Ever since she was fourteen, Haley Skarupa had her eyes set on the Olympics. She was a hockey player practicing and competing with players five years her senior. By the time she was in college, her coaches were former Olympians. During the summers, she would come back home to Maryland and train with the boys' team. By the time she was a college junior, she was on the world championship team. That was her first taste of the elite level, and she developed quite the appetite for it.

By then, in addition to being a college student, she was playing on two teams: her Boston College team and the US team. Many of her competitors on her college team became her teammates on the US team. After college, she continued to play hockey and work toward her goal of making the Olympic team. By 2017, she was training full-time. She went to the selection camp, where the coaches whittled down the forty players to twenty-five, who would then live and train together while the coaches selected the final team. Skarupa prepared for a full year for this one opportunity. The selection camp is a constant evaluation on and off the ice. Your seniority in the sport is of no value; everyone walks in with a clean slate.

It was a grueling week, physically and emotionally and Skarupa decided to take it day by day, drill by drill. She gave it her all. At the end of the week, the coaches would announce who had made the Olympic team. The selected players would stay in Tampa, Florida, to continue the training while those who did not make the team were sent home. Ultimately, Skarupa's name was not on the list. She did not make the Olympic team. Her dream was shattered.

Skarupa was devastated. She had put her life on hold for a year, and everything she had into the training, but had fallen short of her goal. She returned to her family's home in Maryland to recalibrate and decide what to do next. She worked odd jobs such as walking dogs and working at a video production company as she reflected and planned her next move.

One September day, she got a call from the training camp to say that some of the players had been injured and others were not living up to expectations. She was given forty-eight hours to fly down to Tampa for a two-week informal evaluation. Skarupa did not feel that she was at her peak performance as she had not trained rigorously since being cut from the team. She also realized she could not give up on this unforeseen second chance.

Skarupa flew to Florida and did her absolute best at training camp, and at the end of the two weeks returned to her home in Boston. Before she left, Skarupa was told she may or may not hear in three weeks if she should return for a third visit, for a formal evaluation. The stress was palpable. Hoping that she would get another chance to impress and make the Olympic team, she continued her rigorous training regimen upon returning home. She increased the intensity of her gym workouts and played with a professional hockey team to improve her skills. Around Thanksgiving, she got the call for which she was hoping and waiting: the coaches invited Skarupa to return to Florida for a formal evaluation.

Her nerves were raw, and her emotions were jagged. She knew that she could do her best but ultimately, it was out of her control. That is when she made the decision. She knew that she had painstakingly done everything she could do to elevate her game. Skarupa resolved to let go of everything that she could not control and play for the pure enjoyment of the game. She was going to enjoy the experience. She shifted her mindset to focusing on what she could control and letting go of what she could not.

In December, Skarupa was notified that she had made the Olympic team. A month later, she boarded a plane to Pyeongchang, South Korea, and within days, won the Olympic gold medal along with her teammates. Skarupa never lost sight of her goal. When she was told she had not made the Olympic team, she recalibrated but did not give up. In the weeks between her initial tryout, followed by the informal evaluation, and finally, the formal assessment, she ultimately realized that being rejected once does not mean another opportunity might not arise later. When it does, she is going to be prepared. After all, luck is where preparation and opportunity meet.

In Chapter 4, you heard about Commander Peggy Whitson, who for ten years applied to be an astronaut before she finally gained acceptance by NASA. Fellow astronaut Dr. Charlie Camarda applied once, was rejected, and applied again eighteen years later. What they learned from each rejection, false start, and negative result, and how they picked up the pieces from those challenges, is illuminating. It is what makes them extreme high achievers.

Failure and rejection are so routine that Nobel Laureate Dr. Bob Lefkowitz says, "It is our constant companion." When Lefkowitz worked at the NIH, there was a long period when none of his experiments were working:

> I remember what another senior figure told me over lunch one day when I was bemoaning my fate over how barely anything was working.
>
> He said, "You know, Bob, do you know the difference between a really top-flight scientist and the run-of-the-mill guy?"
>
> "No."
>
> "Well, for the run-of-the-mill guy, maybe 1 percent of what he does works. But for the superstar, it could be as high as 2 percent."

After Lefkowitz won the Nobel Prize in 2012, they interviewed one of his mentors from his NIH days, forty years previously. Lefkowitz said that his mentor reported that one of his main jobs was "To keep Lefkowitz out of a deep, dark depression."

Dr. Bert Vogelstein, one of the highest-cited physician-scientists in the world, explained that to succeed, you need to have a personality that can tolerate failure: "That mindset requires a good bit of resolve, a personality that can tolerate failure, a long-term view. You need to have all of those things if you're going to succeed sooner or later. Maybe not sooner…"

Dr. Helen Hobbs, who won the 2016 Breakthrough Prize in the Life Sciences, concurred. She also recommended not clawing on a problem for the wrong reason: "You must be tenacious and not let go of a problem until it is solved; you also need to know when to let go of a problem." Many directors who trained physician-scientists told me that delayed gratification is critical to success. The comments of Drs. Lefkowitz, Vogelstein and Hobbs were so routine that they were echoed in every single interview with the high achievers.

Fear not trying more than you fear failing

High achievers fear not trying more than they fear failing. They likely feel they have nothing to lose, and any advancement, even a small one, would be a step forward. You read about, Haley Skarupa's journey to the Olympics, which was filled with false starts, broken dreams and opportunities grabbed with both hands. She felt with every molecule in her being that she had to try, no matter the outcome. High achievers ensure a high degree of control over many aspects of their work, including the objectives, pacing, content, methodology, and outcomes assessment.

Sometimes you need to take calculated risks. After years of clinical training, Dr. Bert Vogelstein decided to focus on his research in lieu of seeing patients: "In some ways, I was gambling my professional life, because it would be much easier, and still is today, to get a position in a clinical department if I did part research and part taking care of patients. But I thought, if I'm going to try to do it, I'm going to do it with all my might." He felt he had to at least try.

Risks do not work without the fortitude to carry them through. Vogelstein shared, "You have to have the courage to try something revolutionary rather than settle for an evolutionary kind of research." You need to continually increase your knowledge and make connections others do not see. The more you know, the more connections you can make. The risk of trying then trumps the fear of failing.

Control what you can control

High achievers pursue their passions past stated limits. With all the failures and rejections that inevitably come their way, high achievers do not waste time or energy on things that are not within their control. Instead, they focus on what they can control and place all of their energy on that. High achievers do not question if they will overcome a challenge, as they have faith and confidence in themselves that they will. Instead, they turn their focus to how and when to overcome the latest hurdle.

In 2020, Olympic champion rower Caryn Davies was training for her fourth Olympics. postponed by a year due to the pandemic, with still no guarantee that they would take place in 2021. For a fleeting minute, she considered quitting. However, she realized she had no control over what happened to the Olympics; she only has control over what she does every day. With that mindset, she decided to take it one day at a time and keep up with her training for Tokyo: "When the calculation changes, then I'll change what I do. There's no sense wasting your time worrying about things you can't control. Act according to the information you have, and when the information changes, adjust as necessary."

Michiel Bartman is a Dutch rower and Olympic champion. In high school, he started competing in rowing but his training was halted by mandatory military service. He could not get out onto the water, but he knew he could still keep his body in shape. After putting in a full day of work, he went to the gym to work out. That was all he could do at that stage in his life. He could not practice, he could not compete, but he could stay in shape. He controlled what he could control.

Sometimes flexibility is what you need to overcome failures. Nobel laureate Dr. Mike Brown recounts the time when he and his research partner and fellow Nobel prize winner Dr. Joe Goldstein were trying to purify a membrane valve enzyme. They attempted to do this with their students and fellows and were not able to do it. They put the problem aside and returned to it five years later when the techniques and technology had improved. Then they were finally able to do it: "A lot of times, persistence is just so important. You just keep trying different things. One of our fellows has run into a problem, and we've been exchanging emails about crazy ideas to solve it. Sometimes if you do enough things at random, something works." Pretty good advice from a Nobel laureate.

Connect the dots

There is a difference between knowing, understanding, and accepting things. We all know many things and accept them as fact. But pushing the boundaries to understand how things work, or do not work, how things can be done differently or reimagined is what separates high achievers from everyone else. Dr. David Ginsburg, the physician-scientist at Michigan, put it bluntly: "You just need to know how stuff works. Are you comfortable getting in the car, pushing the accelerator, it goes forward, and you don't have any idea what happened? We're scientists, that's unbearable."

Dr. Huda Zoghbi, a physician-scientist at Baylor who won the coveted Breakthrough Prize in Life Sciences in 2017, had a bumpy road to success. Zoghbi, a pediatric neurologist, would not have been today's thought leader on Rett Syndrome if it were not for her curiosity and persistence. Zoghbi, who loved puzzles and challenging cases, did not have her eyes set on being a physician-scientist. She knew that she was curious and enjoyed investigation, but thought she would focus on clinical investigation, dealing with live patients, not basic science, which researches things at the molecular level. In the early 1980s, when Zoghbi was in the midst of her neurology training, she became very frustrated after encountering many patients with devastating diseases. At that time, all they knew was that it was probably a genetic disorder, but they did not know what caused it or what to do about it.

One day, Zoghbi met a child with Rett Syndrome and was both fascinated and perplexed. She could not understand how it could be progressive but not degenerative. Back in the 1980s, if you had something developmental, there was something abnormal from birth. Alternatively, you could be born normal, and then things would degenerate as in Tay-Sachs or Batten disease. "To see something where you're born normal, and then you lose milestones is unusual," says Zoghbi. "You gain milestones first, and then you lose them, but there's no degeneration. To me, just from a clinical standpoint, I had no insights. It was very perplexing."

The next week, Zoghbi had the opportunity to select the type of patient she wanted to examine. She picked a patient with a diagnosis of cerebral palsy. She knew it was likely an incorrect diagnosis as, at that time, neurologists used that diagnosis when they did not know the cause of neurological impairment. Zoghbi walked into the exam room and saw the young patient wringing her hands. Bells went off in Zoghbi's head. She realized the patient must have Rett Syndrome. In one week, Zoghbi went from never seeing a patient with Rett to seeing two. The syndrome had been reported in the literature by Bengt Hagberg but never reported in the United States, and here she was seeing two patients with this enigma.

Zoghbi realized that Rett might be more common in girls. She asked the Blue Bird Circle, a group of volunteer ladies who helped in the neurology clinic, to pull every female patient record with a specific diagnosis. The Blue Birds came back with thirty-five charts. Zoghbi meticulously went through them and found six charts that fulfilled the criteria for Rett Syndrome; she invited all of these patients back to the clinic.

This finding was the dawn of her groundbreaking work. Within a few years, she published her results in the *New England Journal of Medicine*, considered the preeminent medical journal. Once she published her paper on the new disease, patients flocked to her and she received a grant from the NIH to continue her work. Zoghbi realized that the patients were all girls and looked the same, "So there must be a gene causing this disease." Since then she has committed herself to this population. It all started with her being curious and connecting dots.

When working at the NIH during the Vietnam War, Nobel laureates Drs. Mike Brown and Joe Goldstein noticed something very wrong with the two siblings (see their story in Chapter 1). They could have ignored it, but they did not; they could not let it go:

> Curiosity is essential. You have to want to understand things. If you just want to accept things and just exercise principles already known, that's fine. But if you're curious, you want to find the answer, like we did with these children we could have ignored. Wow, this is something extraordinary these kids have. They have this enormously high cholesterol there must be a genetic cause; there must be an answer here.

That curiosity led them down a path of questions that they chased for years... all the way to the Nobel Prize.

Valence of Velcro vs Teflon

The road to success is filled with failures, detours, trials and tribulations. Not a single high achiever had a quick ride to success. Perseverance was a critical component of pushing through the darkest of hours.

On the road to success, there are countless rejections, negative comments, failed opportunities, and even eye rolls. The high achievers learned to develop, what is called in group dynamics, a valence of Teflon. When faced with a challenge, rejected grants, or snide comments, you have a choice. You can choose to have a valence of Velcro. Everything will stick to you. You will stay up at night, worry about things, and your cognitive load will be on overdrive. You might lose sleep, get heart palpitations, or turn inward and become silent and slowly depressed or withdrawn. With a valence of Velcro, every negative comment and action sticks to you. Sadly, after a while, it weighs you down, so much so that you cannot continue at this pace. The weight and cognitive load often cause people to leave the profession or stop aiming for high success levels.

Alternatively, you can have a valence of Teflon. Every negative comment and action will glide off of you and you will not lose a moment's sleep over other people's judgments. Arthur Levitt spent his entire life in a pressure cooker. After sixteen years on Wall Street, he became the Chairman of the American Stock Exchange in 1978. In 1993, President Clinton appointed Levitt to the role of Chairman of the Security and Exchange Commission (SEC), a position he held until 2001, making him the longest-serving SEC Chairman in US history. Levitt, who loved every part of his professional life, is not used to not getting his way. When asked about obstacles and negativity in his career, he replied, "I'm sure there were negative things, but I just let them roll off of me." That's Teflon.

You cannot let other people's opinions and comments stop your thoughts or distract you from your work. One of my former Teachers College, Columbia University classmates, Travis J. Dolan, a Colonel in the US Army, always reminded me, "Nobody died. Keep things in perspective." Wise words that have stuck with me ever since. As I notice people struggle with negative feedback, challenges, or bad news, I tell them, "If they aren't paying rent, don't let them take up real estate in your head." Simply put, I am telling them to adopt a valence of Teflon instead of Velcro.

COACHING QUESTIONS

1 What is one project or idea you believe in so passionately that you are willing to put in the work to see it to fruition?

2 What is one action you can take today to help you deal with failure or rejection?

3 What is one thing you can control right now?

KEY TAKEAWAYS

Failure and rejection are natural parts of any process. Success does not just happen. What you see in a person's success is the tip of the iceberg; it is what is below the water line that makes a high achiever. One of the four elements of success is a strong sense of perseverance, not letting things go, or giving up. If you adopt some of these traits, you will see an increase in your success:

1   Find something that you can sink your teeth into, where you need to see a project through to completion, understand why things happen, and see the magic of your work come to fruition.

2   When someone tells you "no," reframe that in your mind to "not yet." Add the word "yet" to the end of the sentence, and you are now in control of when something is truly over.

3   Understand that failure is a natural part of the process and a learning opportunity. Glean what you can from every challenge and use that as ammunition to improve your future performance.

4   Fear not trying more than you fear failing. If you do not try, you will not have the opportunity to succeed. What is the worst that can happen? Give it a try, for the sake of trying.

5   Focus on what is in your control. Use your energy and efforts to determine how to manipulate what is in your control. When variables and data change, pivot accordingly.

6   Look for ways to connect the dots. Continuously scan and consider which random facts and people can be combined. Consider what people overlook. Find a solution to problems people do not even know they have.

References

Duckworth, A (2016) *Grit*, New York, Scribner, an imprint of Simon & Schuster

Dweck, CS (2016) *Mindset*, New York, Ballantine Books

Gotian, R (2020a) 8 high achievers share how they are managing pandemic-related challenges, *Forbes*, https://www.forbes.com/sites/ruthgotian/2020/09/07/7-high-achievers-share-how-they-are-dealing-with-challenges-caused-by-covid/ (archived at https://perma.cc/W4AR-TWVH)

Gotian, R (2020b) Justice Ruth Bader Ginsburg's best mentoring advice, *Forbes*, https://www.forbes.com/sites/ruthgotian/2020/10/13/justice-ruth-bader-ginsburgs-best-mentoring-advice/ (archived at https://perma.cc/9J7N-J6WH)

Gotian, R (2020c) Why some people don't take 'no" for an answer, *Forbes*, https://www.forbes.com/sites/ruthgotian/2020/11/27/why-some-people-dont-take-no-for-an-answer/ (archived at https://perma.cc/B5XD-42W5)

Heiser, D (2008) Depression identification in the long-term care setting, *Clinical Gerontologist*, 3–18

Young, J (2020) A day in the life of Dr. Anthony Fauci, *Huff Post*, https://www.huffpost.com/entry/anthony-fauci-fighting-covid-19_n_5fc7fed7c5b61bea2b14e3ee?ojn (archived at https://perma.cc/2FCX-JTYQ)

06

Building a strong foundation

If you walk into any karate dojo or studio in the world, you will see the participants doing "katas." These are detailed patterns of movements involving choreographed steps and turns. Regardless of rank, every person who walks on the mat makes these same moves to start their class. It is used to practice form and technique and encourages those on the mat to visualize various movement scenarios. If you are a beginner, a white belt, or a fifth-degree black belt, you are doing the same katas to start your training for the day. If you cannot get these foundational steps absolutely right, you cannot successfully build on them and learn more complex forms and techniques. Practice can often lead you to discover ways to improve that can help you leapfrog forward. The techniques become muscle memory and allow you to make micro changes to optimize your success.

Basketball legend Kobe Bryant was famous for showing up at the gym before sunrise and practicing his drills (Gotian, 2021; Grover, 2021). Bryant likely knew he was one of the greatest basketball players but never rested on his laurels. As one of the top NBA players, he would wake up early in the morning and often not leave until he had successfully made 100 baskets. This practice of early morning workouts with repeated throws to the basket is something Bryant did during high school and continued doing throughout his NBA career. Practicing hard things can result in habitually achieving great things. It is the difference between making something a routine versus a commitment.

In 2019, Sir Peter Ratcliffe received a once-in-a-lifetime phone call. On the other end of the line, the person informed him that he just won the Nobel Prize in Physiology or Medicine. Hours after receiving the life-changing call, the Nobel Prize Twitter account showed that Ratcliffe was back at his desk submitting an EU Synergy Grant application to fund his research (The Nobel Prize, 2019). He wrote grants in the earliest days of his career and continued to do so after winning the Nobel. Receiving the high accolades is nice and affirming, but it is never the end goal. High achievers are always focused on their next goal. To make sure they are in top form and a contender to reach their next milestone, they constantly and repeatedly reinforce their foundational skills. If your base is not rock solid, the empire you build may crumble.

Exemplars are continually working on and strengthening their foundation. Physician-scientists are still designing experiments. Olympic athletes are still doing the same drills you would see in a junior high school auditorium. They always return to square one, reinforce it, build and expand from there.

In this chapter, you will learn how to build and reinforce your foundation by asking the right questions, seeking the guidance of mentors, valuing and cultivating teamwork, and considering the benefits of networking and professional relationships.

Master the basics

Ryan Millar, an Olympic champion volleyball player and three-time Olympian, would argue that the most critical skill in volleyball is ball control. Not jumping or blocking the ball, but controlling it. At age eleven, Millar started playing volleyball in the backyard with his older brother. For hours they would practice a drill called "Pepper." This drill, in its different variations, focuses on the skill of controlling the volleyball. Millar stood several feet apart from his brother. He hit or passed the ball to his brother, who then "set" the ball back to him. Millar spiked the ball, forcing his brother to defend or "dig" the ball back to him. Millar then "set" the ball back, allowing his brother to spike it. This is a repeated cycle where the ball is passed, set, and hit back and forth between the two brothers. Millar practiced this drill when he was a pre-teen, until the sun went down in his backyard, and he continued the same warm-up exercise with his national team as they were preparing for the Olympics.

Take a methodical approach

Basic skills are not just for athletes. Neal Katyal argued forty-four cases before the Supreme Court of the United States, more than any other minority lawyer in American history. Despite this illustrious experience, he says that every case is nerve-wracking. Countless eyes are watching, and he realizes that his reputation is always on the line. To help him prepare to the best of his ability, Katyal has four routines, which he does before every case. He did them before his first case before the Supreme Court, the forty-fourth case, and every case in between. Katyal prepares in a way that leaves no stone unturned. For every case he argues before the Supreme Court, he walks in with a binder that has the answer to every conceivable question. He has never looked at the binder during the case, but having it there is his crutch. Just the rigorous process of developing the content for that binder prepares him to argue the case.

Next, he holds multiple simulated court proceedings, known as moot courts. Before his first case, he had fifteen moot courts. Now, with the experience behind him, that number is down to six. The point is that he still does them. He does not ever walk into a case feeling he knows its content and process and therefore does not need to prepare as diligently. The practice is the same. Perhaps he does not need as many repetitions, but he still goes through the same methodical process.

When he argued his first case before the Supreme Court, Katyal's two oldest children were in preschool. The night before the big case, he would walk into their rooms and, one by one, explain the case to them in terms they could understand. "It forces you to boil down the issues and make them accessible," Katyal said. His children are teenagers now, and he still does this. Katyal feels that he has the psychological benefit of bringing his kids with him to the courtroom on the day of the trial. He often writes their names down on the legal pad in front of him, to ground him to remember why he is carrying on this fight.

Finally, Katyal has a playlist he listens to as he walks to court. It gets him focused, in the zone, and pumped. Distractions fade into the background as he listens to the lyrics and beats. He is ready. Music in his ears and binder in hand, he is prepared to take on his next case before the Supreme Court.

Over all the cases Katyal has argued before the Supreme Court, his preparation methods have not changed. He prepares and walks into every new case with his binder filled with answers to every imaginable question. He practices with repeated moot courts, distills the cases to their most essential elements as he explains them to his children, and listens to his customized playlist to get in the zone. It is a methodical approach that helps him prepare for achieving his next goal.

The greatest skill is a lack of weakness

In 1984, when Scott Hamilton won the Olympic gold medal in figure skating, it ended a twenty-four-year drought of the United States not winning the top spot. Hamilton's road to the Olympics was far from smooth sailing. He almost did not make it. Adopted at six weeks of age, he was very sick as a child. Between the ages of four and eight, he was in and out of the hospital and was not growing. Hamilton received one misdiagnosis after another. Doctors gave him a six-month life expectancy, news his mother refused to accept. Trying to give him a semblance of a normal childhood, his parents enrolled him in ice skating lessons at a new rink that had opened up near their home.

Every Saturday morning, Hamilton went to the rink and skated with abandon. He was so excited to be around healthy children. Every week his skating improved. Finally, after years of being in the hospital and always being the last person selected for teams at school, Hamilton got his first dose of self-esteem. He was good, really good. He was the best in his skating class.

He started skating full-time and ultimately made it to the men's championship. He had a very bumpy start, but his love of skating did not diminish. By the time he was eighteen, Hamilton's mother had died; he was devastated and did not know how to continue without the one person who loved him unconditionally and always had his back. He decided he would work harder than ever and make his mother proud. Hamilton returned to his training with a newfound focus. He was able to complete jumps he never could before; things were looking up.

Hamilton was rated fifth in the world and the top spot, which he wanted badly, was now in view. He was always a better free skater than he was a figure skater, and that was his weakness. Figures are when a skater has to trace circles with their blades so precise that leaning on the wrong side of the skate could result in point deductions. Hamilton decided he was going to find a way to fall in love with what he hated most. "The greatest strength is a lack of weakness," he said. He worked on his figures day and night. It was a core skill, and he was determined to excel at it; he had to, as it was the only thing standing between him and a gold medal. Hamilton saw his figures improve and learned to like it. He had half the ice for three hours every morning, and he worked non-stop on his figures. He knew he had to master this foundational skill if he was ever to win a competition.

Standing on the top spot on the Olympic podium in Sarajevo was a relief. He realized he was the fourth American man ever to win the gold medal in figure skating. In the end, at the Olympics, Hamilton came in first place in the figures, the one skill he initially disliked and which was his weakness. He worked relentlessly on the foundational skill to win gold.

Broadway stars use their entire body in every performance. Being able to sing, dance and act simultaneously and flawlessly means they constantly need to work on their foundational skills to ensure there are no weak areas. Victoria Clark won the 2005 Tony Award for Best Leading Actress in *The Light in the Piazza*. Before taking to the Broadway stage for her award-winning performance, she practiced many of the same warm-up techniques that have served her well throughout her thirty-eight-year stage career. Her warm-ups have evolved as her needs have shifted and her voice has changed, but the goal has remained the same. "The storyteller needs to *open* in order to warm up the channel for the stories to be released," shared Clark. She is keenly aware that her entire body, not just her voice, is her instrument. She does aerobic exercise to increase her stamina, flexibility, and lung capacity. She often talks or sings while walking or jogging to ensure she has the energy to sing and dance simultaneously. As she progressed in her career, her physical flexibility diminished somewhat. In turn, her aerobic warm-up speed decreased, but as she did in her very first year of acting, she is still doing physical warm-ups to get herself ready for the stage.

When she started her career, her vocal warm-ups were complex scales where vowels and syllables frequently changed. She did not stop doing these vocal exercises just because she won a Tony Award, but traded in the complex scale warm-up and evolved to two-note scales on a single vowel, "ah," which serves as a kind of litmus test for her to ascertain where her voice is on any given day. An actor can work their entire career to reach the gilded road that leads to the Tony Awards. They do it by continuing to build and reinforce their foundational skills and working diligently to overcome any real or perceived area of weakness. High achievers know how to pivot and modify or refine their routines to accommodate their new and changing needs.

Whether an Olympian, Tony Award-winning star, or lawyer, all high achievers focus on reinforcing their foundation, paying special attention to overcoming any areas of weakness.

Ask the right questions

When I first embarked on my doctoral journey, my mentor, Dr. Bert Shapiro, gave me sage counsel when I was considering which topic to focus on for my dissertation. "Do something important, not just interesting," he said. That was essential advice that has guided me every day since. As a scientist, he knew that selecting the right question was paramount to success, and his recommendation was right on target. I chose to research the most successful physician-scientists of our generation. That advice all those years ago ultimately led to the book you are now reading, countless keynotes, and articles in such journals as *Forbes*, *Harvard Business Review*, *Psychology Today*, *Nature*, as well as many academic journals.

But how does one determine the right questions to ask, and why is that important? For starters, asking questions helps you find gaps and possible solutions that others might not be aware of or see clearly. Consider where there is missing information, knowledge, understanding, or skills. How can you fill in these gaps? What is the best way to have the greatest impact? Understanding that what you do and say can have the power to make an impact that is far greater than you can help you identify the right questions to ask.

Like many exemplary physician-scientists, Dr. Bert Vogelstein from Johns Hopkins spends six to eight hours a day designing and interpreting experiments. "It is exactly what brought me into research in the first place. I relish doing experiments, designing hypotheses and testing them. I love playing with laboratory toys. I don't like meetings," he said. Surrounded by graduate students and postdoctoral fellows, Vogelstein still has the same practice and outlook on experiments as he did early in his career.

Physician-scientists are continually looking for the right problem to solve; finding it can be the key to your future. Dr. Tony Fauci, America's infectious disease expert, underscored the need to choose something important. Because of this ideology, Fauci is always at the forefront of leading the US response to such viruses as HIV, Ebola, SARS, Zika, and Coronavirus. "[Be sure to] ask an important question. It is nice to be interested in something trivial. It could be a nice little hobby, but I always try to ask a question and get involved in an area that is important. What you are asking needs to lead to an answer that will have an impact," said Fauci.

Be curious

To ask the right questions, you need to be unapologetically curious:

How does that happen?

What would happen if I did this?

Who said that?

Why is this not being done?

Why is it being done this way?

When you start asking yourself, 'Why didn't anyone do this?' you know you are onto something.

After ten years as CEO of Snapfish, Ben Nelson realized he wanted to step down. He knew he could build something impactful from nothing but did not know what his next adventure would be. Mulling over several ideas in his head, he kept returning to education; the problem was he did not know how to turn it into a business. He discussed his interest with his former boss, who asked him several provocative questions. Reflecting on the conversation led Nelson to think deeply about how he would transform education. The son of two academics, he realized that the fulcrum of education is at the undergraduate college level. "If you fix higher education, you fix everything else. High school prepares you for college. It does not matter what high schools want to do; rather, what colleges will accept," said Nelson. He kept wondering how he could reimagine higher education.

Nelson's father, Dr. Nathan Nelson, is a preeminent biochemist who, in his 80s, is still working at his laboratory bench doing research. The younger Nelson felt that while his father is a prestigious scientist, he is not the best educator. His mother, on the other hand, is a scientist and gifted teacher who engages her students in their learning. He wanted to find teachers like his mother to educate the next generation at the undergraduate college level. He was so excited and fueled by the idea that he could barely contain himself. He wanted to build an institution of higher learning, where the level of teaching surpassed the high level of prestige.

With $25 million of venture funding, Nelson launched the Minerva Project, intending to create an elite brand of higher education with substance. He kept asking himself, how could this be done better? What would be more impactful? What is wasteful? Within two years, he had stripped down higher education to its core and built it back up. He reimagined the admissions process and criteria, curriculum content and delivery, and tuition structures. Instead of a traditional campus, the world became their campus. The students start their education in San Francisco, California, and over the next three years, they move to six different cities around the globe. While students are in residence, they are not on any campus. There is no gym or cafeteria. They are learning adulthood.

The Minerva Project started because Ben Nelson asked questions, lots of them. He was frustrated with what he saw and used his skills and network to make it better. He was curious and looking for new ways to make an impact. Asking the right questions is not just for science. In management, consider if you are solving the right problem. Is there an unmet need? Talk to people, ask questions and learn where the gaps are. Then work to fill them.

Cultivate a team of mentors

The data on mentorship is clear. Those who are mentored out-earn and out-perform those who are not (Allen et al, 2004; Eby et al, 2013, 2008). Nobody is born knowing all the answers. More often, we do not know what we do not know. Surrounding ourselves with people who can hear our ideas, help breathe life into them while teaching us how to manage pitfalls, is critical to success. All of the high achievers were mentored, and not by just one person, rather by an entire team of mentors. They would gain guidance from anyone around them who could offer perspective, skill, and ideas. Some were senior to them, some were junior, and some were at their level. They started relying on mentors early in their careers. Long after they achieved success, they continued to return to their mentors for guidance and perspective. Many of the long-time mentors became friends over time. The trust was always there, which kept the relationship going for years. The high achievers found mentors who would support them but never try to develop them into a mini version of themselves. They saw incredible promise in their mentees and helped to guide them to greatness.

Dr. Jeffrey Friedman is an award-winning physician-scientist known for discovering leptin, the hormone that regulates body weight. As he was building his laboratory and hiring people, he often went to his mentor, Dr. Jim Darnell, at the Rockefeller University, for guidance. Friedman's trial-and-error management style worked up to a point, but he realized he needed an additional perspective, and Darnell was always there to listen. The two would chat about managing a lab, motivating people, and science. For years, their labs were on the same floor, and they would have joint laboratory meetings. The relationship evolved and the tenor changed, but the mentoring relationship was always there.

They do not teach you in medical or graduate school how to manage a lab, lead a team, operate a budget or space. Friedman, like all scientists, had to try various approaches, observe others, and seek guidance. Early on, when he first built his laboratory, he did not fully appreciate the importance of selecting the right people. Equally relevant, he underestimated how damaging it can be to get people who could not effectively contribute. Thus, while some of the people he initially recruited made important contributions, others did not. When building his team in the laboratory, Friedman initially assumed that the worst outcome would be that someone would not contribute in a meaningful way. What he had not realized was that people can actually detract from the overall effort in many different ways, for example if their experiments are so poorly done that they need to be redone.

Another way in which people can negatively impact on a laboratory has to do with their effect on the people around them. Even one disgruntled person can undermine the boss and cause a toxic environment that ripples throughout the team. At one point, Friedman felt the graduate students and postdocs in his laboratory were in the midst of a revolt. He was in a perpetual bad cycle. He wanted to hire new and better people but could not. In science, before someone joins a group, they talk to the other members of the laboratory, and that is where the problem escalated. The current members told potential new hires that things were not good, and that they should stay away.

Friedman realized that his career could end for no other reason than losing control of the people in his laboratory. In science, a bad reputation does not dissipate quickly. "It has a legacy because even if someone new comes, a negative reputation extends well past the time when the difficulties took place, and it takes as many as two or even more generations to rebuild," Friedman said.

Friedman streamlined his team and spoke with his mentor. "I've had it. These people can do what they want," he told Darnell. He wrote them off in his mind and sat down with the three or four outstanding technicians who were committed to the project and told them, "These people can say and do what they want. They are not the project, we are." From that day, Friedman took ownership of his laboratory and team. His mentor, Jim Darnell, came up to him afterward and said, "That is the first time I ever thought you were going to do it."

Darnell was giving Friedman an important lesson. He listened but did not give him the answers. Friedman said, "You have to, at a certain point, realize you and you alone are solely responsible for the success of the laboratory." Darnell could have told him that, based on his decades of experience, but until Friedman realized it on his own, it would have had little impact.

I knew many of Friedman's former MD-PhD students as I had run the program for over 20 years. They always returned to Friedman for guidance and perspective, years after graduating from his lab and earning their PhD. He was paying forward the great mentorship he had received as he understood its value. He understood the need to be a guide by the side, helping the mentees see and believe what needs to be done. Mentees need to do the work on their own, and a mentor can help shine a line on the right path.

Look for the non-obvious mentors

Our parents' generation taught us that mentors should be older and wiser and have traveled our desire path. A more contemporary approach is to find mentors who are different than you, so that you can glean diverse perspectives. Not all mentors are obvious or more successful than you. Be open to looking along the fringes for people who can have a positive influence on you and your career.

Joe Jacobi won the gold medal in canoe/kayak at the 1992 Olympic Games in Barcelona. In his late teens, Jacobi met Steve Park, a regular guy from the neighborhood who liked to paddle on the same river as the local competitive team. Jacobi had just finished a training session and was paddling to the "take-out" of the river, where Park was in his boat training alone.

Jacobi was getting out of the boat and off the river with a friend and teammate, Lecky Haller, a World Champion. They watched Park paddle for a few minutes, then Haller turned to Jacobi and said, "Remember, you can learn something from anyone, not just people who are better than you."

Park was older than the other athletes who were training at the river. He had a full-time job and other life commitments. He was in his mid to late forties, decades older than the World and Olympic athletes training on the river. Park was just paddling to get healthier. However, his dedication stood out, even to the World Champions. Jacobi understood that anyone could positively contribute to the performance culture and community and actively worked to widen his circle beyond his coaches and teammates. Years after retiring from competitive racing, he continues to surround himself with a diverse group of people who can have a positive impact on him.

Find mentors who believe in you more than you believe in yourself

Nicole Stott would never have applied to be an astronaut if it had not been for her mentor, Jay Honeycutt, the former director of NASA's Kennedy Space Center. She already had her pilot's license when she finished high school and was itching to fly again when she graduated from college. She learned about NASA and got a job there in the space shuttle program as an engineer at Kennedy Space Center. Stott was there for almost ten years and saw every aspect of what it took to fly a space shuttle. She saw the astronauts coming through as they were getting the space shuttle ready. She recognized that 99 percent of the time the astronauts were on earth, not in space. Just like her.

That is when she started considering being an astronaut. Previously she had thought it was only something other special people got to do, not her. She was never told that she could not do it; it just seemed too unreal, too impossible. Then she saw actual astronauts and considered what they were doing and how similar it was to what she did. She also realized that their educational and work achievements and experiences were similar to her own.

The clincher for her that sealed the deal was speaking to her mentors, who told her to pick up the pen and fill out the application. It was just the push she needed. She realized she was in full control of this one aspect of the process. Without their encouragement, Stott admits, she would never have gone through with completing the application. She feels that her mentors saw more in her than she saw in herself. None of them said, "Are you sure? It is a long shot." They did not question her. They encouraged her to do the one thing she had total control over—fill out the application to become an astronaut. In hindsight, Stott realizes she needed affirmation from someone that she trusted that she could do this. She admits she would not have done it on her own. After her second try, Stott was selected to be an astronaut and spent 104 days in space.

Jay Honeycutt gave Stott a great deal of solid mentorship since he first started mentoring her in 1988. The piece of advice that really resonated with her was his idea that we always need to think, "Here's how we can, not why we can't." Honeycutt taught her that every problem has a solution; it just has not been discovered yet. It is brilliant advice. That attitude allows you to think creatively. It is a way of thinking which Stott finds liberating and used to solve endless challenges and dilemmas in her career. Decades after Honeycutt first encouraged her to fill out the application to become an astronaut, he and Stott are still great friends.

Learn by working with others

Can you play nicely in the proverbial sandbox? Learning to work with others, share, and compromise can be the difference between success and failure. You cannot always have it your way. The path to success is never walked alone. People are there to help you, but to succeed, the vision needs to be aligned. The sooner you realize that, the sooner you can disentangle some of what might be blocking your success.

Avoid being the loudest voice in the room

Daryl Roth has produced over 122 on- and off-Broadway plays, including six-time Tony winner *Kinky Boots* and the Tony-winning revival of *The Normal Heart*. Seven of her productions have earned Pulitzer Prizes. Before a play ever gets to the stage, there are many steps and people who help bring the idea to fruition; the writers, actors, directors, and stage managers are just a handful of the creative team required to get a play to Broadway.

Early in her career, Roth was a producer on the musical *Nick and Nora*. It failed. She noticed that the creative team did not have a shared vision for the show, so ultimately it did not succeed. She learned from that experience and recalibrated. "Being able to collaborate is the most important thing in theater," said Roth. "When you cannot align at the reading table, it shows on the stage."

When Roth looks for a new show to produce, she seeks out themes that are in line with her interests. She looks for a story that resonates with her, is meaningful, and to which she responds. It is the tapestry of her work, and there are common threads. She is very interested in gender, family relations, stories of her Jewish tradition, and strong women. She believes that to be successful, producers need to be passionate about what they are presenting.

The key to great collaboration, Roth feels, is to work with great people and hire experts. "Surround yourself with people who are better than you— lawyers, company managers, directors," she said. She listens more than she talks. She has realized that when she listens to other people's points of view, she finds it more effective than trying to be the loudest voice in the room. This is part of Daryl Roth's strong foundation, which she has reinforced over time.

Develop your power skills

If anyone knows how to collaborate, it is astronauts. Part of what the Chief Astronaut's Office looks for is how well the astronaut candidate can work with others. Dr. Peggy Whitson served as NASA's Chief Astronaut and always looked for people who would help pull the crew together. The collaboration is so critical to the mission that Whitson enhanced the Expeditionary Crew Skills Training, which NASA implemented. The astronauts were not lacking in technical skills but needed to enhance their soft skills, or, as I prefer to call them, power skills. Whitson led the astronauts through training that focused on communication, teamwork, self-care, team care, leadership and followership. Positive and negative examples were given to reinforce the lessons.

Collaboration, teamwork, and strong communication are so pivotal that Whitson and other astronauts attended the National Outdoor Leadership School (NOLS). The astronauts broke up into groups with two instructors, and undertook a seven- to eight-day hike, carrying 75 pounds of gear on their backs. It was physically very challenging. Every night the group would debrief. The two instructors would not tell them what to do unless they were in danger. In NOLS, they focused on communication training. One team had a map, the other did not. They had no choice but to communicate effectively. This replicates how astronauts talk to mission control from space. One team has data, and the other does not.

When Whitson became Chief of the Astronaut Office, she added the Maxwell Airforce Reaction Group to the training. This military officer training, adapted for the conditions astronauts would face, consists of obstacle courses with different constraints and rotating leaders for each obstacle. "Once the team figured out how to work together, the leader did not matter," said Whitson. They are there to fine-tune their leadership, followership, collaboration, and communication skills to solve any issue that arises. In the process, they learn to trust each other—that cannot be taught in a classroom. The training focuses less on how to solve the challenges and more on how to work together as a team.

Build your network as you build your career

All of the high achievers have an extensive network they have been cultivating over their entire career. It is their social and political capital: their currency. Over time, people in their network become good friends and trusted confidants. They continuously meet new people and develop more professional relationships. It is continually evolving.

Dr. Jon Cohen, Executive Chairman of BioReference Laboratories, runs the third-largest Covid testing facility in the United States. During the first half of the pandemic, he doubled the size of the company and BioReference Laboratories won the testing bids for the National Basketball Association (NBA), National Football League (NFL), and many colleges and universities (Gotian, 2020a). Cohen's career has not been linear. He is a physician, a vascular surgeon, and went through many years of rigorous medical training. He became Chair of Surgery at a major medical center by the age of 40, Executive Director of the hospital, and then Chief Medical Officer of the health system. He was a healthcare advisor for presidential candidate John Kerry, ran for Lieutenant Governor of New York on healthcare reform, and ultimately became senior advisor for New York State Governor David Paterson, responsible for all policy and strategy. When he left his government role, he served as a senior executive for Quest Diagnostics before his current role leading BioReference Labs.

Cohen's career has transcended academia, politics, and the scientific industry. From each experience, he has learned new skills and connected with more people. Each role has informed the next, and each opportunity would not have been possible without his previous learned experiences. The number of people he has interacted with or treated well has come around to be helpful in the future. "It is a deep network of well-formed relationships developed over time. People want to be around nice people and work with nice colleagues," said Cohen. Due to his wide-ranging career, he has met many people in different industries. He had views on particular issues, and people knew he stood for something. Cohen reaches out to his network once a quarter just to stay in touch. He makes a point of sitting and scrolling through his contact list as he knows it is important to stay on people's radar.

In all of my talks, I tell the audience that you are never too young or too inexperienced to develop a network. Peers rise together, and you are not going to be a student or junior manager forever. Shortly after Justice Ruth Bader Ginsburg passed away, I interviewed several of her former clerks for a *Forbes* article (Gotian, 2020b). Many of the clerks know each other because every year, Justice Ginsburg would invite them to a clerk reunion. All of the clerks from her entire career would gather together. They were fresh out of law school when they clerked for Justice Ginsburg but continued attending these events for decades.

Judge Paul Watford serves as a United States Circuit Judge of the United States Court of Appeals for the Ninth Circuit. He met Colorado Attorney General Phil Weiser when they clerked together for Justice Ginsburg in 1995–1996. They worked with Justice Ginsburg when she authored the historic United States vs Virginia decision. Paul Watford and Phil Weiser were Supreme Court clerks when they met in their twenties, and are now a Judge and Attorney General, respectively. Peers rise together.

In 2003, Dr. Peter Agre won the Nobel Prize in Chemistry. He told me that the Nobel laureates all know each other and are familiar with one another's work. Every summer, the scientists are invited to the Lindau Nobel Laureate Meeting. While they certainly get to speak with each other and reminisce, they also have the opportunity to talk science with the next generation. Six hundred undergraduate college students, doctoral students and postdocs from all over the globe get to meet one another, and network with each other and the Nobel laureates.

Having a strong foundation that is constantly reinforced is a pivotal element on the path to success. In every industry, the high achievers never rest on their laurels. They work hard to overcome any weakness and build on their strengths, and they do this with the help of others who help guide and support their journey to success.

COACHING QUESTIONS

1 Who can you reach out to today in order to build your network and develop your professional relationships?

2 What is one area of weakness you can commit to working on developing into a strength?

3 Who is one person who believes in you and can serve as your mentor?

KEY TAKEAWAYS

1 No matter your rank or years of experience, you must continuously build and reinforce your foundation. By taking a methodical approach, practice and master the basic skills and do not ever let them get dull. If your foundation is not strong and reinforced, you cannot build a solid career on it.

2 Look for the gaps in people's logic by being curious and asking questions. What is missing or being overlooked? Do not look for things that are interesting; instead, focus on what is important.

3 Those who have mentors out-earn and out-perform those who do not. Cultivate a team of mentors who can help you see different perspectives, encourage you, and help you achieve things you likely would not have been able to do on your own.

4 Learn how to work with others and collaborate effectively.

5 Start developing your professional relationships. Surround yourself with interesting people and maintain contact with your network.

References

Allen, T et al (2004) Career benefits associated with mentoring for protegee: A meta analysis, *Journal of Applied Psychology*, **89**, p 127

Eby, LT et al (2008) Does mentoring matter? A multidisciplinary meta-analysis comparing mentored and non-mentored individuals, *Journal of Vocational Behavior*, **72**, pp 254–67

Eby, L et al (2013) An interdisciplinary meta-analysis of the potential antecedents, correlates, and consequences of protege perceptions of mentoring, *Psychological Bulletin*, **139**, 441–476.

Gotian, R (2020a) How to succeed when you've never done the job before, *Forbes*, https://www.forbes.com/sites/ruthgotian/2020/09/14/how-to-succeed-when-youve-never-done-the-job-before/ (archived at https://perma.cc/C4BT-837Y)

Gotian, R (2020b) Justice Ruth Bader Ginsburg's best mentoring advice, *Forbes*, https://www.forbes.com/sites/ruthgotian/2020/10/13/justice-ruth-bader-ginsburgs-best-mentoring-advice/ (archived at https://perma.cc/9J7N-J6WH)

Gotian, R (2021) Why Kobe Bryant and Michael Jordan kept winning on and off the court, *Forbes*, https://www.forbes.com/sites/ruthgotian/2021/05/18/why-kobe-bryant-and-michael-jordan-kept-winning-on-and-off-the-court/ (archived at https://perma.cc/7DXK-3XKW)

Grover, TS (2021) *Winning: The unforgiving race to greatness*, New York, Scribner, an imprint of Simon & Schuster, Inc

The Nobel Prize (2019) Grant proposal deadlines wait for no-one! Twitter @nobelprize *Grant proposal deadlines wait for no-one! Sir Peter Ratcliffe sitting at his desk working on his EU Synergy Grant application, after learning he had been awarded this year's Nobel Prize in Physiology or Medicine*

07

Learning and growing are never over

For over two decades, I ran a combined MD-PhD programme. For eight years, my students pursued rigorous training to get dual postgraduate degrees. Admission to the program has a 3.5 percent acceptance rate; you would have a better chance of getting into Stanford than into this particular MD-PhD program. The students are the crème de la crème, the best of the best.

One day, a student walked into my office, as they often did. This student in particular had headphones plugged into his ears. "What are you listening to?" I asked, thinking he would tell me about his favorite band or musician. I was wrong and surprised. He was listening to an interview with a famous scientist. He often listened to science-themed podcasts, he informed me. He told me it was how he learned about the work of others, their methods, what worked, what did not, ideas they had, and stumbling blocks they had along the way. I was fascinated.

Many of the high achievers I interviewed for this book finished their formal education years, if not decades ago. Many earned advanced and terminal degrees. A diploma, award, or notoriety was never the end goal of their learning; it was just the beginning. Learning is a continuous process in which you examine further, ask additional questions, and connect more dots. Continuous learning is about learning to think differently, be faster, stronger, or better. For adults, it often does not happen in a formal classroom.

Many high-achieving billionaires such as Bill Gates, Warren Buffett or Mark Cuban are known for consuming new knowledge by reading many hours a day (Gallo, 2017). Yet it is not reading that has made them so successful, but rather that they are not afraid to admit that they can learn from others.

Reading is only one of many ways to learn something new. Many high achievers learn informally by listening to podcasts and attending talks about interesting topics or people. They seek out guidance and additional perspectives from those senior and junior to them and their peers (Gotian, 2020a).

A critical part of learning is seeking additional viewpoints and advice (Yoon et al, 2019). High achievers are constantly striving to make micro changes that will improve their performance and enhance their knowledge (Kluger and DeNisi, 1996). They obtain this by seeking input and feedback. They do not shy away from feedback; they crave it (Gotian, 2020d). Their mindset on feedback is that it is not a criticism, rather an opportunity for enhancement.

High achievers value the perspectives of others and seek guidance from their mentors. They do not just have one mentor; they have an entire team who they can draw upon for advice (Gotian, 2020c, 2020b). Recognizing the great value in this, they put a great deal of time and dedication into mentoring others and paying it forward. They realize that the success of their mentees ultimately measures their success.

This chapter will show you the different ways high achievers learn, usually outside of a formal classroom. Every experience becomes a learning opportunity, and everyone they meet has the potential to teach them something. Whether learning by seeing, doing, talking to others, or relying on past experiences, high achievers recognize there is always more to learn. Equally as essential, they are open and eager to learn more.

Map a learning path

It is impossible to have comprehensive knowledge on every particular topic. There are too many nuances and new knowledge and evidence appearing at an increasingly rapid pace. Figuring out your areas for growth and opportunity (notice, I do not call them weaknesses) is pivotal if you want to be a high achiever.

You might be higher ranked than your teacher

Dr. Christopher Walsh is a physician-scientist at Harvard Medical School and chief of the genetics division at Boston Children's Hospital. He has won numerous accolades from top scientific associations, including election into the prestigious Institute of Medicine. While he obtained both his MD and PhD, his willingness to continuously learn after he completed his formal education, his ability to be vulnerable and learn from others, on top of his natural talent, helped make him successful.

Walsh earned his PhD in neuroscience and then continued his clinical training in a neurology residency. After over a decade of training post-college for his MD, PhD and neurology residency, Walsh did a post-doctoral fellowship and realized he needed to learn molecular biology. He found that the best way to do this was to find the best molecular biologist in the laboratory and "just do everything that person told me to do," he explained. It just so happened that the best molecular biologist was someone who was two years out of college. Walsh, a world-renowned physician-scientist, learned molecular biology from someone more than a decade younger than him. Few people would have done that, but Walsh realized that knowledge can be gleaned from many different sources—you just need to be open to it. He realized that his path to achievement meant filling a knowledge gap and he strategized effectively to fill this need. How he learned molecular biology and the age of the person who taught it to him was irrelevant, as long as he was broadening his fund of knowledge.

Create your own learning development plan

In 2009, Congress confirmed Jonathan Jarvis as the eighteenth Director of the US National Park Service (NPS). This role was the crowning accomplishment of a journey that started in 1976 when Jarvis joined the NPS as a seasonal employee in Washington, DC. He began as a GS4, the lowest rank on the government pay scale, with a $12,000 annual salary. But he loved the work and wanted to pursue a career in the National Park Service, and he knew that to advance, he would have to move around; he ended up moving nine times, each time to a higher-level role.

How did Jarvis, with a bachelor's degree in biology, become the Director of the US National Park Service? How did he learn how to lead 20,000 permanent, temporary, and seasonal employees, 279,000 volunteers, 423 areas covering more than 85 million acres in every state, and a budget of over $2.8 billion?

"The National Park Service did not have a leadership development program, so I created my own," said Jarvis. After a full day of work, he took relevant leadership development evening classes at the University of Washington. Every time Jarvis learned a new leadership theory or skill, he would experiment and try it out on his staff. He rose to become Superintendent by the age of 39 and continued to develop his leadership and management techniques by learning and implementing his new-found skills. Jarvis was hungry for more. He applied to executive training programs at the national government level. Recognizing the value of learning diverse topics and gleaning insights from other industries, Jarvis spent part of his training time outside the organization and government. He went to work in a philanthropic organization, learning how and why people donate money. He also completed a senior fellowship with the Washington State Parks system to study racial inequality.

All of that learning through myriad funnels paid off for Jarvis. After completing the programs, he was selected as the regional director of the park service in the Pacific Northwest and the Islands, including Hawaii and Samoa, where he oversaw fifty-eight national park units. After spending seven years in that role, in 2009, President Obama nominated Jarvis to be the Director of the National Park Service.

Every conversation is a learning opportunity

Talking to others is a great way to learn new ideas, understand how to resolve problems, and learn what opportunities may become available. Before Maxine Clark became founder and CEO of the Build-A-Bear Workshop, she was president of Payless Shoes, the international discount footwear chain. So how did Clark learn to pivot from shoes to stuffed animals? It is said that luck is where preparation and opportunity meet. Clark prepared herself by talking and engaging with everyone around her, learning from everyone along the way. She learned about opportunities, successful and failed strategies, weak links, supply chain, leadership, and management.

After college, Clark went to work at the May department store chain. Within a few weeks, her boss had health issues and she stepped into his role. She realized she had a great deal to learn, and she had to accomplish this quickly. She was brand new to the position and talked to everyone around her, learning about everything from inventory management and supply chain to pressure points and purchasing. Every conversation was an opportunity to discover more, pick up critical details, and identify gaps in processes or understanding. By talking to others, Clark also learned about unwritten rules and traditions, often referred to as the hidden curriculum.

Her successful rookie results were noticed and after a long interview she was offered a job at the headquarters in St Louis, Missouri, as a proverbial "Chief of Staff" for merchandising. She was not necessarily a fashionista, but rather a working woman who understood what women like her wanted and needed. She talked and listened to working women, always having her finger on the pulse of what was in demand, connecting the real conversations to data to better predict trends.

Ultimately, a project she was working on led to the purchase of Payless Shoes. The company's two leaders took Clark under their wing, and she took every opportunity to talk to them, absorbing every piece of their wisdom and learning from their expertise. They taught her everything they knew about the shoe business, introduced her to key stakeholders, all while she asked a litany of questions to appease her curiosity. The more she spent time and asked questions, the more the leadership got to know Clark, her work ethic, determination, and ability to exceed benchmarks. She was not just a name. She was a curious individual who worked hard, produced excellent results, and constantly learned along the way by asking questions and regularly interacting with the company's leaders. Although small in stature, she was impossible to overlook. In 1992, Clark was appointed president of Payless Shoes. When she launched Build-A-Bear, she used the same conversational skills to learn what customers want, and how to branch into the toy market.

Find your community

Candace Cable's life changed at 4 am one early morning in Lake Tahoe at the age of twenty-one. A terrible car collision caused by a drunk driver left her paralyzed from the waist down. At the time of her accident in 1975, she did not know anyone else who used a wheelchair for mobility and felt isolated and alone. In addition, she found it impossible to get around. Two years prior to her accident, the 504 Rehabilitation Act had been enacted, mandating that any establishment that was federally funded is required to create equal access, such as ramps, assisted technology, or language, for people with disabilities. Unfortunately, there was no enforcement and Cable found herself struggling to get basic access. To cross the street, she had to find driveways so that she could get her wheelchair down off sidewalks. Her former positivity disappeared because the lack of inclusion made her feel broken and of no value to society.

Cable enrolled in a local college and went to the office of Disabled Students Services for accommodation support. "That's where I found my people," said Cable. She met students with disabilities different from hers and her sense of loneliness dissipated. She spent time with this new group who were participating in sports, something she had not considered before. Wanting to spend more time with them, she tried out different sports and gravitated toward wheelchair racing. She competed in the 5K, doing the same course, start and finish line as the runners, and felt fully included, finally.

Cable found her community. That feeling of belonging and togetherness influenced her to pursue a career in competitive sports. She did not see it as a competition against others; it was a competition with herself. With the support of her new community, Cable continued to compete and made it all the way to the Paralympic Games. She competed in nine Games in three different sports in both the winter and summer Paralympics: wheelchair racing, alpine skiing, and cross-country skiing. Cable even competed in the Olympic Games when wheelchair racing was an exhibition sport and won two Olympic medals to add to her twelve Paralympic medals, of which eight are gold. She had lots of firsts, including being the first American woman to win medals in the winter and summer Paralympic Games. She now uses her awards and her athletic notoriety as a platform to meet with leaders, and sit on commissions and boards to initiate inclusion change and human rights for people with disabilities. It all started because she spoke to people in a college office.

Approach questions from every angle

Dr. Gary H. Gibbons, a cardiologist and head of the National Heart, Lung, and Blood Institute at the National Institutes of Health, depends on conversing with others to answer his scientific questions. Since his first year as a medical student at Harvard Medical School, Gibbons has asked why African Americans have higher hypertension rates. He looks at this question from every angle, including clinical, scientific, and public health approaches. Gibbons routinely talks to other clinicians and scientists specializing in genomic sequencing and seeks guidance from experts in the field. The more he talks to people, the more likely he is to find answers to his questions or new lines of inquiry. He realizes that every person might have the answer to a small piece of the puzzle. If he can seek out the right people and combine all of the answers, he could be set on the path of solving this issue that impacts millions of people. His talking to people is a matter of national health.

You can learn a lot by watching

People are often so busy talking that they are not listening. There is a magical sense of calm when you do not speak but simply observe and take it all in. Look at the interactions between people, how they present themselves, command a room, or perform a particular skill. Their body language, word choice and tone are all clues.

Christopher Waddell started as an able-bodied skier, competing with his Middlebury College ski team until an accident left him without the use of his lower body. He is now known as a Paralympic sit skier and wheelchair racer who has participated in four Winter Paralympics and three Summer Paralympics, winning thirteen medals, five of them gold. He is also the first paraplegic to climb Mount Kilimanjaro, documented in the movie *One Revolution*.

Waddell grew up in Massachusetts and cannot remember a time when he was not skiing. From the age of six, he was coached by Rob Broadfoot, who would wait on the base of the mountain and give Waddell corrections to improve his performance. Rather than wait forty-five minutes for the ski lift, Waddell and his friends would hike up the mountain, stopping every so often to watch their tween ski idols. Waddell stared at their form, watching for any tips on how to keep his upper body quiet and prevent his arms from flailing. He scrutinized how they went around the red and blue flags along the mountain, trying to figure out how they chose their path through the gates to maintain as much speed as possible. At the starting gate, he watched their form, the way they kicked their skis back. He was creating a kinesthetic awareness. His coach could have given him all of this information, or he could have read about it, but for Waddell, watching those skiers was the way he embedded their every motion in his mind, and he worked to replicate them. Athletes often watch videos of their competitors and their own races to search for areas of improvement. Waddell did not need the movies, as he was watching them live.

He skied competitively in college and loved every minute of it, but at the age of twenty he had an accident on his beloved ski slopes that left him paraplegic. He spent grueling months in the hospital. High-achieving athletes all reference visualizing their races, routines and meets before they ever do them. From his hospital bed, Waddell once again visualized his skiing, his every turn. He knew he wanted to find a way back onto the slopes.

When he returned to school in the spring, Waddell's college ski coach approached him about skiing on a monoski, a unique apparatus for adaptive skiing. Having watched a cancer survivor with one leg on a monoski years earlier, he knew what it entailed. Right then and there, he decided he would become the face of adaptive skiing so that others could see what was possible.

Award winning physician-scientist Dr. Huda Zoghbi, who studies Rett Syndrome, summarized it best when I asked her how she learned new things: "I learned how to do science and I learned how to look and notice everything. I always came to the lab with wide-open eyes. I see things, I observe things."

Learning from experience

If you ever saw the movie *Cool Runnings*, you heard the unlikely story of the Jamaican Bobsledding Team. Four Jamaican men, who had never seen snow, let alone ice, got together and qualified to compete at the Winter Olympics. Three of the four always wanted to be Olympians and had their eyes set on competing in track, a sport Jamaica was famous for dominating. The other member was a soccer player. Two Americans who lived in Jamaica discussed the idea that Jamaican athletes were the best in the world, and decided to test this by seeing how Jamaican elite athletes could adapt to a new sport.

Jamaica was known for having pushcart derbies, which the two Americans thought resembled a bobsled. They also had the idea that you need sprinters to get the ideal push of a bobsled at the start line. None of the Jamaican track sprinters were interested in switching sports, so the Americans looked for athletes within the Jamaican Army. Colonel Ken Barnes knew that Captain Devon Harris, a middle-distance runner, had his eyes set on competing in track in the 1988 summer Olympics in Seoul, Korea. Barnes convinced Harris to try out for the new Jamaican bobsledding team. He made the team, and in lieu of training for a summer Olympics in track, Harris, one of the original Jamaican bobsledders, was training for the 1988 winter Olympics in Calgary. While the movie certainly took creative license, there are some parallels with the truth. With the odds stacked against them, Harris and his teammates had no choice but to learn from their experiences.

As Harris was busy with his military commitments, he did not have enough time to train for the qualifiers properly. "I was army fit, not sports fit," he said. To make things even more complicated, Harris, who used to play soccer and run track, was a distance runner. The bobsledding team needed the explosive power seen in sprinters. Harris badly wanted to make the Olympic team. It was his dream. Every day, he went to the track and practiced his short-distance running.

As bobsledding was a completely new sport in Jamaica, Harris had no idea who would show up to try out. There were no local known names in the field, and the tryouts were the first time he met the other competitors. He was introduced to his other three teammates for the first time at the airport in September 1987, four months before the Olympics. They were traveling together to Lake Placid, New York, to meet their coach and train; that was the first time they saw an ice rink and bobsled.

Six weeks later, they were in Calgary, Canada in a rented bobsled, as they did not even own one. It was the first time the Jamaican team had seen a bobsled track. Harris, who ironically is afraid of heights, climbed into the bobsled behind his teammate, the driver, who had never done this before. There was only one way to find out if they had what it took: they had to just do it. They did three runs on the track that night. "It was terrifying," said Harris. They could have read all the books, talked to all the coaches, and seen all the movies of previous races, but there is no other way to learn how to go down a bobsled track than getting in a bobsled, going down the hill, and doing it yourself. Ultimately, the motley crew had talent and explosive force which could not be ignored. They competed in multiple Olympics.

Lee Cockerell is the former executive vice president of operations for Walt Disney World Resort. His portfolio included leading 40,000 employees, or as they are called at Disney, cast members. He also oversaw twenty resort hotels, four theme parks, two water parks, as well as a shopping and entertainment village. Cockerell created the Disney Great Leader Strategies, used to train and develop 7,000 leaders at Disney. At work, he was known as the "Dobermann" as he was always getting results and being offered promotions: "It took me thirty-five years to become an overnight success."

Cockerell's story is exemplary for many reasons. He had never been to Disney until he started working there and rose through the ranks to become a senior executive despite not having a college degree, which is highly unusual. He grew up poor in Oklahoma, without indoor plumbing. Instead, they had an outhouse. His family had a dairy farm, and Cockerell's chores included milking the cows before school. Education was never a priority in his family or town. He did enter college but did not know how to manage the expectations once he arrived, and left after two years to join the Army.

He was working as a banquet waiter at the Washington Hilton when he decided to apply for a job in the accounting office. While he had received a 'D' in his accounting class in college, he excelled in his new accounting role. "I learn by doing," he said. To supplement his on-the-job learning, he would read and listen to audiotapes with lessons.

He moved from Hilton to the Marriott, where he worked his way up over seventeen years to become vice president for food and beverage, learning everything he could through trial and error.

Disney recruited Cockerell to open the food and beverage department for Disney Paris and before long he was promoted to lead the hotel division. Eventually, he returned to Orlando, Florida to head up all of the Disney operations.

The insecurity Cockerell felt at not having a college degree led him to work longer and harder than those around him. "I learned from good bosses and bad. I watched, listened, talked to people, and learned by trying new things," he said. His career success was defined by his ability to learn everything he needed outside of the formal classroom. Informal learning in the workplace is a common and key factor in future success (Marsick and Volpe, 1999; Marsick and Watkins, 1990).

Dr. Tony Fauci, director of the National Institutes of Allergy and Infectious Diseases at the National Institutes of Health, did not have experience responding to the Coronavirus. He had, however, led the United States' response to countless epidemics and pandemics. This latest threat was not his first rodeo. "You don't learn how to do it. You just do it. It isn't like you can take a class on it," Fauci shared. Experiential learning, the art and science of learning by doing, is a core theory in adult learning (Kolb, 1984; Knowles, 1984; Dewey, 1938).

Mentoring others

Mentorship is such a critical aspect of success that it finds its place in two chapters of this book. While the high achievers benefit from receiving mentorship, they pay it forward by mentoring the next generation. The most successful people of our generation make a habit out of paying it forward. They count their success by looking at the achievements of those they have mentored. They mentor individuals, groups, and run small- and large-scale mentoring programs.

The approaches to mentoring differ, but the end goal is always to help their mentees succeed. Nobel laureate Dr. Bob Lefkowitz spends as much time as he can with his mentees. He lets them watch everything he does, including which problems he chooses to study, his thought process, and how he decides when to stop working on a problem. "I never chair a department, head a program, or was a dean. I love being here in the lab, in the office, and working with my fellows and letting them watch everything I do," he said. He learns from his mentees as well, as they are filled with unbridled curiosity and perspective, which often leads to new lines of questions and discovery.

After the 2003 space shuttle tragedy, NASA engineers developed a methodology and repair kit for identifying problems and substituting heat-resistant tiles while still in orbit. A little-known fact is that this project was developed off NASA premises, in a garage. Astronaut Dr. Charles J. Camarda, senior advisor for engineering development at NASA, was the leader of the project and flew on the next shuttle two years later to test the innovative solution.

Camarda wanted to recreate the innovation, excitement, and creative thinking that occurred in that garage while motivating a whole new generation to love science, engineering, technology and math. He realized that people are stifled by their environment, with their structured rules, processes, and traditions. Understanding that progress will only occur when people can think freely and creatively, Camarda launched an educational non-profit called the Epic Education Foundation (Epic Education Foundation, 2021). He inspires thousands of middle school, high school and college kids worldwide to think differently as they work together to solve epic challenges. The students are mentored by "The Friends of Charlie Network," which includes engineers, physicians, scientists, educators and astronauts. They are taking their decades of experience and helping the next generation solve some of the world's most pressing problems in the most unconventional of ways. In the process, Camarda learns more about the contemporary educational systems, areas of weakness, and opportunities he could address. Not having constraints lets kids develop more radical ideas, which helps seasoned veterans such as Camarda.

When she was helming the Build-A-Bear Workshop, Maxine Clark developed a mentoring program called Huggable Heroes. Following an application process, along with her team, she selected ten entrepreneurs with a social justice interest (Clark and Joyner, 2006). The winning entrepreneurs were awarded $10,000, of which $7,500 was in the form of a scholarship, and $2,500 was donated to a charity of the winner's choice. The young entrepreneurs would get together, go through a day of professional development training, and learn from each other. Over 100 entrepreneurs came through this program, and Clark is still in touch with many of them. "You have to build to get," she says.

In June 2013, Maxine Clark stepped down from her role as CEO of Build-A-Bear to focus on her next chapter in life: mentoring. Clark has a history of relying on her mentors. Before Build-A-Bear, her mentors guided her for years to her eventual role as president of Payless Shoes. These days she focuses her work on mentoring women and minority entrepreneurs and redefining K-12 public education. She is always scouting for potential mentees. Many potential mentees are referred to Clark by her friends and professionals in her vast network. She also actively seeks them out by perusing LinkedIn, Instagram, and various news sources. If she reads an article or sees a post about something she finds intriguing, she will reach out to the entrepreneur.

In 2012, Clark read an article in the paper about three women who were making toys with a technological twist, all unique companies. She searched their website and sent an email explaining who she was, and offered to help. Imagine getting an unsolicited email from the founder of Build-A-Bear! She learned that one of the women was an engineer and was frustrated that none of the toys available to her as a child had encouraged the type of thinking needed to be an engineer. Having been alerted to the problem of too few women engineers, Clark decided to invest in the woman and her company, and leveraged many of her contacts to help her grow her business.

A friend introduced Clark to Jamie, a fine art painter who was looking to expand into different realms of painting. Using a unique technique she had developed, Jamie started to paint custom-ordered wedding bouquets. As Covid hit, weddings moved to the backyard with a handful of people and limited fanfare. Clark saw the opportunity to capitalize on the wedding bouquets and recommended Jamie do the same types of paintings for wedding cakes. Jamie listened to her mentor, the business is growing, and the cake portraits may soon be available.

Jamie lived in San Francisco, California, and the cost of living was prohibitive. With some encouragement from Clark, she moved back home to St. Louis, Missouri, bought a great home and is in process of creating a studio, home and investment all in one! "An integral part of mentoring is encouragement," said Clark. With that idea in mind, Clark became a customer, helped the painter optimize her website, recommended offers she should make to customers, and ways to scale her business. Realizing Jamie needed to train more people in her unique technique so that she could meet the increasing demand, Clark suggested the painter connect with the dean of a local art school so that she could teach the students her style of painting.

"You give encouragement and introduce your mentee to your network so that they can grow their business," said Clark. Today, she actively mentors fifteen young entrepreneurs and helps them grow their small businesses. Clark learns about every new business she helps and is always looking for new ways to connect people to provide something even bigger and better. It was learning about all of those businesses in her previous career that led her to take Build-A-Bear to such great heights.

Michiel Bartman, the Dutch rower with multiple Olympic medals, could have taken any job, including coaching future Olympians. He decided he could make a more significant impact by mentoring college students through rowing. While coaching at Harvard, Bartman and the rowers were on a long bumpy bus ride on the way to their next competition. Bartman sat next to one of the graduating seniors and asked him about his goals for his final rowing season. The student looked at him, confused, and revealed he did not have any plans. Bartman saw this as a mentoring opportunity and pushed the young athlete to develop plans for himself, consider what he wanted to achieve and what he wished to leave behind. At graduation, the student thanked Bartman for encouraging him to develop goals and bring them to fruition. A year later, the recent graduate returned to campus for an alumni row and approached Bartman again. He wanted to thank him profusely for insisting that he develop goals; it was a lesson that kept on bearing fruit. "Being able to pay it forward is so fulfilling. There are so many highs I learned along the way and so many things you need to experience. There are things I wished I had known earlier as it would have made a difference," said Bartman. He tries to teach that to his students, one mentoring lesson at a time. Every day, the students also teach Bartman something new.

High achievers all take an active stake in mentoring others. Along the way, consciously or subconsciously, they are learning something new. They are recognizing opportunities, pain points and stressors faced by the next generation. This informs the high achievers' work on a daily basis. They have a national platform and are not afraid to use it to help others and further a cause.

High achievers crave new knowledge, a new perspective, a new way of looking at a problem or finding a solution. Their quest for new information is an unquenched thirst, as they always look for additional opportunities to learn. Despite their accomplishments, degrees and accolades, they will ask questions, listen to others and read new ideas. They realize that they do not know all the answers and, as such, keep asking questions.

COACHING QUESTIONS

1 Which do you feel is your preferred method of consuming new knowledge?

2 What are two books, articles, podcasts, videos, or webinars you can commit to learning from on a regular basis?

KEY TAKEAWAYS

High achievers do not stop learning when class is over or a degree is achieved; the learning is constant and comes in a variety of forms. They are not afraid to admit when they do not know something. To them, not knowing is worse than not trying to know. They fear not trying more than they fear failing. To enhance your continuous learning and growth, consider these strategies:

1 There are countless opportunities to learn which extend outside of the formal classroom. Look for opportunities to continue learning and consuming new knowledge. Talk to interesting people of varying generations, listen to podcasts, watch TED talks, read books and articles.

2 Engage in conversations with interesting people. You will learn about an organization, its people and processes. It will also offer insight into the hidden curriculum.

3 You can learn a great deal by watching others. Watch the people around you, how they interact, behave and get their point across. Consider what they do and how it is accomplished.

4 Do not be afraid to try something new and let the experience be your guide. Sink your teeth into a new idea or project and give it a try. Ask questions and look for gaps in knowledge. You may learn from each experience.

5 Find your people, those who will motivate and inspire you to achieve more.

6 High achievers benefit greatly from being mentored. In turn, they selflessly mentor others, give back and pay it forward. They count the achievements of their mentees as the litmus test of their success as a mentor.

References

Clark, M and Joyner, A (2006) *The Bear Necessities of Business*, New Jersey, John Wiley & Sons, Inc

Dewey, J (1938) *Experience and Education*, New York, Collier Books

Epic Education Foundation (2021) *Epic Challenges*, https://epiceducationfoundation.org (archived at https://perma.cc/DD7S-M5PM)

Gallo, C (2017) Bill Gates and other billionaires say this 1 habit is the secret to their success, *Inc.* https://www.inc.com/carmine-gallo/bill-gates-other-billionaires-say-this-1-habit-is-secret-to-their-sucess.html (archived at https://perma.cc/7JFL-7BU4)

Gotian, R (2020a) How peer mentors can help you succeed, *Forbes*, https://www.forbes.com/sites/ruthgotian/2020/06/09/how-peer-mentors-can-help-you-succeed/ (archived at https://perma.cc/4F46-TR3Z)

Gotian, R (2020b) How to create your own mentoring team, *Psychology Today*, https://www.psychologytoday.com/us/blog/optimizing-success/202009/how-create-your-own-mentoring-team (archived at https://perma.cc/4FZJ-P75Z)

Gotian, R (2020c) How to develop a mentoring team, *Forbes*, https://www.forbes.com/sites/ruthgotian/2020/07/06/how-to-cultivate-a-mentoring-team-in-five-easy-steps/ (archived at https://perma.cc/9BCK-8PWJ)

Gotian, R (2020d) How to turn feedback into an 'opportunity for enhancement', *Forbes*, https://www.forbes.com/sites/ruthgotian/2020/08/14/how-to-turn-feedback-into-an-opportunity-for-enhancement/ (archived at https://perma.cc/PDH2-VUEM)

Kluger, A and DeNisi, A (1996) The effects of feedback interventions on performance: A historical review, a meta-analysis, and a preliminary feedback intervention theory, *Psychological Bulletin*, **119**

Knowles, MS (1984) *The Adult Learner: A neglected species*, Houston, Gulf

Kolb, D (1984) *Experiential Learning: Experience as the source of learning and development*, Englewood Cliffs, NJ, Prentice-Hall, Inc

Marsick, V and Volpe, M (1999) Informal learning on the job, in V Marsick and M Volpe (eds.) *Advances in Developing Human Resources*, San Francisco, CA: The Academy of Human Resource Development

Marsick, V and Watkins, K (1990) *Informal and Incidental Learning*, London, Routledge

Yoon, J et al (2019) Why asking for advice is more effective than asking for feedback, *Harvard Business Review*

PART THREE

Optimizing your success

08

Finding and making room for your passion

High achievers are 400 percent more successful than the average person (O'Boyle and Aguinis, 2012). If you want a chance at succeeding more, your first step is to identify what you love to do and figure out how to create a job around your passion. As you read the pages in this chapter, you will learn how to figure out what activities you are good at and, equally as important, most enjoy doing. You will then discover how to optimize your time and energy so that you are most effective and finish more than double the amount of work in a fraction of the time.

Conduct a Passion Audit

You might already know what you are good at, but what is your passion? It is crucial to identify this and recognize the difference. Just because you excel at accounting or public speaking does not mean you are passionate about it. Continuing to work on projects you are not excited about will lead you down an isolating road of burnout and resentment. Conversely, pouring in the effort and commitment to something you are good at will increase your likelihood of success (Duckworth, 2016).

You will likely need to try your hand at multiple activities before you find your calling. You might be good at several, but there will be one that really sparks joy in you. Today, Kayla Harrison is a sixth-degree black belt in judo who won two gold medals in consecutive Olympic games. She is the first and only American to win an Olympic gold medal in judo. Her mother enrolled her in dance, t-ball, and a variety of other activities, including judo; that was the one activity that stuck, and Harrison stopped all the others.

She was all in when it came to judo; she loved it, and it loved her back. She won every medal there was to win. However, after her second Olympic gold, she found her passion for judo waning. She knew that to be the best, she had to love what she did with every ounce of her being, so she searched for her new passion. Today, she has found what she calls her mature love, which is mixed martial arts. Harrison enjoys the strategy of the sport, always forcing you to think five steps ahead. She is already the first female champion of the Professional Fighter's League. She loves it and cannot see herself doing anything else.

Once you identify your passion, you need to create the physical and emotional space to pursue it and determine if this is a fad you currently find exciting or something important to get behind in the long term. Learning how to leverage your peak performance energy will help you excel and keep the fire burning as you fuel your passion.

Research has shown that you only need to spend 20 percent of your time doing what you love (Gotian, 2020a; Shanafelt, 2009). Finding what you enjoy requires you to do a "Passion Audit," which I have developed. For starters, take a sheet of paper and make three columns.

Table 8.1 provides an illustration of a Passion Audit, so you have an idea of what it looks like. I have provided a sample blank Passion Audit worksheet in the online resources so you can fill one out for yourself.

TABLE 8.1   Passion Audit

Things I am good at	What I am not good at or do not enjoy doing	What I would do for free if I could
Operations	Grant writing	Social media posts
Networking	Budgets	Interviews of interesting people
Empathy	Forms	Writing
Grant writing	Editing	Talking and helping people, especially women
Talking to people and making them feel valued and heard	Standardized tests	Mentoring, especially women
Mentoring, especially women	Setting up automated emails	Keynote speaking

TABLE 8.1   *continued*

Things I am good at	What I am not good at or do not enjoy doing	What I would do for free if I could
Event planning (the behind-the-scenes details)	Sending invoices, following up	Coaching
Writing	Difficult conversations	Fundraising, especially for a program to help women in the workplace
Getting to someone's why	Operations	
Helping people, coaching, especially women	Crisis management	
Keynote speaking	Excel	

Column 1: List everything you are good at

Column one should be a list of everything you do well. It does not matter if you enjoy doing it; you just happen to be good at it. Are you proficient at writing grants or press releases or developing social media content? Are you the Excel master who loves to analyze data? Perhaps you are an excellent public speaker, teacher, or mentor? Is organizing projects and tasks your superpower, or do you let someone else take that on? Are you the thinker, analyzer, or doer?

As you consider what you are good at, it is important to recognize the circumstances under which you perform best. Other factors to consider in your response in this column include:

- With what types of people do you work best?
- To whom do you best relate—college students, junior managers, or C-suite?
- With which profession do you most connect—accountants, doctors, lawyers, or the marketing team?
- Which conditions optimize your performance?
- Do you work better alone or with a group?

The goal is for you to be able to come up with a statement that encapsulates the conditions under which you perform best. The more specific you can get with listing your activities and behaviors, the better. For example, your ideal conditions may be expressed in the following way: "I enjoy mentoring female college students who are interested in science. I help them in small groups of up to five at a time." Think critically about whether you excel at teaching them new technical skills, opening their minds to different opportunities, or giving them the confidence to succeed.

Column 2: List everything you are not good at or do not enjoy doing

Make a list of everything you are not very good at or do not enjoy doing. Notice I wrote "or" not "and." You might excel at writing grants, which would appear in column one, but if you do not enjoy writing them, also list them in column two. Ask yourself, if you can keep your title and salary but give away the responsibilities you do not enjoy doing or feel you are a master in, what would those be?

As you consider what you do not enjoy doing, it is important to recognize the circumstances as well. Other factors and questions to consider in your response in column two include:

- Which tasks cause you to procrastinate?
- What tasks fill you with dread and deplete your energy?
- Do you prefer to work alone or with others?

As with column one, be very specific. If you do not enjoy the spotlight, giving talks, or being on stage, list it in column two. If writing is not a natural strength, write it down. Are you tired of dealing with day-to-day operations for a department or organization? If group work drives you crazy list it in column two. Conversely, if the sound of silence is deafening, write it down. List all of the things that do not bring you joy and you would rather someone else took them on.

The goal is for you to come up with a statement that summarizes the conditions under which your performance or motivation is sub-optimal. For example, your less-than-ideal conditions might be stated in the following way: "I dislike activities that force me to work alone, devoid of any human interaction. I do not enjoy sitting at my desk all day, staring at spreadsheets or writing standard operating procedures."

Column 3: List what you would do for free if you could

Consider your professional and personal life and list all of the things you would do for free if you could. You likely are already doing them for no compensation or recognition. When you procrastinate with tasks from column two, it is often the functions in column three that you are doing. Maybe you enjoy developing creative content for social media or have PowerPoint slide decks that are the envy of every audience member. Perhaps your enjoyment is organizing an event or masterfully connecting people.

As you consider which activities bring you joy, it is important to recognize which activities you do because you want to, not because you have to. As you develop items for column three, ask yourself the following questions:

- What do you enjoy doing on your day off? This will offer you an unedited view of what you desire.
- How do you spend your time?
- With whom do you spend your time? Is it solitary or with groups?
- Which volunteer committees are you actively participating in both at work and in your personal life?
- Which organizations are you a part of: alumni, religious, advocacy, or parent groups?
- Which are the tasks you jump to volunteer for or feel you can do better than anyone else?
- What do group leaders always approach you to do or lead?
- When you are considering doing something new, from where do you get your ideas?
- Do you execute ideas or run to one person in particular to brainstorm or help bring the concept to light?
- Do you enjoy seeing numbers add up on a spreadsheet?

Pay attention to what you get excited about, and keep a running list for a few weeks.

Now that you have completed this first draft, carry the list around with you and add things and cross them off as they come to you. Ask friends, family and colleagues what they think you are good or even gifted at, and what you tend to put off, procrastinate about or simply not give your all. For a week, pay attention to what topics people come to you for guidance or expertise on.

The goal is for you to come up with a statement that embodies your ideal activities that bring you joy and fulfillment. For example, you may list your optimal activities as: "I really enjoy working with people who I know well and get excited about bringing ideas to fruition. I enjoy and am really good at getting people to rally around a new program by making ideas go viral, especially by creating stellar social media content."

Applying your Passion Audit to your current role

Consider your current work and imagine how you might be able to re-engineer your responsibilities. Are there obligations you could shed to make room for a new passion project? Is there a committee you could join or a commitment you could initiate that revolves around your latest obsessions? For example, if you are a social media maven, perhaps create and maintain digital content for your department, favorite committee, or professional organization. If you love mentoring female youth, is there a program you could develop within your organization to introduce young women to your field? Just spending part of your time doing the things you love will make the tasks in column number two feel less depleting, especially if you can maneuver things to support your projects from column three.

Passions change over time, so do not fear repeating the Passion Audit as often as necessary. Life changes such as a new partner, child, house, illness, death of a loved one, or a global pandemic can impact your priorities and interests. Just as your passions evolve, so should you. The critical part is to identify and label what excites you and fuels your passion.

Identify what you will do next

Now that you have identified your passion, it is time to develop goals and plans to begin your success journey. I never cared for the question, "What do you want to do in ten years?" The job you want likely does not even exist. What many quickly realized during the Covid-19 pandemic was that they were likely reevaluating any long-term goals previously held. Maybe the goal was not realistic or included jobs that have not yet been realized. Case in point, ten years ago, your organization likely did not have a dedicated social media manager. Now they have degrees in the subject and entire departments to handle digital communication.

Perhaps you focused on the wrong goals. Instead of thinking about what you would like to become, consider what you would like to do and which problems you would like to solve. Think of some of the questions that can guide your thinking as you seek to clarify this issue. Some might have been answered in your Passion Audit.

- Do you like to work with people, or do you prefer to work in relative isolation?
- Do you like the background noise of people talking or the hum of fluorescent lights?
- Do you prefer to crunch numbers and see trends or develop something creative like a short video?
- Do you prefer identifying problems, coming up with solutions, or executing a plan?
- Are you the thinker or doer in your work group?

These are the types of questions you should be asking yourself as you begin to craft an idea of what you would like to do in your career. It is less about the title and more about the types of things you would like to do, where you would like to accomplish this work, and with whom you would like to do it.

Develop a role to utilize as many skills and behaviors as possible from column three. Remember, you only need to spend 20 percent of your time doing these things. By doing this, the challenges from column two will not be as daunting. For example, you dislike writing grants, even though you are pretty good at it. But if you had to write the grant to fund your passion project, you would be personally invested in it, and your motivation would thereby increase.

You may not enjoy the spotlight, but if it means getting an interview with a major media company that would give your new group attention and increase donations, you will likely take that meeting. You might even be excited about the potential exposure.

Name it and claim it

Answering these types of questions will help you get out of the starting blocks. The key is not to work on your ultimate goal but to start identifying your *next* goal. Do you want to become a director, partner, or associate professor? Name it and claim it. Do not worry about being a managing partner just yet if there are five other levels in between. Have a laser focus on the next goal you would like to achieve.

Now that you know what promotion you would like next, consider what you would need to achieve to meet your next goal (Gotian, 2020d). Do you need to get another degree? Learn a new skill? Meet certain people? Again, name it and claim it. Once you have identified what you need to do next, make a plan. If you need to get another degree, what kind would it be? Do you need to take a standardized test such as GMAT or GRE to gain acceptance? If so, focus on studying for the test as you begin to identify schools to apply to.

Do you need to learn a new skill? Figure out how you can achieve this. Can someone teach it to you? Can you read a book or watch a video? Perhaps take an online course? Start identifying what you need to do to learn and eventually master this new skill.

Are there certain people with whom you need to connect? Have you thought about how you will meet them? Can anyone in your circle introduce you, perhaps family, friends, or colleagues? Consider also following these choice people on social media and engaging with their content to show interest. Not so much that you are stalking them, but enough that they will repeatedly see your name as someone who is interested in their work (Clark, 2019).

Have you often wondered why it appears that some people accomplish so much and others fail to get out of the starting blocks? The difference in outcomes could simply be the goal on which you are focusing. To add momentum, consider focusing on the next goal, not the ultimate goal, and be methodical in your approach.

Support your goal

Knowing, identifying, and labeling your passion and goals are strategic first steps. Not having time or energy to pursue what you love doing will always make you feel unfulfilled. The next step in achieving success is to create an environment that lets you actively pursue your passion and build the skills that enable you to leverage its potential (Gotian, 2020b, 2020d). Now that you have an idea of what it is, you need to divest all, if not most, of the activities that are not directly aligned with your goals. Get ready for another three-column exercise.

Table 8.2 provides an illustration of a Goal Audit so you have an idea of what it looks like. I have provided a sample blank Goal Audit worksheet in the online resources so you can fill one out for yourself.

Goal: Get promoted to director of a department within my organization.

TABLE 8.2   Goal Audit

List of my activities	Need to resign—does not support my next goal	Good for the heart and soul
Diversity task force	All passive committees	Diversity task force
New hire welcoming committee	IT program beta tester	Women's mentoring group
New IT program beta tester, website reviewer	Website reviewer	Choir
Review new standard operating procedures	Wellness committee	Thursday night basketball league
Wellness committee	PPT reviewer	Women's mentoring group
Women's mentoring group	New hire welcoming committee	
Department liaison with marketing and accounting	Review PPT slides of all department members	
Review PPT slides of all department members		
Member of 12 committees which meet 1–4 times a year. Passive role (no prep needed)		
Attend all budget meetings		
Attend all strategy meetings		
Accreditation task force		

Milestones needed to meet: MBA, hit productivity markers, be known as a subject matter expert by presenting at conferences and writing articles in the industry journal.

Column 1: List everything

Make a list of every activity, committee, task force, special project, and group you are a part of in your professional and personal lives. Be very specific. Even if the group only meets once a year, add it to your list. If the group is virtual and communicates only by email, it gets recorded. Add everything, and I mean everything.

I am pushing you to list every activity, even those you think take just a minimal amount of time. That might be the case, but it requires preparation time, travel, and perhaps most importantly, it will knock you out of your concentration when you happen to be in the zone, the state of flow, working toward your goal you are passionate about. You know that feeling of liberation when you have a day that does not involve any meetings, conference calls or Zooms. It is so rare and precious. You know you can get lots of work done. Find a way to work toward protecting your time at all costs.

Column 2: If it does not align, you must resign

Review your list carefully. There's a good chance you never looked carefully at how many groups, committees, task forces and special projects you show up for and need to remain actively or passively engaged in. I bet it is double digits! It is not practical to be fully present and devote yourself to all of these activities while still carrying out your full-time job and personal pursuits.

Consider which tasks do not align with your goals. If the connection is not imminently clear, you need to either fire yourself from that committee or take a leave of absence. People often agree to serve on committees because they will get to be with an influential crowd. Unless you are an active member of the committee who gets to work with the other members regularly, it might be worth questioning the longevity of your role. Ask yourself, "Would anyone notice if I was not there?" If your presence is barely noted, feel free to resign from the committee.

Some committees are a great stepping stone, but as you move further in your career, you need a new hill to climb, and membership on the previous task force is no longer useful. You can quit that activity as well.

If the group is well-intentioned or disorganized and you find yourself spending most of the time trying to keep its members on task, that is a sign that it is time to move on. If your role on the committee does not leverage your skills and experience, it is time to look for a new challenge.

If you enjoy the group, its mission, activities and fellow members, but feel overwhelmed by all of your responsibilities, do not give up your seat so quickly. Tell the chairs you have a big deadline coming up or a hectic few months, and you will need to take a brief leave of absence while you tie up some loose ends and focus on your big project.

Leaving a group, committee or task force is an excellent opportunity to advance your career by giving yourself time to pursue your passions. It is also a great time to sponsor someone else to take your place. The person you are nominating might not be on anyone's radar. As a sitting member of the committee, recommending someone else often provides the necessary influence to give a new person a much-needed opportunity to learn new skills, meet new people and shine on their own. As you move up through the ranks, be sure to bring up someone else along for the ride.

Column 3: Good for the heart and soul

Not every activity can push your goal forward; sometimes you just need to refuel your tank. Consider which activities from your list inspire and rejuvenate you. Perhaps it is singing with a choir or going to religious services. If that puts a smile on your face and brings you joy, then by all means you should do it. Your goal is important, but so are other things in life, and being happy is at the top of the list.

Spend time with people who make you smile and laugh, see your potential, will always have your back, and are fully supportive. A lunch outing with them can recharge you and be valuable time spent.

Manage your minutes and days

In his book, *Indistractable*, Nir Eyal reminds us that if we do not plan our time, someone else will (Eyal, 2019). One of the most organized people I have ever met is Janice Lintz, the hearing advocate you met in Chapter 4. She is always juggling multiple big projects and is routinely communicating with government agencies and CEOs of Fortune 500 companies. She has multiple balls up in the air at any one time. Her big projects such as getting hearing access in Delta terminals, Apple stores, baseball stadiums, subway stations, and New York City taxis, leave little time for routine tasks, which are essential, yet can be mind-numbing and a time sink. Lintz converted these dreaded tasks into micro-projects and optimizes her small chunks of time between phone calls. The time is too short to take on a big task so she uses those filler times to pay bills, balance the checkbook, or respond to emails. Every minute counts for Lintz. Notifications on her phone are silenced as she focuses on the task at hand.

She has a running list of her projects. She also has a calendar which she uses religiously. If someone asks her to follow up in two weeks, she does not rely on her memory or jot it down on a Post-It note, praying it does not get lost. She sets a reminder on her calendar. If there is something with a due date, such as a call for proposals, she puts that on the calendar with a reminder a week prior. Nothing gets forgotten or overlooked.

Lintz's ability to track the progress of a project is remarkable and makes her stand out to even the most finicky of leaders. When she starts a project, she keeps a phone log. She has a list of each person she spoke to about a project, significant points of the conversation, and her action items identified in red. Anything significant is in bold. She cross-references her calendar and phone log. Nothing falls through the cracks. Her phone log gets converted into a PDF and then sent to the proper authority as proof of her effort to get a problem solved. When trying to make the National Park Service more accessible, she ran into multiple roadblocks. She sent her seventeen-page phone log to the US Secretary of the Interior. She asked what more she could do to make Ellis Island accessible? It worked (Lintz, 2017)! The National Park Service became accessible and developed the National Park Service's Guidelines on Effective Access, which Lintz assisted with, and they acknowledged her contribution. It all happened because she was effective with her time and kept meticulous records. Her tools of choice are red ink, bold typeface, and her calendar.

Manage your energy

Now that you have identified your passions and eliminated any external distractions which move you away from your goals, you need to learn how to leverage the hours of the day when you are most productive (Eyal, 2019). Doing so could more than double the amount of work you produce in half the time. When you finish working on a task, you are more likely to feel inspired instead of exhausted.

Are you a morning person or nocturnal? Do you do your best work before everyone wakes up or after everyone goes to sleep? Being aware of when you are most focused and efficient will help you prioritize working on your passion. If you are like me, you are generally an early riser and do your best work before everyone wakes up. With every hour that passes, the focus begins to wane. By the late afternoon, a project that would have taken you thirty minutes in the morning can take up the entire afternoon.

It is critical to be aware of your peak performance time so that you can manage your energy. Getting this right is more vital than managing your to-do list. You need to control your day so that you can do the work that requires the most focus and cognitive attention in the hours when you are at your peak. As a morning person, I do my writing, editing and budgets, which require an intense cognitive focus, in the earliest parts of my day. Tasks that require less concentrated attention, such as meetings, either in person or virtual, responding to emails or telephone calls, making appointments, or paying bills, occur in the afternoon.

To leverage your peak performance hours, list the time of day you are most alert and creative. Think about whether you are a morning person or a night owl. Your peak hours are when you get your best work done, so you need to recognize when that is and reserve your cognitive skills for that part of the day. Doing so will save you hours of work and frustration. If you have any control over your calendar, reserve your high-performance hours for your cognitive work and the other parts of the day for the tasks that require less focused attention. Just as college professors have scheduled office hours, try to condense your meetings into the non-cognitive blocks on your calendar. It is not as simple as managing your time; you need to calibrate your energy within time blocks.

Get into a rhythm

Now that you know the hours of the day when you are most effective and can separate your tasks accordingly, you need to get into an effective flow during your peak performance hours. My favorite tool has always been the Pomodoro Technique (Cirillo, nd). This approach, developed by Francesco Cirillo in the 1980s, allows you to work within an allotted time instead of fighting against it. The Pomodoro Technique consists of six steps:

1 Select the task on which you wish to focus and work. Whether it is a big or small task is irrelevant. What is important is that this is the one project you want to focus on and give your undivided attention to.

2 Set the alarm on your phone for 25 minutes. This is just long enough that it is not overwhelming. Shut off all of your email and social media notifications. You are going to focus on this one assignment for less than half an hour.

3 Immerse yourself in the task for 25 minutes. Give it your full attention. During this time, if you think of anything, write it down and get to it after your 25 minutes are up. Remember, you have devoted 25 minutes to this one task.

4 When your alarm goes off, you did it. Congratulations! You have just spent 25 uninterrupted minutes on one task. When was the last time you were able to do that?

5 Take a short five-minute break. Grab a coffee, a bite to eat, or take a brisk walk. The respite from the intense focus is just what your brain needs. Make sure the break is not work-related. Do not check your email or call someone from work.

6 After four Pomodoros, take a more extended break of 30 minutes. You need this time to recharge.

The Pomodoro Technique is heralded by many, including me. There are various apps and variations of this theme so choose what works best for you. Anything can be your timer. During the Coronavirus pandemic, I often used the washing machine cycle as the timer (Gotian, 2020c). For the length of one cycle, I would focus on my work. I took a break to put the clothes in the dryer while listening to a podcast and would repeat as necessary. As a self-proclaimed morning person, I always did these intense Pomodoro writing and editing sessions in the morning. I tried to concentrate, whenever possible, all of my Zoom meetings in the afternoon.

Jump when opportunities present themselves

Every high achiever I have spoken with took chances: lots of them. They tried something new and often outlandish on a regular basis. A unique opportunity was the possibility of an adventure for them. As always, they feared not trying more than they feared failing. They figured they had nothing to lose, so why not try?

Dr. Scott Parazynski is a physician and astronaut. He participated in five space shuttle flights and seven spacewalks and is in the US Astronaut Hall of Fame (NASA Kennedy Space Center Visitor Complex). He was the first person to both fly in space and climb Mount Everest. Parazynski always has exciting and lofty goals. If someone says "it's impossible," he gets more excited. "There's probably a way. Let me figure it out," he tells himself. That mindset led him to climb into a lava lake "in the name of science," and led him to the Olympics while a medical student at Stanford.

Bonny Warner, a member of the 1984 Olympic luge team, was a Stanford student with Parazynski. She was actively recruiting students to the sport of luge and held a one-day clinic to introduce people to the sport of going down an icy hill at ninety miles per hour, feet first. Parazynski decided to see what the cause was for all the excitement. He tried it out, quickly became mesmerized, and became a self-proclaimed "luge junkie." At age 24, he was selected to participate in a winter training session at the Olympic Center in Lake Placid, NY. During his final three years of medical school, he simultaneously studied medicine and trained for the Olympics.

In 1988, he made it to the Olympic trials and did well, but was not one of the top four to make the Olympic team. As that door closed, though, another opened. A luger from the Philippines needed a coach, and Parazynski stepped into the role, taking advantage of yet another opportunity. Before he knew it, he walked in the Winter Olympic Games opening ceremony behind the Philippines' flag. He made his goal of making it to the Olympics, just not as he had originally intended. When the opportunity presented itself, he grabbed it with both hands.

Parazynski always knew he would be a physician and astronaut and was well on his way to seeing those goals come to fruition. Luge was a passion, and this was the time in his life to pursue it. It was a once-in-a-lifetime opportunity, and he was going after it. Being a physician, astronaut, and Olympic-level luger might not be your objective, but there are many lessons you can adopt from this journey about pursuing multiple goals:

1 Open your mind and be aware of new opportunities. Look for things within and outside the apparent parameters. Be sure to look beyond the obvious.

2 Be bold enough to try new things. Deviations from your plan will come when you least expect it. Do it anyway. That led Parazynski to compete in luge and coach at the Olympics.

3 Challenge yourself. If you always stay within your comfort zone, you will never learn anything or experience new things. You will get bored, and your work will suffer. Learning occurs outside your immediate comfort zone.

4 Find a challenging environment. If you are the smartest person in the room, find another room. You can learn from everyone around you if you are open to it. Consider people who are senior or junior to you and even your peers. Look for people who are within and outside your industry. You can learn new skills and ways of viewing problems and solutions.

Taking these actions will prevent you from having an either/or mentality. It will encourage you to pursue multiple streams of interest until you find the right one, where your genuine passion shines. Managing your time and energy, and leveraging opportunities can aid in sustaining your level of fulfillment.

COACHING QUESTIONS

1   What is one modification in your current job you would consider making to support your passion?

2   What is one thing you can do to help you meet a milestone toward your next goal?

3   What is one thing you can do today to get better control of your time, focus, and energy?

KEY TAKEAWAYS

1   Conduct a Passion Audit to determine what you excel in, what you enjoy, what you procrastinate about, and what you would do for free if you could.

2   Identify what you will do next so that you have something clear on which to focus. Instead of thinking about what you would like to become, consider what you would like to do.

3   Name it and claim it. Identify your next goal, give it a label and vocalize it. Let people know what you want to work on next.

4   Support your goals. Now that you have identified your goals, label them and make sure that everything you do and the responsibility you accept aligns with your goals. Remember, if it does not align, you must resign.

5   Manage your energy and focus your cognitive work during those hours of the day when you are most alert.

6   Get into a rhythm and consider using a system to push you to do focused work without distractions, with small breaks in between.

7   Act when opportunities present themselves. Most importantly, keep your eyes open for circumstances where you would be slightly out of your comfort zone. That is where real learning occurs.

References

Cirillo, F The Pomodoro® Technique, https://www.huffpost.com/entry/how-an-ordinary-person-ca_b_7756394 (archived at https://perma.cc/U4WB-FXWK)

Clark, D (2019) How to reach out to someone whose career you admire, *Harvard Business Review*, https://hbr.org/2019/07/how-to-reach-out-to-someone-whose-career-you-admire (archived at https://perma.cc/3WZU-N7SM)

Duckworth, A (2016) *Grit*, New York, Scribner, an imprint of Simon & Schuster

Eyal, N (2019) *Indistractable: How to control your attention and choose your life*, Dallas, TX, Ben Bella Books

Gotian, R (2020a) Do what you love: but first find out what that is, *Forbes*, https://www.forbes.com/sites/ruthgotian/2020/06/05/do-what-you-love-but-first-find-out-what-that-is/ (archived at https://perma.cc/4VMD-ZN8E)

Gotian, R (2020b) How to stop your New Year's goals from going up in smoke, *Psychology Today*, https://www.psychologytoday.com/us/blog/optimizing-success/202012/how-stop-your-new-years-goals-going-in-smoke (archived at https://perma.cc/M64D-SSNB)

Gotian, R (2020c) A new spin on the Pomodoro Technique. How doing laundry can improve productivity, *Forbes*, https://www.forbes.com/sites/ruthgotian/2020/12/22/how-doing-laundry-made-me-more-productive/ (archived at https://perma.cc/Z5DK-PHMW)

Gotian, R (2020d) Stop dreaming and learn how to turn your goal into a reality, *Forbes*, https://www.forbes.com/sites/ruthgotian/2020/11/24/stop-dreaming-and-learn-how-to-turn-your-goal-into-a-reality/ (archived at https://perma.cc/PJ4L-VP2X)

Lintz, JS (2017) How an ordinary person can change the world, well at least start the process... *Huff Post*, https://www.huffpost.com/entry/how-an-ordinary-person-ca_b_7756394 (archived at https://perma.cc/U4WB-FXWK)

NASA Kennedy Space Center Visitor Complex, U.S. Astronaut Hall of Fame https://www.kennedyspacecenter.com/explore-attractions/heroes-and-legends/us-astronaut-hall-of-fame (archived at https://perma.cc/4BVP-YRZW)

O'Boyle, E and Aguinis, H (2012) The best and the rest: Revisiting the norm of normality of individual performance, *Personnel Psychology*, **65**, pp 79–119

Shanafelt TD et al (2009) Career fit and burnout among academic faculty, *Archives of Internal Medicine*, **169**

09

Finding a mentor

In this chapter, I explain what mentors do, where you can find one, when you should look for a mentor, what you can and cannot expect from your mentoring relationship, and lastly, how you can be the mentee everybody wants. You will learn who to consider as a mentor, what you can do to be a great mentee, how to set up meetings with a mentor and, overall, how to maintain a positive mentoring relationship that is sustainable. This chapter will focus on some overlooked places to find a mentor and provide scripts to approach a potential mentor successfully.

I discuss mentorship quite a bit in this book with good reason. All the high achievers attributed much of their success to having and listening to mentors. Colorado's Attorney General, Phil Weiser, said, "Part of my blessings in life has been having a series of mentors, starting with AP History in high school, college, law school, and clerkships." AG Weiser clerked for US Supreme Court Justice Ruth Bader Ginsburg and admitted to having learned a great deal from his former mentor, including "the ability to let things rub off of you and respond with dignity and grace" (Gotian, 2020f).

Recognizing the enormous impact and potential, all the peak performers found ways to pay it forward by mentoring others. Successful people like to develop and surround themselves with other successful people. That is why over half of Nobel laureates trained with previous Nobel winners, and many Olympians choose former Olympic athletes to be their coaches (Zuckerman, 1995). High achievers are not intimidated or threatened in any way by the success of their mentees. Quite the opposite; they wear the success of their mentees like a badge of honor. They take great pride in developing raw talent and seeing them reach the highest pinnacle of success. The high achievers I interviewed beamed as they recounted the achievements of their mentees.

A dedicated mentor can take on the crucial task of helping you advance and provide much-needed support when you question your professional worth. The road to extreme high achievement is long and often isolating. Triumphs, hurdles and challenges fill the long and windy path to peak performance. When we see the successes and accolades, that is the tip of the iceberg. It is everything and everyone below the waterline that helps create the success that everyone ultimately sees and admires. The mentor plays such a critical role in this. Not only do they open endless doors for the mentee, they help you when you are feeling down, questioning your ability to get the job done, even if you wonder whether you are cut out for your chosen field. Mentors provide the necessary challenges and scaffolding to ensure your success. In Chapter 7, I discussed how high achievers learn informally from others; mentors are a critical part of that pillar of success. Peak performers continually consume new knowledge from their mentors. They crave their guidance and listen intently to their words of wisdom, knowing that they are always given with the intention to offer support.

The research on mentorship is explicit. Those who have mentors out-perform and out-earn those who do not (Allen et al, 2004; Eby et al, 2008). A recent study showed that 76 percent of people think mentors are critical, yet only 37 percent have one (Olivet Nazarene University, 2020). But where does one find a mentor (Gotian, 2020b)?

Whether in person or virtually, potential mentors are all around us, some-times in the most unlikely of places. Often they are right in front of us, but we have not given them any attention. When seeking a mentor, forget about their title or rank. Instead, focus on someone who can provide you with guidance, support and perspective, and introduce you to people in their network who can help you achieve your goal.

The value of mentors

Dr. Kathy Kram, a Professor in Management Emerita at Boston University, has spent her entire career studying mentorship. Her research underscores two essential roles of mentorship: one of career development and the other of psychosocial support (Kram, 1988, 1983). The professional development functions assist the mentee in learning the intricacies of organizational life and politics while preparing them for advancement opportunities. The mentor can offer career support by increasing the mentee's exposure and visibility, offering them challenging work assignments, sponsoring them for opportunities, and protecting them from people and tasks that can derail their careers. Career stalling tasks include office housework, citizenship tasks, and work that needs to be done but is not considered promotable (Armijo et al, 2020; Grant and Sandberg, 2015; Williams, 2014).

The psychosocial functions build the mentee's competence, confidence and effectiveness in their professional role. The emotional supporting functions can include role modeling, the proper way of dealing with challenges and successes, acceptance and confirmation of the mentee, counseling, and friendship. Empathy helps the mentee when they are dealing with defeat, failed experiments, or missed opportunities. Mentoring gave astronaut Nicole Stott the boost to fill out the NASA application to become an astronaut. She had toyed with the idea previously, but her mentors encouraged her to fill out the application. It was just the push she needed.

We all need help with both the professional and psychosocial functions. We benefit significantly from the professional push to keep our careers progressing, helping us develop a plan of action and introducing us to the right people. Psychosocial support is needed to encourage us when we do not believe in ourselves; it can help us through the challenging times when we think our work is meaningless, will never amount to anything, or when we suffer one loss or rejection after another. The mentor can keep the big picture in mind, know that defeat is temporary and see the potential we have yet to see in ourselves.

Like many others who work in the mentoring space, Kathy Kram emphasizes that mentoring has evolved and now encourages people to have a network of mentors, or as I call them, a team of mentors, which you will hear more about in Chapter 10 (Gotian, 2020a, 2020c, 2020d). You cannot wait for someone to spontaneously notice you and offer mentorship. Kram recommends being proactive in initiating mentoring conversations. "Regularly assess and ask yourself, who would it be helpful for me to talk to and interact with to help me move through a major career change?" she said. Kram suggests that any significant change in your life, such as a new job, degree, or partner, should be a trigger for launching a self-assessment and reviewing your mentoring network. Even without disruption to your life, you should check your mentoring team annually. She suggests asking yourself three questions: ·

1 How is my current network serving me? Are there any holes?

2 Is there anyone in my network with whom I want to develop stronger relationships?

3 Is there anything in front of me that would benefit from greater assistance?

When looking for a mentor, Kram suggests considering the following points (Gotian, 2021a):

1 Expertise is not sufficient to be a good mentor.

2 Test the mentor's availability.

3 See if they are interested in being helpful.

4 Do they want to devote time, and do they have the bandwidth?

5 Test the waters before jumping in.

Most people realize that a mentor can help them succeed. Hopefully, this will assist you in finding more than one member of your mentoring team (Gotian, 2020c).

Who is a mentor?

Traditionally, a mentor was considered someone older, with more experience. If you find the right person, by all means ask them for guidance with your career. Mentors do not need to look like you, be in your department or even your industry. The goal is to think and look broadly for mentors who can give you different perspectives and support you and your career.

As we go through the list of potential sites to find a mentor in the next few pages, I want you to realize a few things that a mentor is and is not. A mentor can be, but does not need to be older and more experienced. They can be of different ages, races, ethnicities, genders, or religions. A mentor is not necessarily someone you worked with on a project or co-authored a paper with. A mentor is someone who provides career guidance and offers support when it is needed. As a mentee, you need to come to your meeting ready to learn and succeed. Be prepared to meet with your mentor armed with a goal and a plan, and the mentor should help you refine that plan and introduce you to people who can aid in seeing your goal come to fruition.

Before we discuss who should be your mentor, I would like to mention who should not. While your boss seems like an obvious choice of mentor, I caution against making them your only one (Gotian, 2020h). While your direct supervisor wants you and your department to succeed, if you leave, even to another division within the organization, replacing you is expensive and a great deal of work. The boss needs to recruit a successor who will undoubtedly have a steep learning curve and may not fully understand or appreciate the culture. If your successor does not arrive before you leave, your boss may need to pick up the slack, train the new person, and simply manage one more thing in their growing list of obligations. Subconsciously, and without ill intent, your boss might be stopping you from moving ahead by not effectively mentoring and sponsoring you for opportunities (Gotian, 2020g, 2021b). Many bosses are superb and mentor the people on their team with aplomb. I am not advocating that a boss should not be your mentor; instead, they should not be your *only* mentor.

How to be a good mentee

At the core of mentorship is a relationship. It is a vital foundational concept if you are to succeed. You want to build and nourish the relationship over time and not make it transactional. That last part is worth repeating. If every time you interact with your mentor, you ask them to do something or save you from something, you will quickly find yourself without a mentor. They will resign from the role, and the mentoring relationship will be short-lived. You will frustrate them. Instead, prove your worth, show your curiosity and give more than you receive. Engage with the potential mentor in person, virtually, and on social media. Engagement shows you are interested, underscores what topics are meaningful to you, and showcases your work. Share the good news, keep your mentor up to date on projects you are working on, articles you read that you think they might find interesting, or a photo from a vacation. Nothing exhausts a mentor more than receiving an email from a mentee who only wants something; worse yet, if they never listen to the advice they are getting. After a while, your mentor will stop responding to your emails if their only purpose is to solve yet another problem for you. Remember, a mentoring relationship should not be transactional.

If you really want to stand out as a mentee, mentoring advocates, and the authors of *Athena Rising* and *Good Guys*, Drs. Brad Johnson and David Smith strongly encourage seeking and excelling at stretch assignments to show what you are capable of achieving (Smith and Johnson, 2020). In their book *The Mentoring Guide*, physicians Drs. Vineet Chopra, Valerie Vaughn and Sanjay Saint recommend that when taking on projects, mentees should under-promise and over-deliver (Chopra et al, 2019). Doing so repeatedly will make a mentor want to help you as you are setting yourself apart.

Mentors are looking for diamonds in the rough, those who have the raw talent and desire and want to learn more and take charge of their career. They are happy to help them and see them succeed. Dr. David Ginsburg, the physician-scientist you met in Chapters 4 and 5, is still in touch with most of his former mentees and meets up with them in person when he can. Looking back, he realizes that they were all standouts and special in their own way.

Where to find a mentor

Hopefully, by now, I have convinced you of the benefits of finding a mentor. Now it is time to put your plan of finding a mentor into action. There are steps you can actively take to make this pursuit interesting and fun.

So, where does one find this great mentor? It is not as elusive a concept as you may think. Good mentors are everywhere. Work, conferences, personal life, in-person and online mediums are excellent places to find a mentor. There are three main wells where you could find potential mentors: your work, personal life, and overlooked random places. Each has unique benefits.

Mentors at work

Work seems like a prominent place to find a mentor as people understand what you do, why and how you do it, and your professional reputation.

SENIOR LEADERS AND RETIREES
Many have come before you, and there is a great deal to be learned from their experiences. They have climbed the ranks, perhaps taken advantage of opportunities, found shortcuts, or are in the know regarding best-kept secrets. Approach senior members of your organization or industry and strike up a conversation about any random topic. Look for a shared connection such as your alma mater or favorite food, color, sports team, or vacation destination. After a while, ask them for their perspective on an idea you've had or a project you are working on. At this point, they will know you as a person, and the foundation of trust and a relationship is built. Look

for people both inside and outside your department. Consider break rooms and workplace cafeterias as a potential place to meet senior members of the firm. You never know who you might meet at the salad bar.

You have likely heard about the group of guys who play golf together, and they are the ones who get the choice projects and promotions. What is important to realize is that they built a relationship where their colleagues know them over a shared non-work pastime. They joked and laughed together and commiserated over a missed shot. They got to know each other as people. As a mentor, when you know someone and have an idea of their work ethic, morals, and how they get along with others, you are more likely to pitch an opportunity and want to see and take part in their rise to leadership roles. If you did not get a chance, it is not because people do not like you; they just don't know you. If golf is not your sport, or you were not invited to that gathering, who is stopping you from starting your own gathering and inviting other people? Consider organizing a group dinner, trips to go apple picking, white water rafting, wine tasting, or an outing to see a show. Start organizing a few events and have the organizational role rotate. Invite leaders from your organization to join in. Before long, you will start a movement and find your own mentors who get to know you outside of the office.

Do not forget retirees as possible mentors. They have been at the institution for a significant time, and know the politics and pressure points. In the most unfiltered way, which can be refreshing, they will tell you who will have your back and who will stab you in the back. They may also have more time to sit and talk with you about your career and have a more comprehensive network, built over decades in the industry, of people to which they can make introductions. Reach out to a retiree by phone or email. Introduce yourself, and let them know that you have heard about their work and you were curious about XYZ. Ask to take them out for coffee or lunch if they are in the area, or set up a video call if they are not local. They might have the time and appreciate the opportunity to reminisce. Get to know them, share the projects you are working on, and find a common interest.

COMMITTEE MEMBERS

There is a good chance you will have to join a committee task or force, or collaborate on a special project at work or within your volunteer pursuits. Often these groups bring in people from different divisions and departments, and it is an excellent way for you to showcase your motivation, work ethic, curiosity, attention to detail, and persistence. Pay attention to how everyone else works, the questions they ask, and the opportunities they share. Are they doing their work and thinking in isolation, or do they work in a group? Does your thinking align with theirs? Do you have any shared chemistry with them? If so, that person can be your mentor. Look at the chairperson of the committee. Why do you think someone hand-picked them for the role? Talk to them outside of the committee meeting. Follow up on something that you heard or an idea you had.

Every organization has committees and teams that are working on special projects. Do not forget to consider your regional and national organizations as well, as they are always looking for volunteers to work on new initiatives. This is an excellent opportunity to broaden your reach, meet people outside your immediate circle of influence, expand your network, and find mentors with a more national or global view.

CONFERENCES

In-person and virtual conferences are a hotbed of potential future mentors. Not sure where to start? It is quite simple: you need to make a connection and not ask for anything. Speakers, panelists, and fellow audience members are all people who can guide you in your career. The key element is to strike up a conversation and quickly get to a topic that is common to both of you. It could be your alma mater, hometown, a common person you know, or a favorite pastime. You are giving them a reason to like you. They have enough people who are interested in their professional role and who bring that up as a point of commonality. You will stand out by talking about something different, which they often do not hear.

As soon as the speaker roster is announced, reach out to the person by email or social media and let them know you are excited to hear their talk. Most importantly, let them know why their topic is of interest to you. Follow up with them on social media and engage. Engage not so much that you are stalking them but enough that they know who you are after a while. Every two to three weeks is plenty. Most people check their own social media, so there is a good chance you will reach the intended person directly.

If you did not get the opportunity to reach out to the speaker before their presentation, go to their talk 20 minutes early or log onto the virtual conference before the start time. Often, the speakers arrive early to do their soundcheck and ensure their audiovisual needs are functioning correctly. After that, they are standing around without anything to do, so they often get engrossed in their phone. That is a great time to introduce yourself, tell them you are looking forward to their talk and why. There likely will not be anyone else there fighting for their attention. Bring up your common thread, such as saying you were a student at their alma mater, and watch their eyes light up. You can talk about your favorite professors, or the dorm you each lived in. It is a private language between the two of you. Now you are someone who is interested in their work but understands something from their past. It is a shared connection.

Conversely, after the presentation, there is usually a long line. If you do get the opportunity to chat with the speaker, you will feel rushed, and the speaker will likely not remember you. For virtual meetings held on Zoom or any other virtual platform, I strongly encourage you to turn your camera on and chat with the presenter and organizers. You will have their undivided attention for at least ten minutes. That is longer than any other opportunity you will get.

After their presentation, reach out again and remind the speaker of the common thread. Also, let the speaker know what precisely from their talk resonated with you and why. Start to have a dialogue about it via email. After some time, you can reach out to ask a question, such as "How did you deal with…?" It is best not to ask for any favor, introduction, or insight in the initial communication. You will scare the person away. Your goal should be to develop a relationship, not to make the conversation transactional. This same process can be utilized in both in-person and virtual conferences as well as to keynote speakers, panelists, and break-out session leaders.

If a fellow audience member made an incredibly insightful comment or asked a good question, reach out to them and let them know. Getting up in front of other people can be nerve-wracking, which is why most people refrain from doing so. Let the person know that their comment resonated with you for a particular reason. This confirmation supports them while helping you make a meaningful connection with a curious thinker. As you would do with a speaker, connect with them on social media and engage with their content. If there is an article you read or podcast you heard about a topic that you think would be of interest to them, email it to them and attach a short note letting them know why you thought they would find it intriguing. Consider introducing them to people in your network who might be able to assist them with projects in which they are involved. Not sure if this would work? Simply turn the tables. Imagine you went up to the microphone in a crowded conference room and asked a question. Now envision someone approaching you during the break to tell you how much they enjoyed your comment and how good they thought your question was. Would you not feel great? I think it would make you stand a bit taller.

For virtual conferences, pay close attention to the chats. People tend to be much more communicative there. As you would for an in-person conference, reach out privately to a fellow participant and let them know that you found their comment to be of interest. You can also reach out to someone if they made a statement that is aligned with something in your life. Perhaps they referenced a previous shared employer, same hometown, alma mater, or that they are a yogi. Find anything to make the connection and build a relationship. A conversation over curly hair led one student to become my mentee. She called me her mentor—that is not a title one gives to oneself.

Coffee breaks and bathroom lines might seem like a reprieve from a conference, but they can be the most productive places if you leverage your time standing in line. These places turn into great opportunities to strike up conversations with people. You need to be ready to initiate a conversation with any random stranger so that you are not tongue-tied when you meet someone you wish to talk to. A solution is to have starter sentences ready (Gotian, 2020e). These are benign conversation starters such as:

"What was your favorite session so far?",

"Where are you based?"

Or when commenting on a unique accessory, you could say "What a cool…".

I was once at a conference cocktail reception and a woman walked by with a purse in the shape of a clock. I had to remark on its uniqueness as it was truly remarkable. "What an interesting design for a purse!" I exclaimed. Turns out, the woman was Susan Silver, author of *Hot Pants in Hollywood*, and one of television's first female comedic writers. She wrote for *The Mary Tyler Moore Show*, *Maude*, and other network favorites. She told me the story behind the purse, I found out about her non-profit work that she embraced after retiring from writing, and we found alignment in those causes. She proceeded to introduce me to many of her friends at the conference. It all started with a comment on her purse.

After the conference is over, do not forget the airports. If anyone is holding a conference bag or is a recognizable face from the meeting, approach them. Say, "Did you just attend the XYZ conference?" Wait for a reply. Then respond, "I was there too. I am [say your name and organization]." Wait for a response. "What was your favorite session?"

Now you are off and running. The conference was the common ground for both of you, and you can chat about your favorite talk, the most inspirational message you heard, the rubbery chicken at dinner, or anything else as you wait to board. Be sure to follow up within 24 hours of landing.

Mentors from our personal lives

Our family, neighbors, children's schools, the gym, faith-based organizations, and volunteer organizations are all places from within our personal lives where you might find a mentor. They are often filled with other professionals from varying industries, allowing you to diversify your mentors and hear how problems are approached and solved in other industries.

FAMILY

When you think of your family, think broadly. Consider your immediate family as well as the distant members such as uncles, aunts, second cousins once removed, and those who you know are part of your family, but no one is sure where the connection lies. If you want to be a doctor, but the only member of your family who is a physician is a distant cousin, contact them. Perhaps someone in your family works at a medical school, or has a college roommate who is now a physician. The critical thing to realize is that you need to be clear with what you are seeking. Do not only look for apparent connections. Even indirect associations might prove to be helpful; the important thing is to keep an open mind.

If you have not spoken to this family member in a long while, this might be an excellent opportunity to rekindle the relationship over the common bond of a shared love for a particular occupation.

NEIGHBORS

Do you know your neighbors? You might be surprised at the industries they work in and the guidance they can provide. You already have the common bond of living in the same building or neighborhood and can have an untold number of conversations about snow removal, garbage collection, public transportation availability, or the prices in the local supermarket. You may see your neighbors when they are out of their usual business attire and professional persona. You might run into them in the elevator, laundry room, or grocery store. Knowing what field they work in and building a relationship with them can set the groundwork for a strong mentoring relationship.

CHILDREN'S SCHOOL

If you have children in school, do you know the other parents? While you may not have the time, patience or bandwidth to sit on the parent-teacher organization, you can join the parents' social media group and take a more passive role of reading what others post. You will get insight into what other parents do, what issues are important to them, and how they react. As you would at a conference, reach out privately to those whose messages have a tone and content that aligns with or challenges your way of thinking. The common thread that unites you is your children's school, favorite teachers, pediatrician recommendations, or balancing work and family.

If you are sitting through an assembly, play or sports game, talk to the other parents and understand what industries they are in. Get to know them as people and build that relationship. Offer to introduce them to people in your network. As always, give more than you receive. A friend watched her son play baseball and was sitting on the cold bleachers as the wind was blowing. She overheard a conversation between two other parents where one said he was looking to hire a new junior person for his finance office. Another parent chimed in and said she knew someone who was looking for a job in that industry. That led to a conversation about the work they each did, their roles, and hiring practices. On the cold metal bleachers, watching their kids play baseball, they got to know each other as people.

GYM

If you go to a gym or play any organized sport, how well do you know the other members of your gym class or team? Have you spent time talking to them about what they do and where they work? With the common thread of staying fit, consider asking them such questions as:

"Are you new to this class/gym?"

"How long have you done Pilates?"

"How many times a week do you take cardio classes?"

"Do you prefer free weights or the treadmill?"

The variety of benign starter sentences is endless. The point is to engage in conversation with them and get to know them as people. Before long, you will start discussing each other's professional lives. When I was researching high achievers for this book, I was trying to locate a specific person and reached out to my network. One friend mentioned that he knew the person I was seeking to speak with as "he has the locker next to mine at the gym."

VOLUNTEER ORGANIZATIONS

Where and with whom do you spend your weekends? What organizations do you belong to that align with one of your interests? Think of the various religious, political or social groups to which you belong. Who are the other members, and what do they do? In which fields do they work? Who do they know? Even if you are not familiar with the field, ask them, "What is new in the legal field this month?" You will get insight into what projects they are working on, the people they are interacting with, and how they overcome challenges. It is an open-ended question that discloses critical information about a field and its key players. Follow up and keep searching for where there is alignment between what they do and who they know. It is always there, you just need to gently dig.

RANDOM PLACES

Work and personal interests are some of the more obvious and popular places to find mentors. Still, there is a potpourri of other opportunities to meet people who can help guide your career and ascension to peak performance. Think of your past history and those who helped form your identity and ignite your passion in a field. Were there teachers from high school who inspired or supported you? What about professors in college whose classes you loved? Were there classmates who you always felt had their act together? Reach out to them. Let them know what you are up to, and start rekindling that professional relationship.

Has someone written a book you enjoyed or an article you found interesting? Reach out to the author and let them know why the book or article was so meaningful. Let them know what resonated with you and why. Many authors do not hear from their readers and are often writing in a vacuum. Reaching out to them will make you stand out as it is not a common occurrence.

When you meet anyone new, a good rule of thumb for following up can be summarized as 24/7/30 (Lopata, 2020). Follow up with the person within twenty-four hours after speaking with them, and then shoot them a quick email or LinkedIn request seven and then thirty days later. Let them know how you are implementing something the two of you discussed.

A mentor is a title that is earned, and it is the mentee who bestows that title. You are not a mentor until your mentee calls you one. Both sides put in the work and have a relationship based on trust and the ability to see greatness in each other. To have a fully developed and robust mentoring experience, I encourage you to get a team of mentors from a variety of industries and levels of the hierarchy.

How to set up a meeting with your mentor

Breaking another mentoring myth, meetings with your mentor do not need to be scheduled or scripted. Many believe you need to meet with your mentor every other Tuesday at 4 pm with an agenda and have a contract before conversing for the first time. I don't know about you, but I certainly would not wish to start a mentoring relationship with a binding contract. Trust and common purpose are the foundations of any relationship, not a letter of agreement. It is fluid with an almost unrecognizable on- and off-ramp. Anyone can exit this partnership at any time.

Meeting at a fixed day and time makes little sense in today's rapid, ever-changing world. Things come up that need immediate attention. Alternatively, what if there is nothing new to discuss? Do you make things up just because you have the time allotted? If a mentor is giving of their time, there should be something productive to discuss. If you only have a quick question, do you need to wait until your scheduled time to have a conversation? In today's ever-evolving world, what a mentor/mentee relationship looks like is unrecognizable compared to the traditional definition.

COACHING QUESTIONS

1   Who are people who you respect and regularly turn to for guidance?

2   What are one or two things you could do to leverage this relationship?

KEY TAKEAWAYS

1   Look for mentors within your professional vicinity. Consider senior leaders, retirees, people at conferences and work-related committees.

2   Consider potential mentors from your personal life, including your family, neighbors, parents from your children's school, the gym, and volunteer organizations in which you partake.

3 Be open to reaching out to people from your past, including former professors and classmates, as well as people you have never met before, including authors.

4 Be ready to initiate a conversation by having starter sentences that you can draw upon whenever you meet someone new. For example, consider the following starter sentences:

   a What was your favorite session?

   b I hear you are a fellow (name your school) alumnus.

   c I loved what you said about... It really resonated with me because...

   d I love the design on those socks!

   e I really appreciated what you said about...

   f I understand you work on XYZ. I am in that field at ABC company. Did you also have a hard time with (insert challenge in the industry)?

5 In virtual meetings, utilize the chat function to interact privately with people who made comments that resonated with you.

6 Follow up and engage with people on social media. Let them know what in their post resonated with you and why.

References

Allen, T et al (2004) Career benefits associated with mentoring for protegee: A meta analysis. *Journal of Applied Psychology*, **89**, p 127

Armijo, P et al (2020) Citizenship tasks and women physicians: Additional woman tax in academic medicine? *Journal of Women's Health*

Chopra, V, Vaughn, V and Saint, S (2019) *The Mentoring Guide: Helping mentors and mentees succeed*, USA, Michigan Publishing.

Eby, L T et L (2008) Does mentoring matter? A multidisciplinary meta-analysis comparing mentored and non-mentored individuals, *Journal of Vocational Behavior*, **72**, pp 254–67

Gotian, R (2020a) Follow these 5 steps to develop a mentoring team, in S Jain and D Kim (eds.) *Women In Medicine Compendium: An evolution of empowerment*, Wiley

Gotian, R (2020b) How do you find a decent mentor when you're stuck at home? *Harvard Business Review*, https://hbr.org/2020/08/how-do-you-find-a-decent-mentor-when-youre-stuck-at-home (archived at https://perma.cc/JNS4-9T5J)

Gotian, R (2020c) How to create your own mentoring team, *Psychology Today*, https://www.psychologytoday.com/us/blog/optimizing-success/202009/how-create-your-own-mentoring-team (archived at https://perma.cc/4FZJ-P75Z)

Gotian, R (2020d) How to develop a mentoring team, *Forbes*, https://www.forbes.com/sites/ruthgotian/2020/07/06/how-to-cultivate-a-mentoring-team-in-five-easy-steps/ (archived at https://perma.cc/9BCK-8PWJ)

Gotian, R (2020e) How to start a conversation with a stranger, *Forbes*, https://www.forbes.com/sites/ruthgotian/2020/09/29/how-to-start-a-conversation-with-a-stranger/ (archived at https://perma.cc/PFX7-JGB8)

Gotian, R (2020f) Justice Ruth Bader Ginsburg's best mentoring advice, *Forbes*, https://www.forbes.com/sites/ruthgotian/2020/10/13/justice-ruth-bader-ginsburgs-best-mentoring-advice/ (archived at https://perma.cc/9J7N-J6WH)

Gotian, R (2020g) Why you need a role model, mentor, coach and sponsor, *Forbes*, https://www.forbes.com/sites/ruthgotian/2020/08/04/why-you-need-a-role-model-mentor-coach-and-sponsor/ (archived at https://perma.cc/NV3T-7FGS)

Gotian, R (2020h) Why your boss shouldn't be your mentor, *Forbes*, https://www.forbes.com/sites/ruthgotian/2020/10/16/why-your-boss-shouldnt-be-your-mentor (archived at https://perma.cc/8973-CZX8)

Gotian, R (2021a) How to find the perfect mentor to boost your career, *Forbes*, https://www.forbes.com/sites/ruthgotian/2021/01/26/how-to-find-the-perfect-mentor-to-boost-your-career/ (archived at https://perma.cc/M9G3-GEMZ)

Gotian, R (2021b) Role model, mentor, coach, or sponsor—which do you need? *Psychology Today*, https://www.psychologytoday.com/us/blog/optimizing-success/202101/role-model-mentor-coach-or-sponsor-which-do-you-need (archived at https://perma.cc/8RC2-HGP8)

Grant, A and Sandberg, S (2015) Madam C.E.O, Get Me a Coffee, *New York Times*, February 6

Kram, K (1983) Phases of the mentor relationship, *Academy of Management Journal*, **26**, pp 608–25

Kram, K (1988) *Mentoring at Work: Developmental relationships in organizational life*, Lanham, Maryland, University Press of America

Lopata, A (2020) *Connected Leadership*, UK, Panoma Press.

Olivet Nazarene University (2020) *Study Explores Professional Mentor-Mentee Relationships in 2019*, https://online.olivet.edu/research-statistics-on-professional-mentors (archived at https://perma.cc/TW23-2Z58)

Smith, DG and Johnson, WB (2020) *Good Guys*, Boston, MA, Harvard Business Review Press

Williams, JC (2014) Sticking women with the office housework, *The Washington Post*, https://www.washingtonpost.com/news/on-leadership/wp/2014/04/16/sticking-women-with-the-office-housework/ (archived at https://perma.cc/UL3U-T5D6)

Zuckerman, H (1995) Gender and Science, in WT Golden (ed.) *Scientific Elite: Nobel laureates in the United States*, Routledge

10

Your mentoring team

If one mentor can help you achieve success, imagine what an entire team of diverse mentors can offer. They can help you tap into more perspectives, different experiences, and new networks, which might have previously been out of your reach. However, these are not random people you assemble. As Dorie Clark mentions in her book *Reinventing You*, consider this collection of people as your personal board of directors (Clark, 2013). This group is pivotal as they can make or break your career. Relying on one person within your organization is risky as you are suddenly without a mentor if they leave the company (Claman, 2010). When you have a group of people, you are not stuck when abruptly one departs. Who doesn't want an entire group of people guiding them toward professional success? This chapter will provide you with insights and tools to develop your own mentoring team and help you strategize who its members should be so that you are not left with blind spots.

Perception of perfection

The first thing to overcome when searching for a mentor is the perception of perfection. If you are looking for the perfect mentor, stop (Gotian, 2021b). He or she does not exist. When I ask people if they have a mentor, they often tell me they have not found the right person—a case of analysis paralysis. Perfection is toxic, and you will never get out of the starting blocks if this is all you seek. Face it, nobody is perfect, including you and me. Nobody has the skill set, patience, temperament, network, and time combination you seek. Nor do they have matching identities and cultural upbringing with which you were raised. But there is good news. You can find a close cousin of perfection by encasing yourself in a group of people, each of whom can offer something unique.

Mentoring pitfalls

No one person can give you everything you need. You also need a clear out if a mentoring relationship is not living up to expectations. There are endless tales and sagas of mentorship that went sour. Physicians Drs. Vineet Chopra, Dana Edelson and Sanjay Saint call this "mentorship malpractice." Sadly, some of the most popular stories include the following pitfalls (Chopra et al, 2016):

- the mentor who is never around;
- the mentor who claims your idea as his own and takes all of the credit;
- the mentor who insists on seeing all of your work but has an enormous lag time with feedback and needs constant reminders and follow-ups;
- the mentor who does not have your back and will not go to bat for you publicly or privately;
- the mentor who tries to shape you in their image, effectively trying to create you as a "mini-me."

The benefit of having several people guide your career is that if one person sours, is too busy, or takes on any of the aforementioned pitfalls, others can seamlessly step in to help. One person cannot be all things to even one person, let alone multiple people. There will always be hurdles and challenges. We are human, after all. You can get different things from a diverse group of people, and there are still ways for you to offer to help. More on that when we discuss junior mentors later in this chapter. The best mentoring relationships are so fluid that you often forget who is the mentor and who is the mentee. Both parties learn from each other. Not because they have to, instead they want to.

Collapse the gaps

Being dependent on one person puts you at significant risk and leaves gaping holes in the career guidance you should be receiving. You are going to need different things in your career, which will evolve. Since no one has accomplished precisely what you intend to, under identical circumstances, it would behoove you to widen your circle and develop an entire team of mentors (Gotian, 2020d). You will not find perfection with one person, but you can create a model with multiple diverse people, representing different facets of what you need. As Dr. Adam Grant suggests in his book *Think Again*, they will challenge you to rethink conventional wisdom, look for opportunities and sharpen your curiosity (Grant, 2021). Between them, the sum of all of their parts, you can find someone with the ideal characteristics you seek.

When thinking of who you want on your mentoring team, if everyone looks like you and comes from a similar background, you will have tunnel vision. All the guidance will be similar and undifferentiated. If you have a diverse group of mentors with varying experiences and backgrounds, you will receive enlightening and discerning guidance. When identifying who should be on your mentoring team, consider:

- Which skills you need to develop.
- Does their presence calm you or send you into a frenzy?
- Do you feel inspired or depleted after you talk to your mentor?
- What is their mentoring track record?
- Do they give selflessly in public and in private?
- Will they introduce you to people who can further assist you?
- Will they give you constructive information to enhance your work? (It is an opportunity for enhancement, not feedback (Gotian, 2020f).)
- Their mentoring style. Does the mentor give you an article to read, tell you to look something up, or talk you through a challenge? Which is your preference?
- Will this person sing your earned praises when you are not in the room?

Granted, the last one falls into the sponsorship category, how the mentor amplifies their mentees' work (Gotian, 2020b, 2020i). While you may never know what happens behind closed doors, you can look for examples of how they shine a light on others. Listen to how they refer to others' work in a meeting, on Zoom, and on social media. Those are all important clues. If your mentor seems envious of your success, walk away. A dedicated mentor will measure their success by your accomplishments: if you succeed, they succeed.

Research has proven time and again that those who are mentored out-perform and out-earn those who are not. They have higher salaries as well as more significant salary growth. They get promoted more often, report lower burnout rates and have greater loyalty to the organization (Allen et al, 2004; Eby et al, 2013, 2008). However, having just one mentor is extraordinarily limiting; having a team of mentors puts you in the driver's seat.

You can dip into different areas of expertise. A silver lining is that if one mentor is busy or has substantial differences of opinion, you can approach other members of your mentoring team. It is essential to have a carefully crafted personal mentoring team (Gotian, 2019, 2021b). This collective, which has your best interests at heart, has to be selected carefully and strategically. There are layers of different types of people who can help your career, many you might not have considered but ought to.

A mentoring team offers a diversity of thoughts, perspectives, skills, and social capital. The more diverse your team, the greater your reach and potential. I always encourage those I work with to curate mentors from divergent industries and geographies so they can learn and appreciate new ways of thinking and approaching problems. Do not limit yourself to one industry or organization: think globally. To truly get a wide array of outlooks, make sure those in your mentoring team do not all look like you. Aim for a cross-section of genders, ages, and ethnicities. My team of mentors includes people from a wide range of industries, including medicine, science, education, law, sports, and the military. I have learned countless tips from each one of my mentors and have grown my network exponentially. My mentors led me to publish in major journals, taught me how to develop mentoring circles in my organization, and helped me get face time with key people when traveling to their institutions. You are the common denominator in your team. While you can reach out to any team members, they do not all need to meet together. There is a good chance they will not even know of each other's existence. That is entirely acceptable. You can cherry-pick which mentors to approach at different times for your specific needs.

When considering who should be on your mentoring team, think carefully about who can give you new perspectives, teach you the technical skills needed for your work, and help you expand your network. Who is the person that can be your sounding board as you identify new thoughts, ideas, and plans? Look for people with wildly different strengths. Consider which areas of your job you need to do regularly, which you wish to grow in, and the skill set needed for the following two job levels. Consider who can help you develop those skills. Be as encompassing as you can. Think of who is a good writer, a financial whiz, a master on multiple computer platforms, an expert networker, and whatever else you might need. You want these people on your side so you can learn everything you can from them and have them be your guides. You will want to consider people in and outside your field and industry, people at various levels of the organization, and those with similar project experience.

Start by looking within

There is nothing new under the sun, my mentor once told me. You might think that your work is incredibly unique, and no one has ever experienced what you are going through, but at the end of the day, it is not so new. Sales, marketing, finance, and leadership development have all had the same structure for decades. Change happens slowly, and there are scores of people who have lived through fluctuations in the organization and industry. Listen to what others share with you and learn from their experiences. A mentor may not teach you something that you cannot learn independently, but they can certainly save you time. Conversations with those within your department and professional association can teach you valuable lessons about their path, including challenges and time-saving techniques. Find out what lessons they learned along the way and are willing to share with you so that you do not need to reinvent the wheel. There are veterans in your industry who have a wealth of knowledge. You will do yourself a disservice if you do not reach out to them and develop a rapport.

One important thing to note is not to limit yourself to your department. Even individual units within an organization have their deep-rooted traditions (Lindstrom, 2021). Consider reaching out to the other departments within your organization to learn about their operations and pain points. You can learn about problems and possible solutions and potentially be the change agent. You might even be the person who dares to cross the silos to find opportunities for problems people did not realize they were having. By learning how other departments view issues and solutions, you are getting a more profound knowledge of how things work at the organization. This view will afford you insight as you move up the hierarchy and you will know something that others have yet to figure out.

In 2017, United States President Donald Trump appointed James "Hondo" Geurts as Assistant Secretary of the Navy for Research, Development and Acquisition. With this new role, he brought a wealth of experience from his time in uniform and as a civilian, having served in all levels of acquisition leadership positions. Geurts previously served as the US Special Operations Command Acquisition Executive, where he was responsible for all special operations forces acquisition, technology and logistics. Prior to Senior Executive Service, Secretary Geurts served as an officer in the US Air Force, retiring after 22 years of service. While in uniform, he served as an acquisition program manager, assigned to engineering and program management leadership positions, throughout his career.

When the new administration took over in 2021, Geurts continued his life of public service, this time performing the duties of Under Secretary of the Navy. In his most recent role, he served as the deputy and principal assistant to the Secretary of the Navy and the Chief Operating Officer and Chief Management Officer for the Department of the Navy. His jurisdiction included intelligence-related activities, special access programs, infrastructure, and classified activities for the US Navy and Marines. He oversaw an annual budget in excess of $200 billion (US Navy, 2021).

Geurts was informally known as the "Pentagon Mayor," in reference to his daily walks around the famous corridors, speaking to all who crossed his path. He is naturally curious and finds talking to people is a great way to build relationships and learn new things. As the Navy's head of innovation, he was always looking for something new. At the core of innovation is taking two things that you would not ordinarily think about putting together and combining them to make something new. The best way to do that, according to Geurts, is to find out what is happening all around you. Get out of your office, talk to people, find out what they are working on and what challenges they solve. "I'm not that smart. I'm a poacher," said Geurts. "The fastest way to learn something is to take what is already there and adapt it for your use. That is how you get innovation at scale." In Geurts' case, he did it by talking to people all around the Pentagon. Talking to people within his organization is a practice he has adopted throughout his career. Along the way, he has found several people he can count on as sounding boards for new ideas and opportunities.

As you consider people within your organization and industry, be sure to look at other departments and all of your associations for your field. Consider regional, national and international associations. Start working on building professional relationships. Do not ask for anything, just maintain contact. Interact with people within all of these groups to maximize your potential for finding appropriate people for your mentoring team.

There's a whole world outside your company

If you lock yourself into finding mentors simply within your organization or industry, you are severely limiting yourself. There might be a solution in another industry that yours has yet to understand or rectify. You can save yourself a great deal of time, effort and heartache by understanding how others approach challenges and opportunities.

When Anne Wojcicki founded and became CEO of the personal genomics company 23andMe, she reached out to Facebook COO Sheryl Sandberg, fashion designer Diane von Furstenberg, and media mogul Arianna Huffington. Although Sandberg works in technology, von Furstenberg in fashion, and Huffington in media, they offered Wojcicki sound counsel throughout her various career stages. Launching and running a new company can be extremely overwhelming, and you cannot help but want to be involved in every decision, solve every problem, and meet every new face. As Sandberg taught Wojcicki, you cannot know every detail of what is happening within your organization, and you need to learn to be okay with that. There was also simple operational advice that helped Wojcicki feel good about making her employees feel special. "Sandberg taught me not to do things that cannot scale. If I celebrate every employee's birthday, I will buy a cake every day," said Wojcicki. That would not feel special and very quickly can feel like a chore instead of a reward. "Instead, Sheryl taught me to celebrate anniversaries." That was a practice she quickly adapted and is an excellent example of an idea that is transferable across industries.

The thrill of learning new skills

If your latest project requires you to learn new skills, find someone who knows how to do it and learn everything you can from them. Be a sponge and absorb everything you can. Find out what works, what does not, what is a waste of time, and what can save you time. Determine which are the right tools and resources to use and which processes and people to avoid. Be open to who you are approaching. The expert in the room might be right under your nose.

In Chapter 7, you learned about Dr. Chris Walsh, a physician-scientist who learned molecular biology from a recent college graduate. James Geurts, performing the duties of the Under Secretary of the Navy, did not think twice about approaching anyone and everyone to learn new skills, a new perspective, or simply a new idea.

When putting your mentoring team together, consider three levels of people: those who are senior, junior, and your peers. Do not forget retirees.

Senior in rank

Those who are senior to you have a strategic view. Those higher up in the hierarchy know what has been tried and what plans and opportunities are on the horizon. They might be privy to information and decisions that have yet to be released. They have a well-developed mentoring network that provides social and political capital that can be leveraged as needed. It is not just who they know, but who those people know and their influence. These can be people in the C-suite and those who are one or even two levels above you. They were once in your shoes and can empathize with your situation. You can learn from their experiences, failures and successes.

When I give talks on mentorship, people always tell me they have a fantastic mentor: their boss. Your supervisor as a mentor sounds great, but is it? Your boss can see your potential and any areas of opportunity and can help you succeed in the workplace, and many do. But who is checking for your boss's blind spots?

During my doctoral studies, I recall chatting with friends about people's reactions to their pursuit of higher education while working full time. One classmate told me that her boss, who she always got along with splendidly, had said, "You don't need a doctorate for what you want to do." Ironic that he should say that, as he had no idea what her career goals were. She excelled at her work, and he assumed that if she attained a higher degree, she would eventually seek a role further up in the hierarchy, leaving him with a critical role to fill. Moreover, he would be saddled with the extra work until someone new was hired and brought up to speed. He was right.

As discussed in Chapter 9, while your boss may be a good mentor, I caution you against having them as your *only* mentor. So how can you move ahead in your career while optimizing your mentoring relationship with your boss?

Identify your next career goal

Meet with your boss and let them know what your next career objective is so that they are not caught off guard when you suddenly leave for a new job. Do not worry about the "where do you want to be in 10 years" goal, as that may change several times. Focus on your next immediate goal, then consider your one-, three- and five-year goals.

Develop a plan

Develop a plan to help you meet your goal. Consider the five-year goal, and then work backwards. What would you need to accomplish by year three and year one to meet your target? Ask your boss/mentor what they think you should do to develop that goal. Is there a course they suggest you take? Is there a subject matter expert with whom you should connect? Do not worry if you do not know them. There are strategic ways to approach people you do not know (Gotian, 2020e); you can also ask for an introduction.

Identify a successor

What can you be doing now to develop a successor so that they can seamlessly slip into your role when the time comes? Let them know that by doing this, there is a higher likelihood you will stay in the organization and will be there to answer questions long after you leave the role. You will also be developing other people within the organization, which illuminates your ability to find and develop promising talent (Gotian, 2020c).

If you look good, they look good

Remind your boss that their success as a mentor is directly related to the success of their mentees. In other words, if you look good, that makes them look good. Your boss should be one of the people on your mentoring team, but not the only one. Ask your boss who else they think should be on your team. If they know the person, ask for an introduction. Remember, when you meet this new person, work on developing a relationship. Do not ask them upfront to be your mentor (Gotian, 2020g). If you do, you are asking them to take on another obligation, and you have yet to prove yourself to them.

Many bosses are great, fantastic even. They recognize that they can play a small part in your success. Having several diverse people guide your career can eliminate blind spots, leverage opportunities, and develop collaborations. Your boss could and should be one person on your mentoring team, but nobody should have a mentoring team of one.

Retirees

Those who retire have lived a full life. They have seen and experienced a great deal. Just because someone has retired from the organization does not mean they should be put out to pasture. They are a goldmine of information and often an overlooked resource. Retirees have usually spent a great many years at the organization, know what works and what does not, who is trustworthy and who is not. Finished with the daily hustle, bustle and stress of everyday work life, they often find themselves in a position where they want to give back but have trouble finding the path to do so (Gotian, 2021a, 2021c). It is why you see so many retirees volunteering in various capacities. There are many organizations, including Eldera, who match elders or retirees with mentees (Eldera.ai, 2021).

When Dr. Charles Camarda, the astronaut profiled in Chapter 4, retired from NASA in 2018, he wanted to give back and train the next generation to solve complex challenges. He credits much of his success to the mentors who helped him throughout his career, starting in college. Camarda wanted to do the same for others and scale the mentoring he could offer. He recruited twenty of his friends, including former NASA astronauts, engineers and educators, to serve as mentors. Fresh in retirement, he launched the Epic Education Foundation (Epic Education Foundation, 2021). Together, they create high-performance teams blending children and professionals to solve "epic" challenges using advanced science, mathematics, and engineering techniques. In the midst of the pandemic, they mentored 200 mentees; since the inception of the program, they have reached 5,000 mentees.

Peer mentors

Too often, people look far and wide for a mentor, when excellent mentors are right under their noses. Most people forget that their friends and colleagues can also be mentors. They understand the pressures of someone at your career stage, can best empathize, share resources and opportunities. They might hear about job opportunities, calls for articles, potential speaking engagements, requests for podcast interviews, and proposals. Peers are too often overlooked as a potential source of mentors when they have so many good qualities. They are patient, have your best interests at heart, and expect nothing in return. I will talk much more about peer mentors in Chapter 11.

Junior in rank

There are many lessons to be learned from those who are junior to us. Many have touted the benefits of learning new technology, becoming proficient in social media and learning about new areas of possible collaboration. The younger they are, the more they read and start seeing the possibility of connecting the dots. They have friends they are close to with different areas of interest.

James Geurts, performing the duties of the Under Secretary of the US Navy, would approach the most junior people at the organization for guidance. "You have to go pretty deep in the organization so that it won't change their outlook," said Geurts. He would share with his junior mentors how he was thinking about a problem or contemplating communicating something. He would ask them how they felt it would be perceived. They taught him things such as how to use Twitter and what gets perceived as authentic or not. He learned how they think.

Stop looking for people who look like you

I often hear that women and underrepresented minorities have trouble finding mentors. To help alleviate these challenges, stop looking for people who look like you. As David Smith and W. Brad Johnson report in their book *Good Guys*, there are simply not enough women and minorities in senior ranks (Smith and Johnson, 2020). Those limited numbers cannot take on the obligation of mentoring every person who matches their gender or ethnicity. It is not fair to them or you. They will be too busy, they will not be able to give you or your career sufficient attention, and ultimately their work will suffer. If their work deteriorates, they will not be able to serve as anyone's mentor.

You have many identities, with your gender and race/ethnicity being just two of them. You might also be a first-generation college student, immigrant, oldest child, young parent, recently married, recent homeowner, new manager, or the first business leader in your family. These are all circumstances that make up who you are. It is essential to understand that no one person can match all of your identities. You are a unique individual. Finding a multitude of people to fit different parts of your identities is the first step.

Developing your mentoring team

How do you identify who should be on your team? A simple five-step process can help you determine who can help guide your career and serve on your *Targeted Mentoring Team*. The underscoring idea is not to collect random people to serve as your mentors. You need to be strategic and consider who can help you in the various facets of your professional life and ultimately optimize your success. Before you get started identifying people, you need to consider your goals and plans seriously. A worksheet is available with this book to help you structure your mentoring team.

Step 1: Your goal—name it and claim it

What do you want to do in ten years? I am not a fan of that interview question. During the Covid pandemic, you may have reevaluated your longstanding objectives. Maybe the distant goal was not realistic. Your current long-term plan may not include jobs that have yet to be created. Case in point, ten years ago, your organization likely did not have a dedicated social media manager. Now they have degrees in it and entire departments to handle digital communication.

You might be focused on the wrong goals (Gotian, 2020h). Reexamine the questions you are asking yourself, and put a focus on the tasks and environment instead of the title. Instead of thinking about what you would like to become, consider what you would like to do. The same questions used to guide your "what next" questions in Chapter 8 can be utilized again to guide your thinking:

- Do you like to work with people, or do you prefer to work in relative isolation?
- Do you like the background noise of people talking or the hum of fluorescent lights?
- Do you prefer to crunch numbers and see trends or develop something creative like a short video?
- Do you prefer identifying problems, coming up with solutions, or executing a plan?
- Are you the thinker or doer in your workgroup?

Reflect on these questions as they will give you great insights as you begin to craft an idea of what you would like to do in your career. Remember to focus less on the title and more on the types of projects and ideas you would like to work on, under what conditions you would like to accomplish this work, and with whom you enjoy working.

Answering these types of questions will help you get out of the starting blocks. The key is not to work on your ultimate goal but start identifying your *next* goal. Do you want to become a director, partner, or associate professor? Name it and claim it. Do not worry about being a managing partner just yet if there are five other levels in between. Have a laser focus on the next goal you would like to achieve.

Why does it appear that some people accomplish so much and others fail to get out of the starting blocks? The difference between success and stagnation could rest on the notion of which goal gets your attention. To add momentum, consider focusing on the next goal, not the ultimate goal. Be methodical in your approach.

Another approach is to work backward and reverse engineer your goals (Friedman, 2021). It sounds complicated, but it is not. Think about your five-, three- and one-year goals. Do not look past that, as so much can change, including your situation and interests. Start with your five-year goal and work backward to determine what you would need to achieve at the three- and one-year marks to stay on course. Once you figure out your one-year goal, that becomes your immediate objective and the locus of your attention. How would you describe this goal? Is it to get promoted to vice president or associate professor? It is essential to identify and label your attainable short-term goal. Knowing what you want to achieve and where you want to go will help dictate the path you should follow. The reason for not choosing a long-term goal at this point is that as you develop new experiences and skills, you might find your long-term goals change.

Step 2: Become a fan of the plan

French author Antoine de Saint-Exupéry once said, "A goal without a plan is just a dream" (de Saint-Exupéry, 1943). Naming your goal is a critical first step. To prevent your goal from just being a fantasy, identify what you need to do in the short term to achieve your goal. Do you need to land a big account or publish more articles? Be very specific about what the next steps are.

Now that you know what promotion you would like, next consider what would you need to achieve to meet your next goal. Do you need to get another degree? Learn a new skill? Meet certain people? Again, name it and claim it. Once you have identified what you need to do next, make a plan. If you need to get another degree, what kind would it be? Do you need to take a standardized test such as GMAT or GRE to gain acceptance? If so, focus on studying for the test as you begin to identify schools to which you would like to apply.

If you need to learn a new skill, figure out how you can achieve this. Can someone teach it to you? Can you take an online course? Start identifying what you need to do to learn this new skill.

Are there certain people with whom you need to connect? How can you meet them? Can anyone in your circle introduce you to them? Consider also following them on social media and engaging with their content to show interest. Not so much that you are stalking them, but enough that they recognize your name after a while, as someone who adds value to a conversation.

I recommend listing three to five achievable plans. Break them down into actionable steps to make them more attainable and increase your probability of achieving success. As you lay out your ideas and create a blueprint for your career, avoid listing too many steps. Failure to do this will make everything quickly become overwhelming and will prevent you from starting at all.

Once you have these steps identified, you can begin building your mentoring team. This is the group of people who will help you actualize your plan, provide insight, and connect you with the right people. You are developing your *Targeted Mentoring Team*. Envision a bullseye with a total of three circles, one inside the other. In the middle of the bullseye, write your name, as this is all about and for you.

Step 3: Your inner circle

List the names of people who know you best. They see you when you are tired, hungry, deprived of caffeine, and maybe even cranky. They could be your partner, family, closest friends, roommate, perhaps even your children. Even if they are not in your industry, these people will tell you the truth, even if it hurts. They know the "personal" you.

Step 4: Your middle circle

This circle, right outside your inner circle, includes your closest work colleagues. Those you work closely with have seen you under the pressure of a deadline, crises, or the stress of being understaffed. Having seen you up close in a professional context, they are attuned to your work ethic and professional reputation. Your work colleagues might be senior or junior to you or right at your level. They know the "professional" you.

Step 5: Your outer circle

The outer circle will take the most work but is the critical component of your mentoring team. These people can see far into the future and help make it a reality, starting today. It includes acquaintances and people who work in or outside your field. You may not know them directly, but you know of them. They may consist of people you have heard speak and those whose work, position, or reputation you admire. They are people who, with one or two introductions, you can connect. They do not need to be in your primary industry. If you are having trouble with negotiations, having a master negotiator on your team from any industry is paramount. If you need to do quite a bit of writing in your current or future role, consider whose written work you have always gravitated toward.

Unlike a graduate school dissertation defense, your mentors do not all need to meet together in the same room. They may not even know of each other's existence. These potential mentors can be approached remotely (Clark, 2016; Gotian, 2020a). You can cherry-pick which mentors you call upon for which projects.

This list might need to be tweaked a bit, but the bones are there for you to work with. Start with the inner circle and work your way out. Tell people what your goal and plan is. Mentors will emerge with guidance and connections to their network. Build on that and ask for introductions to your outer circle if need be.

The circles are permeable. Being a mentor is not a life sentence. Add and remove names of potential mentors as needs arise and your circumstances change. Before long, those in the outer circle will move toward the middle circle and new names will be added to the outer layer as you advance in your career. Your mentoring team, if chosen carefully, will help you ascend and achieve your goal.

You can certainly try to move ahead in your career alone, but surrounding yourself with a team of carefully selected mentors will save you time and frustration while opening up new avenues of opportunity. The team structure is flexible and you can add and subtract people as your career evolves. If you are lucky, many of your mentors will turn into life-long friends.

COACHING QUESTIONS

1 Who are three people you can identify for your mentoring team?

2 What is an area of expertise where you feel you have a gap in knowledge?

3 Who could help you fill that gap?

KEY TAKEAWAYS

1 Appreciate that no one is perfect. Instead of looking for the ideal mentor, surround yourself with a group of advisors who can help with the different facets of your career. Develop your own mentoring team.

2 Look for a diverse group of mentors, including those within and outside of your organization and industry.

3 Consider having three layers of mentors: those who are a. senior in rank; b. junior in rank; c. peers.

References

Allen, T et al (2004) Career benefits associated with mentoring for protegee: A meta analysis. *Journal of Applied Psychology*, 89, 127.

Chopra, V, Edelson, DP AND Saint, S (2016) Mentorship Malpractice, *JAMA*, **315**, PP 1453–54

Claman, P (2010) Forget mentors: Employ a personal board of directors, *Harvard Business Review*, hbr.org/2010/10/forget-mentors-employ-a-person (archived at https://perma.cc/QZR3-P82K)

Clark, D (2013) *Reinventing You*, Boston, MA, Harvard Business Review Press

Clark, D (2016) Networking with people you can't meet in person, *Harvard Business Review*

De Saint-Exupery, A (1943) *The Little Prince*, New York, Reynal & Hitchcock

Eby, L et al (2013) An interdisciplinary meta-analysis of the potential antecedents, correlates, and consequences of protege perceptions of mentoring, *Psychological Bulletin*, **139**, pp 441–76

Eby, LT et al (2008) Does mentoring matter? A multidisciplinary meta-analysis comparing mentored and non-mentored individuals, *Journal of Vocational Behavior*, **72**, 254–67

ElderaAI (2021 *Eldera* https://www.eldera.ai (archived at https://perma.cc/ JSH7-BM4N)

Epic Education Foundation (2021) *Epic Challenges* https:// epiceducationfoundation.org (archived at https://perma.cc/DD7S-M5PM)

Friedman, R (2021) *Decoding Greatness*, New York, Simon & Schuster

Gotian, R (2019) Why you need a support team, *Nature*, **568**, pp 425–26

Gotian, R (2020a) How do you find a decent mentor when you're stuck at home? *Harvard Business Review*, https://hbr.org/2020/08/how-do-you-find-a-decent-mentor-when-youre-stuck-at-home (archived at https://perma.cc/JNS4-9T5J)

Gotian, R (2020b) How to amplify the voice of your mentees, *Forbes*, https://www.forbes.com/sites/ruthgotian/2020/06/15/how-to-amplify-the-voice-of-your-mentees/ (archived at https://perma.cc/7HMA-Q73R)

Gotian, R (2020c) How to attract, retain, and lead high achievers, *Forbes*, https://www.forbes.com/sites/ruthgotian/2020/06/29/how-to-attract-retain-and-lead-high-achievers/ (archived at https://perma.cc/Q69D-47YE)

Gotian, R (2020d) How to develop a mentoring team, *Forbes*, https://www.forbes.com/sites/ruthgotian/2020/07/06/how-to-cultivate-a-mentoring-team-in-five-easy-steps/ (archived at https://perma.cc/9BCK-8PWJ)

Gotian, R (2020e) How To start a conversation with a stranger, *Forbes*, https://www.forbes.com/sites/ruthgotian/2020/09/29/how-to-start-a-conversation-with-a-stranger/ (archived at https://perma.cc/PFX7-JGB8)

Gotian, R (2020f) How to turn feedback into an 'opportunity for enhancement', *Forbes*, https://www.forbes.com/sites/ruthgotian/2020/08/14/how-to-turn-feedback-into-an-opportunity-for-enhancement/ (archived at https://perma.cc/ PDH2-VUEM)

Gotian, R (2020g) Looking for a mentor? Why you shouldn't use the 'm' word, *Forbes*, https://www.forbes.com/sites/ruthgotian/2020/07/31/looking-for-a-mentor--why-you-shouldnt-use-the-m-word/ (archived at https://perma.cc/ PAS3-ZU99)

Gotian, R (2020h) Stop dreaming and learn how to turn your goal into a reality, *Forbes*, https://www.forbes.com/sites/ruthgotian/2020/11/24/stop-dreaming-and-learn-how-to-turn-your-goal-into-a-reality/ (archived at https://perma.cc/ PJ4L-VP2X)

Gotian, R (2020i) Why you need a role model, mentor, coach and sponsor, *Forbes*, https://www.forbes.com/sites/ruthgotian/2020/08/04/why-you-need-a-role-model-mentor-coach-and-sponsor/ (archived at https://perma.cc/NV3T-7FGS)

Gotian, R (2021a) Do you want to mentor? The new matchmaking program for mentors and mentees, *Forbes*, https://www.forbes.com/sites/ruthgotian/2021/01/01/do-you-want-to-mentor-the-new-matchmaking-program-for-mentors-and-mentees/ (archived at https://perma.cc/5XSJ-V2VK)

Gotian, R (2021b) How to find the perfect mentor to boost your career, *Forbes*, https://www.forbes.com/sites/ruthgotian/2021/01/26/how-to-find-the-perfect-mentor-to-boost-your-career/ (archived at https://perma.cc/M9G3-GEMZ)

Gotian, R (2021c) Why do people at the top of their field become mentors? *Forbes*, https://www.forbes.com/sites/ruthgotian/2021/01/05/why-do-people-at-the-top-of-their-field-become-mentors/ (archived at https://perma.cc/ED8S-KJQN)

Grant, A (2021) *Think Again*, USA, Viking, an imprint of Penguin Random House LLC

Lindstrom, M (2021) *The Ministry of Common Sense: How to eliminate bureaucratic red tape, bad excuses, and corporate bs*, Boston, Houghton Mifflin Harcourt

Smith, DG and Johnson, WB (2020) *Good Guys*, Boston, MA, Harvard Business Review Press

US Navy (2021) James F. Geurts: Under Secretary of the Navy (Performing the Duties of) https://www.navy.mil/Leadership/Biographies/BioDisplay/Article/2236405/james-f-geurts/ (archived at https://perma.cc/YX8Y-JS5M)

11

Finding your people

Have you heard the saying, *It is not what you know, it is who you know*? This chapter will focus on finding and effectively connecting with people, so that your relationship lasts long after the introduction. You will learn how to engage with people with similar goals or interests, develop your community of practice or affinity group, and learn how to reach out to people, find commonalities, and engage in conversation (Gotian, 2019). These groups are essential as many jobs, collaborations, and opportunities develop through active participation in them. The key is to be involved so that people know who you are. Finding your people is a critical success factor and this chapter will offer you some tips on where to find your people.

When Justice Ruth Bader Ginsburg (RBG) died in September 2020, over 100 of her former clerks came to Washington, DC and stood in formation on the steps of the United States Supreme Court. These clerks had all worked with Justice Ginsburg at some point during her forty years on the bench. They gathered to bid their former boss and mentor goodbye. For an article I wrote for *Forbes*, I asked several of them how they got the call to action to gather in Washington (Gotian, 2020b).

Justice Ginsburg's office kept a detailed list of all her former clerks. When she passed away, they quickly communicated the idea of standing on the Supreme Court's steps for their final farewell. They had well-established lines of communication with her office and between each other. While they worked for her as clerks when they were in their twenties, they did not stay clerks forever. Today, many are judges, attorneys general, partners in prestigious law firms, and solicitors general.

When she was alive, every five years, Justice Ginsburg would invite all of her former clerks for a reunion on a weekend afternoon. There were no lectures or workshops at the reunions. They were sit-down dinners in the

Great Hall of the Supreme Court, preceded by a cocktail hour. Spouses and significant others were always invited. At the dinner, there would usually be anywhere from two to four short speeches, one of them by Justice Ginsburg. A clerk would usually speak, often while presenting a small gift to the Justice. When her husband Marty Ginsburg was alive, he sometimes spoke as well. The entire clerk reunion lasted about four hours.

As former clerks would travel with their families to Washington, DC for the reunion, there would often be ancillary events before or after the reunion. One year, there was a screening of one of the RBG movies. The reunion would offer a wonderful opportunity for former clerks to get to meet each other and learn from one another. Judge Paul Watford is a US Circuit Judge of the US Court of Appeals for the Ninth Circuit. He clerked for Justice Ginsburg during the term of her famous United States vs Virginia case, which struck down the Virginia Military Institute's exclusion of women. Judge Watford loved clerking for the Justice in 1995–1996 and would travel cross-country to attend the clerk reunions. "They allowed us to meet an ever-expanding group of fellow clerks, all bound together by the common experience of having worked for the Justice, and to spend at least a little time speaking with the Justice herself," said Judge Watford.

Colorado's Attorney General, Philip J. Weiser, clerked for three judges, including Justice Ginsburg. Each held a reunion, which he treasured. "They were all special, and the opportunity to build and renew relationships with a special peer group is one I treasured. For me, the opportunity to learn about and observe a range of career paths and life choices was very special."

Find your community of practice

Individual mentors with experience and social capital are critical, but other essential groups of mentors are equally vital yet often overlooked. Those in our age bracket, profession, or industry, with shared experiences, understand the pressures, empathize and can offer perspective. In adult learning, this powerful support group is called a "community of practice."

First named in 1991 by Jean Lave and Etienne Wenger in their book *Situated Learning*, a community of practice can be organic or deliberate, local, regional, national, and international. It offers the free exchange of knowledge, information, and opportunities where group members at every level of the hierarchy learn from each other while developing professionally and personally (Wenger and Snyder, 2000). Very often, when people look to hire someone from their team, they will look within their community of practice and reach out to those who they know, like, and trust.

Communities of practice are an integral part of the workplace. I strongly encourage you to actively participate in several such groups based on their specialty and uniqueness, such as marketing, insurance, or healthcare. There are organizations based on rank, as CEOs would have different needs, concerns, and opportunities from junior faculty members or mid-level managers. Gender offers options, such as the Association of Real Estate Women or the Group on Women in Medicine and Science. There are groups based on race and ethnicity, such as the Student National Medical Association and National Bar Association. Do not forget the alumni association of your school or department. They can notify you of jobs, exciting lectures, and connect you with people in the same field. Joining such groups offers a valuable opportunity to connect with like-minded people over a common purpose. A community of practice can help you navigate the hidden curriculum, those unwritten rules, of a new job while setting you up for success with benchmarked processes and mentors (Alsubaie, 2015).

Traditionally, communities of practice meet in person, such as at conferences, or communicate virtually through such mediums as an email listserv, discussion board, text messages, or group platforms such as Zoom. These groups are formed both within an organization and nationally. The underpinnings of these groups are shared experiences, people, and goals (Stamps, 1997).

In addition to your community of practice, do not overlook your friends and colleagues. Peers rise together, so finding people in your niche is critical. Peer mentors are a vital ingredient in the path to success (Gotian, 2020a). These are the people who are of your generation, working in the same industry and often at the same level. These communities of practice can be sliced and diced in every imaginable permutation. You can create these groups by gender, ethnicity, occupation, or geography. Peer mentors can empathize with your challenge, alert you to new opportunities, and share information on what they have tried before that may be relevant to your situation. They can be a group as small as two people and as large as thousands. They may include people you know socially and professionally (Gotian, 2019).

Learning to fit in

When joining a new profession, moving to a new location, or joining a company, learning the organization's rules, traditions, and culture is critical for survival and success. Just because you know how to do your job does not mean you know how to do it well within these new parameters. You do not see what opportunities exist, the expectations, or ways to acclimate to your new surroundings. There are unwritten rules and traditions, known as a "hidden curriculum" that you are expected to know, understand and follow (Alsubaie, 2015). Peer mentors can help you fit in, feel like a team member, teach you about the expectations, set you up for success, and save you a great deal of time and stress.

Zaza Pachulia started playing basketball at the age of nine. By sixteen, he was playing in the pros. At nineteen, he was drafted into the National Basketball Association (NBA). He retired in 2019 after winning two back-to-back championships with the Golden State Warriors in 2017 and 2018. He played for the NBA for sixteen years, on six different teams and in over 1,000 games. "I ran a lot of miles on the court," Pachulia said.

In his office, Pachulia has a bobblehead of each of the teammates who influenced him somehow. He was a teenager when he came to the United States, and everything was foreign to him. It was his fellow non-American NBA players who Pachulia first turned to when he joined the league early in his career. There was a common bond among them. The veterans took him under their wings and shared words of wisdom.

It was Pachulia's first time living in the United States. The American and NBA cultures were entirely new for him: it was a new world. He needed the advice of people who had walked the path before him. As Pachulia spent time learning and training with the NBA, his circle widened, and veteran American players constantly offered him guidance.

In his freshman year with the Orlando Magic, NBA player, and now co-owner of the Atlanta Hawks, Grant Hill, spent quite a bit of time with Pachulia, as did Juwan Howard, another NBA player and current head coach of the Michigan Wolverines. They helped him get acclimated on and off the court. Tony Kukoc from Croatia played with the Chicago Bulls and won several NBA championships. He was nearing the end of his NBA career when Pachulia started playing professionally and had the benefit of perspective. He offered a wealth of information for Pachulia and focused his guidance off the court over countless dinners.

The trio gave Pachulia tips, such as how to effectively approach every single practice, productively prepare for the games in terms of proper nutrition and resting, and lifestyle recommendations. They shared many stories, which helped Pachulia save a great deal of time and frustration. On the court, they guided Pachulia on how to excel both defensively and offensively. Kukoc was a great passer. "I loved playing with him because I knew I could score easily if he passed to me," Pachulia said.

The veterans also educated him about financial needs, expenses and regulations. Pachulia was not familiar with the US tax system, and it was his teammates who first explained the financial intricacies to him. The veteran NBA players were an endless source of support to him throughout his career, and he honors them each with a bobblehead in his office. "These are the people who inspire me every day," said Pachulia as he spoke fondly to me of his teammates.

Friendtors

Can friends be mentors? Absolutely! "Friendtors," friends who become mentors to each other, are a magical pairing. They have known you the longest, understand when you are upset, empathize with your stress, and are ecstatic when you succeed. They will give you untarnished feedback as they are not envious of your achievements and want you to reach even higher levels of success. They might hear of opportunities that have not yet crossed your inbox, have an idea for a collaboration, or help you prepare for a job interview.

Dr. Erika James, the Dean of the Wharton Business School at the University of Pennsylvania, and Dr. Lynn Wooten, the President of Simmons University, have been friends and friendtors since graduate school at the University of Michigan in the 1990s. Wooten was a year ahead of James and they overlapped their studies during a research methodologies class with an eccentric professor. It was a huge classroom where the number of seats far outnumbered the number of students. James and Wooten, realizing there were very few Black students in the class, tended to sit together. That is how these two academic powerhouses met. They were in their twenties, sitting in an auditorium waiting for a notoriously late professor to show up.

"There was a core group of students who would interact socially after class, over dinner, or a game of cards," shared James. Wooten and James would see each other in these groups, and the friendship flourished. Before long, their professional and academic interests aligned.

After graduation, James was teaching at Tulane and reached out to Wooten with an exciting proposition. In 1994, there was a significant discrimination suit against Texaco, often referred to as the Jelly Bean Suit, referencing the derogatory references to minority groups which they called "jelly beans" (Eichenwald, 1996). James's student collected interesting data, and she was wondering if Wooten wanted to collaborate on a project and paper. Wooten agreed and the two young assistant professors dove into a new field of crisis leadership related to diversity.

It was an exciting partnership as each could bring something new to the table. James brought in the micro-level organizational psychology lens, and Wooten brought in macro-level strategic thinking. Each complemented the other's work seamlessly. "The Texaco case was a defining moment for us," said James. It cemented their friendship, and their peer-mentorship escalated; they became "friendtors."

The more they combed through the data and saw how executives responded in times of crisis, the more the idea of crisis leadership became more prominent in their thinking. That was the catalyst for their joint work in crisis leadership. While it started in the diversity area, it quickly spread to include every other type of crisis, including hurricanes and the BP oil spill. "Crisis management has always been about reactions. We wanted to focus on forward-thinking responses," said Wooten. Together, they created a paradigm shift in the crisis field from management to leadership with a focus that went far beyond communication. That field might not have developed if not for their endless conversations and working together, where they balanced out each other's strengths and challenges.

Many of their ideas would come up organically through informal conversations. Their lives became more and more aligned both in thinking and practice. Wooten and James have kids that are roughly the same age, with two of their children just five days apart. Every day, on the way to work, they would call each other. To this day, they are on the phone with each other five times a week. Annually, they take a mother/daughter trip together. Wooten and James are both only children who think of each other as sisters. It is a friendship and professional partnership that has stood strong for 30 years and counting.

Although they are both working in academia and were both business school deans searching for jobs simultaneously, they never competed with each other for the same roles. On the contrary, they supported each other fully and helped each other calm their nerves through endless interviews and challenges.

When one wants to launch a new initiative, they often run it by the other to get feedback and support. Wooten and James both started their jobs as president and dean, respectively, on the same date, 1 July, 2020. James wanted to bring in more diverse speakers to Wharton and had some trepidation about it. She knew she wanted to do it but recognized that change often makes people uncomfortable. She reached out to Wooten for guidance and to help ease her anxiety. Wooten was energized by James and moved in a similar direction in her presidential role, bringing diverse speakers. "There is power in partnerships," said Wooten. "People see us as partners. We approach things so gently that people do not feel threatened. We want people to feel included and psychologically safe."

They recognize the value in their partnerships and still work together. When I interviewed them, they were working on another book together. They laughed as they recognized each other's strengths and how much they valued that in each other. James loves Wooten's ability to have multiple social circles, while Wooten craves James's ability to stay intently focused while asking for help when she needs it. There is not one dominant mentor in this pairing. Each helps the other without any judgment. It has made them both stronger and more successful, and ideal 'friendtors.'

Finding your people

Every industry has its professional association. Those are your people. These are the people who understand your daily struggles, pressures, and competing commitments. They also know where to find opportunities. Joining such a group is a fantastic opportunity to learn from others. See what they have tried in the past and are working on right now. Imagine all of the new people you can meet and the potential this offers to expand your network.

The peak performers are all members of multiple communities of practice and underscore their joy and need to be a part of a group of like-minded people. They tell me that these people simply get each other. They understand what they have been through, what obstacles might be in their way, and how to prepare for whatever is coming next.

Many of the astronauts are members of the Association of Space Explorers, which represents astronauts from all around the world

(Association of Space Explorers, nd). It was founded in 1985 by a small group of international astronauts, and today proudly boasts a membership of 400 flown astronauts and cosmonauts from 38 nations. The astronauts understand that space exploration is a costly endeavor and they can save much time and effort by learning from each other. Their website proudly states that membership in the group resulted in "a series of high-level discussions which have resulted in new opportunities for space cooperation in the changing global political environment" (Association of Space Explorers, nd).

This organization provides networking opportunities for astronauts from all over the globe, holding conferences throughout the world where they meet in a city and spend time in workshops learning from each other. They take time to explore the town together and get to know each other in the process. Like all of the high achievers, they find ways to give back. The astronauts and cosmonauts visit schools in the conference's host town. They hope that by visiting with the students, teachers, and parents, they will inspire a new generation of scientists and engineers.

Being an Olympian and training for the Olympic Games is a multi-year focused commitment. It is filled with endless work, multiple challenges, and compromises. In 2017, a new initiative was unveiled for people to recognize the Olympians' dedication to their sports. To celebrate the incredible achievement of reaching the Olympic participation level, the World Olympians Association launched an initiative for Olympians to post the letters OLY after their name on any official documentation, similar to how people list their terminal academic degrees of PhD, EdD, or JD (World Olympians Association, 2017). It is a way for people to recognize their commitment, incredible hard work, and for the Olympians to recognize each other.

When I told Olympic fencer, Iris Zimmermann, that I wanted to speak with Olympic and Paralympic champions for this book, she posted a message in the private Facebook group of 1,200 American Olympians. I met several more who, in turn, introduced me to others. This Facebook group aims to facilitate social interaction among Olympians and Paralympians who represent the United States. Regular posts include updates on Olympians, job opportunities, and obituaries. While Olympians and Paralympians generally know the people in their own sport, this group helps them meet others from varying sports in summer and winter Olympics and the athletes from different generations.

American Olympians are part of the United States Olympians and Paralympians Association (USOPA). USOPA assists members upon retirement, connecting them with each other through the national office, their regional chapters, the Athletes Services area, a secure Facebook page, or LinkedIn, to name just a few ways. They also have a very robust mechanism to share job, scholarship, and schooling opportunities. They assist their members with resume writing and have a significant commitment to the athletes' mental health and well-being. This show of support among Olympians can be translated to any group or industry.

Many of the Nobel laureates know each other and are familiar with one another's work. They attend the invitation-only annual LIndau Nobel Laureate Meeting, which hosts lectures, discussions, masterclasses and panel discussions (Lindau Nobel Laureate Meetings, nd). Led by Countess Bettina Bernadotte af Wisborg, the President of the Council for the Lindau Nobel Laureate Meetings, thirty to forty Nobel Prize winners get together in Lindau, Germany, every year. Like the astronauts, they look for ways to connect with the next generation of high performers. For a week, they gather alongside 600 undergraduates and doctoral students to share an exchange of ideas and for mentorship. To date, more than 430 Nobel laureates have attended the meeting. Dr. Peter Agre, the 2003 Nobel Prize winner in Chemistry, says that he looks forward to this meeting every year. He especially enjoys meeting and mentoring the next generation of scientists. At the Lindau Nobel meeting, the Nobel laureates encourage the budding scientists to have the courage to ask difficult scientific questions and develop the stamina needed to succeed. In informal ways, often through picnic lunches or strolls around the grounds, the Nobel laureates openly share their journeys. It is meant to inspire the young scientists while letting them know that while the path to success may be challenging and isolating, others have been there before them who can empathize and help them along (Lindau Nobel Laureate Meetings, 1951–2020).

Attending this conference was so transformative to the attendees that they launched an alumni network, which today has thousands of members. They enjoy a private online community, webinars, special projects, and local events.

Find out which professional organizations exist for your industry and join them. Attend their meetings, sign up for their emails, and join a committee or two if you can. You will get insights and perspectives that can help you in your job and career. You will also find mentors in this group who will want to help and guide you through your career and introduce you to others.

In addition to your national organization, consider joining the local chapter for your industry. Joining these local groups in addition to the national association will increase and improve your ability to connect with others, learn additional skills, and discover new opportunities. As they are closer in proximity, you might be able to meet in person on a more regular basis.

The sudden halt of travel due to the Covid-19 pandemic caused a sharp increase in online communication. Facebook and LinkedIn groups and the new social app Clubhouse exploded in popularity. Connect with the speakers and fellow audience members. Let the person know why you are connecting. Was it a comment they made that resonated with you, or a question they asked which got you thinking? Perhaps it was something completely random that they mentioned, such as a favorite movie, food, sports team, or travel destination. Look for the common thread between the two of you.

If one does not exist, create your own

What if a community of practice in your field does not exist? The answer is simple: create your own. Do not sit and complain about a lack of support or wait for anyone else to do something. Simply start a group. You can start small and build as you grow. Follow the steps below to launch your group.

Step 1: Find your topic

What is a common yet overlooked group that needs attention? You can think of your profession, gender, location, or rank. You can develop a group for female accountants within a firm, region, or industry. They can be female accountants at Company X. You can break it down by region such as the northeast of the United States. Alternatively, you can focus on a specific industry, such as accountants in healthcare. There can be various permutations of the same idea. Try it for your specialty.

While ordinarily we are encouraged not to bring our work home with us, this is one time where it might be beneficial to blend your work and family. You can create a community of practice around the combination of your two worlds. Perhaps you are interested in creating a group for young professionals new to London, people who are doing leadership coaching as a second career, keynote speakers on a specific topic, young parents, or people in your field who are also part of your religion. I know people who organized groups to help people in their field with their personal branding through social media. People who attended a specific conference can also be part of a group.

Step 2: Set up your group

At the beginning of the Covid-19 pandemic, I read a post on a private Facebook group to which I belong. The people who are part of this group are high achievers who attend an invitation-only leadership conference, to which I was invited and had previously attended. The message stated that the host was looking for a distraction from the pandemic and was opening a Zoom for any previous conference attendees who wanted to socialize. It was an instant hit. Everyone introduced themselves, laughed, and shared pandemic survival tips. Within weeks, on a rotating basis, several members of the group would teach the rest of us about their specialty. That Saturday night group became everyone's lifeline during the scariest and most isolating parts of the pandemic. Although they are all high achievers, they checked their egos at the door before logging onto Zoom. The group continues to meet every Saturday night and has not missed a single week since the pandemic began. It forged tight friendships, mentorships, collaborations, and co-authored papers and presentations among the attendees, whose professional backgrounds often varied. If one person had a big keynote, they often invited others from the group who came virtually to lend their support. A few published books and a home-grown fan base helped to amplify their masterpiece.

Setting up a group simply means you need a platform. You can create a Facebook group, email listserv, Slack channel, Clubhouse room, or your own conference. All you need is a way for people to meet each other and share ideas. The platform is not nearly as important as the frequency and depth of the engagement. Start with one channel for virtual communication, and you can always build from there. Do not organize a conference until you know you have an active and engaged audience who will show up.

Step 3: Start the conversation

If you want people to join your group, give them a reason. What is the common thread that unites all of you? How would you communicate and share ideas? Laying some ground rules, such as mutual respect, no judgments, and ensuring a safe space, is always advisable.

Give people prompts to get them to interact. You can have a "New Members Monday" where you list all the new members who joined the group the previous week and ask them to introduce themselves. At the end of the week, you can have a "Friday Flaunt" where each member can list their achievement for that week. Before long, everyone will welcome the newcomers and congratulate the fellow group members on their small and large achievements.

Once people are familiar with each other on a one-dimensional digital post, you can take it up a notch by organizing a Zoom, centered around a specific topic. You can ask someone to give a short presentation on a topic of interest or give tips that offer universal good advice, such as how to stand out on Zoom, how to network in the digital age, or how to increase your social media following. Ensure you utilize break-out rooms so that people can benefit from the smaller groups and get to know each other better. It is always a good feeling to be able to put a personality to a name and face.

Develop a way for people to be able to chat in real time. It can be an email listserv, Slack channel, or Facebook Messenger. If someone has a question or is wondering if anyone in the group has used a particular vendor, they can post their question and get responses in real time.

You are likely a member, or could be, of multiple communities of practice. Find and join them. If one does not exist, create the group; build it, and they will come. Do not discount your friends and peers as they can be great sources of mentorship. They have proven their support and loyalty and are not your competitors. Peers rise together; it is never too early or too late to find peer mentors.

COACHING QUESTIONS

1 What is one organization you are currently a part of?

2 What is one way you can be more active with this group?

3 Is there a group you would consider creating?

KEY TAKEAWAYS

1 Entering a new situation, such as a school, industry, company, or department, is filled with angst. Trying to find your way can be made much easier if you find people who understand your pain points, ambitions and will help you seek opportunities. They will help you fit in as you find your place and rhythm.

2 Your friends can be your mentors or "friendtors." Peers rise together, so it is never too early or too late to find peers who can serve as your mentors, and you can return the act of kindness.

3 Groups of people with a common thread are called "communities of practice." Join the national and local chapters and be sure to engage in conversation with their members.

4 If a community of practice does not exist, take the initiative to start one.

References

Alsubaie, MA (2015) Hidden curriculum as one of current issue of curriculum, *Journal of Education and Practice*, **6**

Association Of Space Explorers (nd) *Delivering the Astronaut Perspective*, https://www.space-explorers.org/ (archived at https://perma.cc/6U2R-8GYN)

Eichenwald, K (1996) Texaco executives, on tape, discussed impeding bias suit, *The New York Times*, November 4

Gotian, R (2019) Why you need a support team, *Nature*, **568**, pp 425–26

Gotian, R (2020a) How peer mentors can help you succeed, *Forbes*, https://www.forbes.com/sites/ruthgotian/2020/06/09/how-peer-mentors-can-help-you-succeed/ (archived at https://perma.cc/4F46-TR3Z)

Gotian, R (2020b) Justice Ruth Bader Ginsburg's best mentoring advice, *Forbes*, https://www.forbes.com/sites/ruthgotian/2020/10/13/justice-ruth-bader-ginsburgs-best-mentoring-advice/ (archived at https://perma.cc/9J7N-J6WH)

Lindau Nobel Laureate Meetings, https://www.lindau-nobel.org/ (archived at https://perma.cc/CHD2-3HZR)

Lindau Nobel Laureate Meetings, Educate. Inspire. Connect. 1951–2020

Stamps, D (1997) Learning is social. Training is irrelevant? *Training*, 3, 35–42.

Wenger, E and Snyder, WM (2000) Communities of practice: The organizational frontier, *Harvard Business Review*

World Olympians Association (2017) OLY post-nominal letters to honour Olympians https://olympians.org/news/983/oly-post-nominal-letters-to-honour-olympians/ (archived at https://perma.cc/8QLN-QURC)

12

Degrees are starting lines

Sitting in a classroom all day is not an ideal learning environment for most adults. This chapter will focus on how you can learn through informal learning mechanisms, which can inspire and motivate you, instead of the formal classroom, which can deplete your time and energy. Understanding your learning style and leveraging it to maximize the effectiveness of your learning is critical. Suppose you circle in on your preferred learning style. In that case, you will also note that you look forward to enhancing your knowledge on a particular topic, because finally, the teaching medium is an appropriate fit for you. There really is something for everyone, and all of these learning opportunities will help you leverage your success.

Despite their long list of accolades and terminal degrees, high achievers never stop learning. On the contrary, they crave new knowledge and know that any fresh morsel of information can improve their outcome. They actively seek it out and embrace it when they stumble upon it. Moreover, they engage in learning about a wide array of topics, not solely focused on their industry. The high achievers are always looking to potentially advance their work with newfound knowledge. High achievers learn differently than you might expect. They are not in the classroom, and for a good reason.

We have all had the experience of sitting in a classroom, eyes glazing, wholly disconnected from what we are hearing. The professor is standing in front of the room, droning on and on, spouting out a hailstorm of information. Furiously, we scribble down notes, trying to make sense of what is being taught. In practice, we are getting increasingly frustrated at our inability to organize the information coherently in our brains. In his book *The Pedagogy of the Oppressed*, Paolo Freire, the Brazilian educator and philosopher, called this idea "banking" (Freire, 2000). The teacher stands in front of the room depositing new knowledge into our brain, and we, as the learner, need to determine in which accounts to store the information. Not an easy task (Gotian, 2021a; Kolb and Kolb, 2005).

Adults have multiple conflicting demands on their time. Sitting in a classroom for eight hours a day while an expert professes from the front of the room is simply not realistic. Many billionaires read for three to eight hours a day. They view it as a way to learn new things and get inspired. Reading for them is a compounded interest. The knowledge they are gaining builds on itself. The stories of Bill Gates, Warren Buffett and Mark Cuban reading for hours every day that you heard about in Chapter 7 are legendary (Levin, 2017; Rampton, 2017). They make it a priority in their day. While reading works for these three billionaires, there are other ways to learn new things, gain insight and increase your knowledge. It was not just reading for hours a day that propelled Gates, Buffett and Cuban to their success. Instead, it was being open to learning new things and the transfer of knowledge.

David Kolb, the educational theorist whose work focuses on experiential learning, developed an adult learning style inventory composed of four elements that outline the significant ways in which adults learn (Kolb et al, 2002; Kolb, 1984a, 1984b, 1984c):

1 Concrete experience.
2 Observations.
3 Formation of abstract concepts based on reflection.
4 Executing the new concepts.

This learning style inventory is not based on auditory, visual, or tactile learning forms. Instead, it looks at how adults process information based on their experiences. When presented with a challenge, do you look at the problem from all sides, consider every alternative, or do you work things out based on trial and error? Knowing this will help you identify if you learn best by reading, watching videos, building prototypes, or just executing the suggestions. Some adults learn best through solitary reading, while others learn by talking through ideas with colleagues or friends. According to Kolb there is no right way, just your preferred way. We are all capable of all four learning styles but will have a strong preference for one of them.

Read like a billionaire

Gates, Buffett and Cuban consume new knowledge every day, and so can you. It offers you insights, perspectives, and might get you thinking about a new idea or strategy to leverage your success. When I interviewed Apolo

Anton Ohno, the most decorated winter Olympian, he had an entire row of books behind him on the topics of psychology and peak performance. He read everything he could get his hands on. While he knew he could train harder, get better gear and the best coaches, his performance would not be optimal if he was not in the right headspace. He needed to find a way to free himself from any self-imposed obstacles and found reading as a way to learn new methodologies and mindsets.

Reading physical books is one effective way of consuming new knowledge, but there are additional formats and reading options available, many of which let you multitask. For those who do not like to carry books because of their weight, electronic books or e-readers are a great alternative. Multiple devices such as an iPad, Amazon Kindle or Barnes and Noble Nook are all options for storing hundreds of books. The benefit is that the device weighs just a few ounces, and you can enlarge the letters and brighten the backlight as you deem appropriate. Audiobooks—what used to be called books on tape—are another alternative. Long commutes can be mitigated by listening to books on such apps as Audible. Someone is reading the book to you.

For any book you purchase in any of the available formats, if you enjoy the book, such as the one you are reading now, leave a rating and review, as it will help more people find it, thanks to the algorithms of the big sellers such as Amazon. Authors, myself included, will appreciate this and very often enjoy reading the reviews.

Shorter, bite-sized reading opportunities can be found in articles. Every major journal has 500–1,000-word articles on every imaginable topic, including interviews with luminaries, time-saving tips, and ideas on how to overcome imposter syndrome. The periodicals publish multiple articles per day, so there is always something new to learn. For professional development nuggets, take a look at Forbes.com, Inc.com, Entrepreneur.com, FastCompany.com, and HBR.org. If you are a new manager, take a look at HBR Ascend (hbr.org/ascend), which is geared toward those early in their leadership journey. For a broader psychological overview of success, consider reading *Psychology Today* (psychologytoday.com). Magazines and websites for your particular niche likely have a careers section as well, such as *Nature* (Nature.com/careers) and ChiefLearningOfficer.com.

Many of your favorite thought leaders are regular contributors to these sites and have their own columns. I write regularly for *Forbes* and *Psychology Today* on many of the topics discussed in this book and have published several pieces in *Nature, Chief Learning Officer* and *Harvard Business Review*. If you have a favorite author whose topics and writing style resonate with you, subscribe to their column. You will automatically be notified when they have a new article published. In addition, follow them on social media as they often post their latest articles to inform their readers of the latest publication.

Blogs and newsletters are another great way of reading and consuming new knowledge. If you have a favorite author or management thinker, subscribe to their newsletter. New content will find its way right into your inbox. Many executive coaches, such as Dr. Marshall Goldsmith and Dorie Clark, have weekly newsletters that they are religious about sending. Others, such as marketing expert Seth Godin, have daily blog posts, which vary in length from one paragraph to two pages long. Do not subscribe to too many as they will clutter your inbox, and you will not read any of them. Instead, select the few who resonate with you most and read the pearls they are sharing.

Podcasts

Years ago, a student walked into my office plugged into his earphones. I expected this 20-something year old to tell me he was listening to music. I was surprised when he informed me that he was listening to a podcast. A famous scientist whose research he was interested in was being interviewed and he was learning more about his journey and how he made his discoveries.

I realized then that podcasts were the perfect opportunity for informal learning, leveraged by the fact that you could multitask while listening— taking a walk, driving, making dinner, or doing laundry while also learning. There are podcasts on every imaginable topic. As of April 2021, there are 1.9 million podcasts with over 47 million episodes (PodcastHosting.org). Over 155 million people in the United States listen to podcasts, and most listeners are loyal, affluent and educated. They subscribe to seven shows on average and listen to 80 percent of each episode. During the second quarter of 2020, people listened to an average of six hours and forty-five minutes of podcasts each week (Buckner and Warren, 2020). That is a 30-minute increase over the previous quarter. The audience for podcasts is growing at an exponential pace, both those who are listening and those who are launching podcasts.

Listen to a few different podcasts and see which ones resonate with you. Consider if you like the style, host, guests, and knowledge that is being shared. Listen to several episodes. If you enjoy it, subscribe, and a new episode will automatically appear in your library. If you want to get noticed by the host, leave a rating and review. They will really appreciate it.

Videos

There is an entire industry based on teaching through video, which you can leverage at both the individual and organizational levels. Videos are an effective method for one person to reach many through the art of story-telling. Curated TED talks and the more local TEDx talks are based on ideas worth sharing, with a duration of no more than 18 minutes. TED talks can serve to ignite a spark and get you thinking about new ideas.

After Google, YouTube is the second most searched engine. With these videos, you can learn how to do anything, ranging from properly knotting your tie to developing your executive presence. You can find countless interviews with luminaries on YouTube; while not interactive, it is an endless hive of topics.

Your organization may provide video learning platforms at no cost to you. Many companies subscribe to an online teaching library through such companies as LinkedIn Learning or Skillsoft. Subject matter experts are brought in to teach you an endless list of skills varying from mastering Excel to branding yourself. If your company subscribes to these learning mediums, you can log into the courses with your work email and start learning new skills at your own pace. If your employer does not offer this benefit, you can sign up for LinkedIn Premium, which includes the LinkedIn Learning courses. When you finish a LinkedIn Learning course, you can then upload it to your profile, showing your followers that you are constantly learning.

If you need to study for a standardized test that will help you meet the next qualification for your job, Khan Academy (khanacademy.org) has many courses available for free, such as LSAT prep, as well as professional development courses on personal finance and developing a growth mindset.

If you are a reader, you might enjoy Rise.com, which launched in April 2021. It takes the books from the Next Big Idea Club and allows organizations to manipulate the content and deliver bespoke courses based on bestselling books (Gotian, 2021a). Adam Grant, Susan Cain, Malcolm Gladwell and Daniel Pink curate two books every quarter which are added to the Next Big Idea Club. Rise.com offers a video from the author to kick off the course, followed by a variety of activities to cement the main points from the books. Whoever manages professional development at your organization can customize the content based on the needs of the employees in your department or organization.

Listen and learn

Ian Siegel, CEO of ZipRecruiter, finished college with a bachelor's degree in sociology, psychology and English with plans to work in Hollywood. After a year spent on the Warner Brothers lot, he realized this was not the career for him. He worked at other companies, and before long he found himself overseeing engineers and computer scientists. The only problem was that he was not an engineer or computer scientist: he was an English major. He felt like a fish out of water. Trying not to make a fool of himself, he told the engineers he worked with, "Tell me what you need, and I will do it." It was that simple. The engineers spoke, and he listened. He looked for patterns, problems and ideas. It was that same listen and learn mentality that sparked the idea for ZipRecruiter, the online application portal that connects job seekers with employers.

Avoid the temptation to speak first. I know this is contrary to much of the guidance that is generally offered (Chen, 2015). While speaking first can help reduce anxiety, you can exponentially elevate your value to an organization and your executive presence if you listen more than you talk. Hear everything that is being said, look for patterns and gaps and summarize the information for the group. Many people like to hear the sound of their own voice and are not listening to what others are saying, therefore missing the opportunity to address a real need. If you can share the common thread or an idea based on what you are hearing, you will bring significantly more value. As a meeting starts to wind down and everyone is done speaking, state, "What I am hearing is…". Then follow up by summarizing the common themes and areas of opportunities you heard shared during the discussion. James "Hondo" Geurts, then performing the duties of the Under Secretary of the Navy, told me that innovation starts by listening to what other people are doing and applying it in a new way—that's innovation.

You can learn a lot by watching

Observing, making connections, processing the new information, and reflecting on it are core foundations of adult learning. This is also what high achievers do, either consciously or subconsciously. For example, Nicole

Stott, the astronaut, and aquanaut you met in Chapter 1, always loved everything about aeronautics. She had an insatiable curiosity and wanted to know how rocket ships flew. She worked at NASA for ten years and watched the astronauts as they were preparing for their missions. By observing them so closely and realizing that their education and background were similar to her own, she started considering being an astronaut herself.

Dr. Bob Lefkowitz, the Nobel Prize winner you met in Chapter 1, learned how to inspire the people in his lab by observing a football coach who motivated his players during halftime. The Paralympic champion from Chapter 7, Chris Waddell, knew that he would ski again, despite his injury. Years before his accident, he saw someone on a monoski, and the vision remained embedded in his mind. That memory reminded him that skiing was still possible for him, albeit differently than before. Supreme Court Justice Ruth Bader Ginsburg's former clerks learned so much by watching the Justice in action. By observing her, they learned how to work effectively with people with whom they disagree and get their point across without losing their composure.

The examples are endless. By observing others, you can see what is possible and you are no longer limited by preconceived notions of what can be done.

You can learn a great deal and get ahead by simply observing and looking for patterns. While watching what is happening around you, ask yourself such questions as:

- Where is the gap? How can I turn this into an area of opportunity?
- What is causing my boss stress? How can I alleviate that stressor?
- What is the main issue my boss's boss is facing? Problems flow downward, and eventually they will reach you and your department. If you can get ahead of it, you will be the hero.
- Which departments have a revolving door, as noted by a high turnover of employees? Why?
- What are the credentials of those in the positions I hope to attain? What do I need to do to earn those credentials?
- Who are the power players in the organization? Who seems to be all smoke and mirrors and, therefore, untrustworthy?

Knowledge of the people and projects that deserve your consideration can be gained by simply paying attention to what is happening all around you. Watch for gaps and patterns and consider how you can fill those needs.

You don't need to be an influencer, but you do need to engage

If you are not on social media, I encourage you to create an account. Some of the most popular ones include Facebook, LinkedIn, Instagram, Twitter and Clubhouse. While being active on all of them can be a full-time job, I encourage you to pick one or two platforms that you wish to concentrate on and delve deeper into their offerings. There is a vast amount of information you can learn, groups you can join, and events you can participate in, all of which you can find on social media. But you need to be part of the online conversation to know of its existence.

Facebook, LinkedIn, Twitter and Instagram each have a unique flair. Facebook tends to be more social but allows you to have groups based on specific interests. LinkedIn has more professional content and underscores the need for that level of networking and engagement. You post your resume on this platform, share articles of interest, job opportunities, and posts related to your work or profession. Social posts are frowned upon. You will not find vacation photos on this site, although there is significant humble-brag—the polite self-promotion of new jobs, advancements, awards and articles. This is critical information as you can congratulate them, or comment on their article. This will help you learn something new, find out about a new opportunity, and get known by the author.

Twitter underscores the need for brevity as the maximum post length can only be 280 characters. On this platform, you can create lists by interest or company, which helps you curate a refined list of people you wish to hear from, and blocks out other social media noise.

If you are seeking visual sharing then Instagram should be your preferred platform. Personal and professional photos and short videos are commonplace here. You can leave a brief message and use hashtags to look for posts around a particular theme. Anything from vacation photos to affirming quotes can be found regularly on this platform.

Clubhouse is the newest addition to the social media family and is only audio. Clubhouse is similar to a radio station where you can listen, and then raise your hand to ask a question or offer a tip.

The good thing about Clubhouse is that you can multitask while listening to the audio. You can passively listen or actively engage by raising your hand. Either way, you are learning. The more you engage, the more people will follow you and you will also see more interesting content, thereby learning more.

If you want to save your sanity and improve your productivity, shut off the notifications so that are not alerted every time you receive a message, or someone engages with one of your posts (Eyal, 2019). Instead, block off time during the time of day when you are most drained and therefore less productive anyway. Reserve a set amount of time to read or post content to maximize your learning.

Webinars

The Covid-19 pandemic has seen an explosion in webinars—live video instruction where you can ask the speakers questions and have them answered in real time. This takes learning from a passive act to an active one as you engage with the content, and has opened up an opportunity to learn from some of the greats. Many webinars are completely free and can be seen live via such platforms as LinkedIn Live, Instagram Live, and Facebook Live. In these live webinars, only the speakers and panelists are on the screen. This is in contrast to a regular Zoom presentation with one or two speakers and hundreds of participants staring at you from their one-inch by one-inch squares, completely disconnected from the speaker. To enhance engagement, many people and organizations use the webinar version of Zoom, StreamYard or similar platforms where only the speakers are seen on the screen, and everyone else can ask questions via the chat, which get answered by the speakers or moderators.

The increased use of webinars allows you to enjoy the benefit of learning content that you would typically have to pay thousands of dollars for at a conference. You can do this without leaving your home or office, and it usually does not cost you a dime. If you are unable to join live, the webinars often appear on the host's website or social media channels. Beware though—sometimes they are only posted on these sites for a limited duration, so if you are interested, watch the webinar sooner rather than later. Webinars are a fantastic form of active video learning.

Talk and listen

Pablo Carrillo is a lawyer who spent almost fifteen years working with US Senator and presidential candidate John McCain, most recently as his chief of staff. Out of law school in New Orleans, Carrillo worked in a boutique law firm in his home state of Louisiana. In connection with one case, he would occasionally travel to Washington, DC. Every time Carrillo went to the nation's capital, he met with people and talked to them. He leveraged every relationship he had, going all the way back to high school.

When he learned that the chief of staff to a Louisiana Congressman was an alumnus of his high school, Carrillo used that common thread to reach out for his support in helping him find a great fit. Carrillo was very interested in working for a person or committee of influence and impact and spoke to anyone he could to leverage every opportunity. He wanted to be able to contribute. Talking to people around him and listening for opportunities helped Carrillo find a job that he loved. After almost three years working with that committee, Carrillo was hired by Senator McCain, who became Chairman of the Senate Commerce Committee when Republicans took control of the Senate. He was looking for investigative counsel. Carrillo ran over with his resume, interviewed for the job, and started two weeks later. It was a great match as they worked together for almost fifteen years.

James "Hondo" Geurts, who you met in Chapter 10, talks to everyone from the front desk receptionist to the Secretary of the Navy. He knows he can learn something valuable from each of them and talks to anyone and everyone. This includes those inside and outside of his organization and industry. You should not believe that people are too high or too low in the organization and therefore not approachable. Just the opposite: talk to everyone. Do not limit yourself only to those who are senior to you. Your peers and those who are junior to you can have helpful information for you as well.

When someone puts in their notice letting their boss know they are leaving their job, it can take Human Resources weeks to get the job posted. If you can hear about the opening before it ever gets published, you can be the first to apply by reaching out to the hiring manager in the department and expressing your interest in the position. The smaller pool of applicants when a job is first posted puts you at a great advantage (Siegel, 2021). If they like you, the job might not even be published. Seventy percent of jobs are never posted, and this may very well be the reason (Kaufman, 2011). Even if the information cannot help you directly, you may use this new knowledge to help someone else.

You do not and should not start every conversation trying to get something out of it. Your focus should be to build a relationship. People like to work and help those they know, like and trust, so give them a reason to enjoy your company. Offer to help them or introduce them to someone in your network. Do not make the conversation transactional. Learn everything you can about those around you. Find out what they enjoy, their habits and hobbies.

Meals are a great place to talk to those at your table. Everything from a holiday family meal to a business lunch are all opportunities to speak to those around you. Start the conversation by discussing a topic of mutual interest—the common thread I keep referencing.

Even Zoom can be used to talk to people by utilizing the chat function. If someone says something that resonates with you, reach out to them via chat and let them know why you appreciated the comment. Engage, engage, engage.

Eighty percent of jobs are filled through personal and professional connections (Fisher, 2020). If you want to get on people's radar, you need to engage in conversation with them (Gotian, 2021b, 2019; Turnbull and Gotian, 2020). This can be done in person or via electronic mediums such as email or text. Engaging with their social media content is another way to get noticed. The critical point is to engage, build relationships and give more than you receive.

Learn while you gather

Conferences, while expensive, are a great way to enhance your informal learning. What you learn in the ballroom is carefully curated, and usually an expert is brought in to speak. Soak up everything you can. Arrive at the conference room a few minutes early to talk with the presenter. Usually, the speaker arrives 30 minutes early to make sure their audio-visual equipment is working. That only takes a few minutes, so the rest of the time they are just standing there waiting for their turn to speak. This is the perfect time to introduce yourself. After the talk, there is usually a long line of people waiting to talk to the speaker, so you will only get a fraction of the time and half of their attention. After the talk, follow up with the speaker via email or social media and let them know what you enjoyed about their speech. You will get noticed if you post something positive about them and their presentation on social media. Just be sure to tag them in your post.

Don't just walk by

While the keynotes and breakout rooms in conferences are a rich source of informal learning, do not discount the hotel lobby, coffee line, or even your time waiting for an available bathroom. Have a mental list of starter sentences that you can pull out at any time. These are benign conversation starters meant to spark a conversation. Consider the following sentence starters:

- I really enjoyed your talk, especially the comment you made about...
- I related to what you said about...
- Where are you based?
- What an interesting (when commenting about something specific such as a bag, hat, or brooch).
- What was your favorite session so far?
- Did you have to travel far to get to this conference?

Each one of these questions can lead to answers, which in turn can lead to a whole new line of inquiry. Be sure not to pepper your new friend with questions without offering some information about yourself. Otherwise, it will feel like an interrogation and they will want to get as far away from you as possible. The conversation needs to be like a ping pong match. Ask a question, wait for a response, give some information about yourself, ask another question or comment, and so on. Remember, every piece of information they are sharing is a form of informal learning which you pack away in your brain and can pull out when needed.

Being ready to start a conversation at any time is what helped Scott O'Neil, the former CEO of the Philadelphia 76ers and New Jersey Devils, rise to success. Shortly after he graduated from college, O'Neil had an entry-level job as a marketing assistant with the NBA team, the Brooklyn Nets. He was in the office on a Saturday morning when the president walked by and asked him what he was doing.

"I'm fixing the copier," O'Neil answered.

"Why?" asked the president.

"Because it is broken," said O'Neil.

The president promoted him on the spot. "He gave me a chance," O'Neil said. There was hardly anyone else in the office that Saturday morning, so they had an opportunity to chat. If O'Neil had just ended the conversation and walked away, he never would have had many of the opportunities that led to his success.

These conversations can also happen at work as you are waiting for an elevator or grabbing your coffee. Talk to those around you. Find a topic of common interest or something unique about what they are wearing. When speaking with doctors wearing the same-colored scrubs, I find myself looking at their funky socks with unique designs as a source for a conversation starter. It works every time.

Emails

Most of us get countless emails every day. We read the important ones and glaze over the others. You are probably subscribed to more newsletters than you have the time or patience to read. You might wish to take a closer look at your emails as there may be some opportunities for informal learning sitting in your inbox. Presentations, interesting articles, or a new professional development opportunity might all be there. You might learn about a call for papers, requests for nominations, or grant opportunities. You might hear of new people joining the firm with a unique expertise or learn of someone who is leaving. Perhaps someone had a new invention or figured out how to use the latest software program you are encouraged to use. Take a closer look; there are opportunities in your inbox you might be overlooking.

COACHING QUESTIONS

1 What are two starter sentences you would feel comfortable using when meeting someone new?

2 What are some of the places you might have overlooked that could offer opportunities for continued learning?

3 Where or with whom would you feel comfortable investing some time to learn something new?

KEY TAKEAWAYS

There are countless ways you can continue learning, none of which require a formal classroom, expensive tuition or enrollment in a degree program. They are flexible, and many can be done from the comfort of your own home. The critical issue is to constantly keep your mind open to everything around you and absorb any new knowledge that you can. Learning is not about a certificate or diploma; it is about constantly being open to the transfer of new knowledge. Some ways you can continue learning include:

1   Reading books, articles, and blogs to gain insight into a new topic.

2   Surround yourself with interesting people and listen to what they are sharing. Stories of joy and pain points will present themselves. Hear what they are saying and remember it. You do not need to know everything, but you should surround yourself with people who can advise you. Do yourself a favor and listen to what they are saying.

3   Watch what everyone around you is doing. Look for gaps and opportunities. Consider the challenges being faced by those who are one and two steps up the chain of command. Identify ways you can help alleviate that challenge, and offer your expertise.

4   Podcasts are on the rise and are a wealth of information on every conceivable topic. Interviews with luminaries and deep discussions about topics of interest can be heard while you multitask, such as during your commute.

5   YouTube is the second most popular search engine after Google. Millions of videos are available to learn about any topic you might find interesting and wish to learn more about.

6   Social media is here to stay. There is an endless hive of information on various platforms. Join some of the groups you identify with, read posts to learn what topics are important to people, and engage with their posts. Shut off notifications so that it does not become a distraction and carve out time to read the latest posts.

7   Like videos, webinars offer content and interviews, which often you would have to pay thousands of dollars for if you attended them in person. The webinars are often live, and you can ask the speakers questions via the chat function. This converts your learning from being passive to active.

8   Talking to people is a great way to learn more about them, what they value, and strategic information that might be helpful in the future. Talk

to everyone around you, including those who are senior and junior to you and your peers. Everyone has something important to share.

9 Conferences offer the ability to learn from curated luminaries who are subject matter experts. Keynotes and workshops provide excellent opportunities to learn new things or a new application of something old, thereby making it new again.

10 Hallway conversations both at conferences and at work offer a perfect opportunity to meet new people. Be ready for a conversation by having starter sentences that you can pull out and use when the situation presents itself.

11 Although emails flood our inbox, they can also provide helpful information. Most people do not read broadcast messages. When you do, look for patterns about challenges and opportunities. If you do, you might find information about a job opportunity, grant, call for papers, or request for award nominations.

References

Buckner, H and Warren, R (2020) How podcasts offer new audiences during the pandemic, *PR Daily*, https://www.prdaily.com/how-podcasts-offer-new-audiences-during-the-pandemic/ (archived at https://perma.cc/SYQ3-MZY2)

Chen, R (2015) Three strategies for introverts to speak up in meetings, *Fast Company*, https://www.fastcompany.com/3052599/the-top-3-reasons-introverts-dont-speak-up-in-meetings (archived at https://perma.cc/S7KW-P4NG)

Eyal, N (2019) *Indistractable: How to control your attention and choose your life*, Dallas, TX, Ben Bella Books

Fisher, JF (2020) How to get a job often comes down to one elite personal asset, and many people still don't realize it, CNBC

Freire, P (2000) *Pedagogy of the Oppressed*, Continuum International Publishing Group.

Gotian, R (2019) Networking for introverts, *Nature*, **571**, S50

Gotian, R (2021a) When your favorite book becomes a course for work, *Forbes*, https://www.forbes.com/sites/ruthgotian/2021/04/06/when-your-favorite-book-becomes-a-course-for-work/ (archived at https://perma.cc/X6Z4-F3N6)

Gotian, R (2021b) Why you only need to meet 40% of requirements in job descriptions, *Forbes*, https://www.forbes.com/sites/ruthgotian/2021/03/23/why-you-only-need-to-meet-40-of-requirements-in-job-descriptions/ (archived at https://perma.cc/2WHY-N97Y)

Kaufman, W (2011) A successful job search: It's all about networking, NPR, *All Things Considered*

Kolb, AY and Kolb, DA (2005) Learning styles and learning spaces: Enhancing experiential learning in higher education, *Academy of Management Learning and Education*, **4**, pp 193–212

Kolb, D (1984a) *Experiential Learning: Experience as the source of learning and development*, Englewood Cliffs, NJ, Prentice-Hall, Inc

Kolb, D (1984b) The process of experiential learning, in *Experiential Learning: Experience as the source of learning and development*, Engelwood Cliffs, NJ: Prentice Hall

Kolb, D (1984c) Structural foundations of the learning process, in *Experiential Learning: Experience as the source of learning and development*, Engelwood Cliffs, NJ: Prentice Hall

Kolb, DA, Boyatzis, RE and Mainemelis, C (2002) Experiential learning theory: Previous research and new directions, in RJ Sternberg and LF Zhang (eds.) *Perspectives on Cognitive, Learning and Thinking Styles*, Mahwah, NJ: Lawrence Erlbaum

Levin, M (2017) Reading habits of the most successful leaders that can change your life too, *Inc.* https://www.inc.com/marissa-levin/reading-habits-of-the-most-successful-leaders-that.html (archived at https://perma.cc/WP8T-6JRX)

Podcasthosting.org, 2021 *Global Podcast Statistics, Demographics & Habits*, https://podcasthosting.org/podcast-statistics/ (archived at https://perma.cc/5JDG-82YW)

Rampton, J (2017) 9 everyday habits of the average millionaire, *Entrepreneur.com*, https://www.entrepreneur.com/article/304219 (archived at https://perma.cc/4NMQ-5FBX)

Siegel, I (2021) *Get Hired Now!*, Hoboken, New Jersey, John Wiley & Sons, Inc

Turnbull, Z and Gotian, R (2020) Five steps for networking during a pandemic, *Nature*, https://www.nature.com/articles/d41586-020-03567-9 (archived at https://perma.cc/JD4V-FPKB)

Conclusion

Congratulations! You have now learned the four-pronged path to success and are ready to start your journey forward. It is not easy or painless, but now it is no longer opaque or hidden. You know what needs to happen; you just need to actually do it. I have revealed the route to success, with plenty of ways to implement best practices. The next steps are up to you and only you can decide what they will be. Instead of talking about one day, make today day one.

I never believed that anyone wakes up in the morning aiming to be average in life. I always accepted that people wanted to achieve more but did not know what was available to them or how to succeed. They had the potential but needed a plan. I have lifted the veil and offered you proposals to consider if you wish to achieve more. If you read this book, I have to believe that you want to accomplish something bigger, that you wish to obtain the success factor. You now have a plan and have run out of excuses. It is time to roll up your sleeves and put into practice the four elements that lead to success. You can succeed, and now you have the tools to do so. Go back and see which technique within each component works best for you at the current stage of your life. Revisit it every time you feel stuck, need inspiration, or are going through a life transition.

As a reminder, extreme high achievers ranging through such luminaries as astronauts, Nobel Prize winners, Olympic and NBA champions, and NFL Hall of Famers all had four elements which they constantly undertook in unison:

1 Intrinsic motivation

2 Perseverance

3 Strong foundation

4 Informal learning

Intrinsic motivation

The high achievers all found an area in which they excel, and they have a passion for and purpose of improving continually. It is the reason they wake up every morning, eager to get to work. They love what they do and would do it for free if they could. It is for an internal curiosity and joy that they continue to pursue this passion rather than external validators such as a degree, award, or promotion.

The awards, as fancy and difficult to achieve as they might be, are one chapter in their journey, not the entire story. The high achievers constantly want to see what is next. They love everything about what they do and feel fortunate that they get to work in their chosen profession.

Perseverance

When I interviewed the extreme high achievers, I always told them that I was less interested in what I could Google about them, which I considered the tip of the iceberg, and more enticed by what it took to get there, what was below the waterline that most people cannot see. Nobel Prize winners, astronauts, Olympians, and CEOs all have a mile-long list of things that did not go their way. Their road to success, like yours, is long and filled with many challenges, hurdles, and potholes. For them, these were not viewed as failures; instead, they considered them learning opportunities to improve their craft. The high achievers never doubted *if* they could overcome the challenge, as they always believed they could. Instead, they concentrated on *how* to overcome the latest problem. The shift in mindset allows them to become laser-focused on the solution. They work incredibly hard and do not give up simply because something does not go their way today, this week, or this month. They recognize that with extra effort, they will eventually find the answer they are seeking. Giving up is not in the lexicon of a high achiever.

Strong foundation

High achievers always go back to the basics. They have a solid foundation which they are constantly reinforcing. What worked for them early in their careers did not go away when they became successful. They are still utilizing the same techniques that made them successful long after they achieved notoriety. They do not give up on their foundational skills; instead, they reinforce them. Granted, they do the same techniques with better and sometimes more expensive equipment, but the process, drills and procedures are exactly the same. Many, such as two-time Olympic champion in judo, Kayla Harrison, told me that what paved the road to her numerous national, world, and Olympic titles were techniques she learned in the first six months of her training. "I am the queen of the basic drills," said Harrison.

Informal learning

Despite getting all of their awards and accolades, extreme high achievers continue to consume new knowledge. They are constantly talking to people, reading, watching videos, or listening to podcasts. Each had their medium of choice, but the bottom line is that they realized there is always more to learn, and someone, somewhere, can teach them something new. They surround themselves with a team of mentors, an entire group of people who believe in them more than they believe in themselves. They motivate, inspire and teach them new things. Equally as necessary, the high achievers soak it all in. Even if they cannot use the information today, they store it and retrieve it as needed.

I hope the astronauts, Nobel Prize winners, Olympic champions, and other luminaries illuminate and inspire your path to success. Use the lessons and stories you read as a guide and inspiration. Download the Passion Audit, Goal Audit and Mentoring Team worksheets to accentuate and beam light on your areas of opportunity and growth. Let your journey begin and may it be filled with excitement, energy, and hope for the future.

If you enjoyed this book, I would appreciate it if you would leave a rating and review on Amazon to help others find this book and start their journey to success. The world is big enough for all of us to succeed.

INDEX

NB: page numbers in *italic* indicate figures or tables.